WH[...]
WE QU[...]

NIGEL REES

BLANDFORD

First published in the UK 1989 by Blandford Press
An imprint of Cassell, Artillery House, Artillery Row, London SW1P 1RT

Copyright © Nigel Rees, 1989

Distributed in the United States by
Sterling Publishing Co. Inc.,
2 Park Avenue, New York, NY 10016

Distributed in Australia by
Capricorn Link (Australia) Pty Ltd
PO Box 665, Lane Cove, NSW 2066

British Library Cataloguing in Publication Data
Rees, Nigel, *1944-*
    Why do we quote?
    1. Quotations
    I. Title
    080

ISBN 0-7137-2161-4

Typeset by Litho Link Ltd, Welshpool, Powys Wales
Printed and bound in Great Britain by Mackays of Chatham Plc

PREFACE

The short answer to the question posed by the title of this book is: because other people have said things memorably and well in such a way that we would rather repeat their phrases than mint new ones of our own.

But that is not really what the book is about. If it answers the question 'Why do we quote?' at all, it does so by demonstrating how the quotations it deals with arose in the first place and how they have been used subsequently. The very fact that these sayings have passed into the language, however fleetingly, shows that they have some special quality of memorability, usefulness and even of irritation.

Anything written or said which gets repeated may be described as a quotation, but clearly there must be something more to it than that. How is it that a group of words acquires quotation marks around it, visible or invisible on the page, audible or inaudible in conversation? And how is a quotation different from a mere saying or catchphrase or idiom?

Well, it would be possible for a group of words to be each of these things at the same time, but (although I have repeatedly ignored the distinction in selecting phrases for inclusion here) a quotation might be defined as an attributable saying. In other words, it was said by an identifiable person (if only we can identify him) or it comes from a specific work, whereas a catchphrase or proverb might well have no firm origin and have simply grown out of popular speech.

My sole criterion for selection has been: is there anything interesting to say about the origins of a particular phrase (and never mind how we should categorize it)? I have allowed myself to broaden what we mean by a 'quotation' by looking at the origins of a number of jokes. I have tried not to overlap with my previous forays – *Sayings of the Century* (George Allen & Unwin, 1984) and *Why Do We Say . . . ?* (Blandford Press, 1987) – except where I have new information to put forward.

Much of the material contained here has come my way during more than a dozen years compiling the BBC Radio programme *Quote . . . Unquote*. I must say at once that this has provided me with an invaluable indicator of what people do like to quote and what quotations people are interested in. I must also acknowledge what a priceless research tool it has given me. In the business of 'phrase detection' what better way could there be of answering a question of origins than by putting it to an audience of some millions all over the world? Someone, somewhere, will know the answer to almost anything.

What is the alternative? To find answers to the questions, 'Who said such-and-such?' and 'When did people first start saying . . .?', the only thing to do is to read widely, on the off-chance that you will stumble over the information. The established reference books never seem to have just what you are looking for!

Very recently a new and invaluable tool has become available to the phrase detective: the computer database with its magically fast ability to fish out words or phrases from among the many millions stored on it. Alas, very few books are so stored at the moment; the first British newspapers and magazines only began to be systematically retained in this way about five years ago, and the first American ones not until the late 1970s. There is very little retrospective building up of databases from the printed word. It is obviously a pipe-dream that everything ever published will one day be available in this form.

So, research into phrase origins is, for the most part, a very rough and ready process. The findings and conclusions contained in this book are therefore offered tentatively. Tomorrow, the reader may well come across evidence that will contradict what is written here. For the moment, I keep repeating the golden rule I have laid down for myself on this subject: it is very dangerous ever to say that a particular person coined a phrase or that it came about in a definite way. There is almost always an example of earlier use. The furthest it is safe to go is to say that a certain person has popularized the phrase at a certain time.

It is inevitable that an air of pedantry at times hovers over this book. You cannot be in the business of pointing out common misquotations or popular fallacies without it. In mitigation I can only say that I am not one of those people – I am thinking of self-appointed guardians of our grammar and language – who feel that any breach of the 'rules' should be a capital offence. I merely find it *interesting* when people get quotations 'wrong', and want to find out why they do it. It is no purpose of this book to represent a pedant's revolt against unfeeling users of language – 'popular' language, at that.

I do find, however, that there are plenty of other people as obsessed as I am about the origins of phrases. Barely a day passes without someone writing to me wanting to know where a saying comes from, usually claiming first to have drawn a blank with the obvious reference books. These days I try to harness this spirit of inquiry through regular circulation of a quotations 'newsletter' among a wide circle of (I hope) benign pedants and honest seekers-after-truth. As I have mentioned already, listeners to *Quote . . . Unquote* also find themselves being drawn into the hunt, as do viewers to the Channel 4 series *Countdown*. I am most grateful to the many many such people who have responded to my queries. In return, I hope I have been able to put some of them out of their misery by providing answers to what has often long puzzled them.

In writing this book I am particularly grateful to the following for asking or answering or attempting to answer specific questions: Peter Allwood; Linda Baxter; Paul Beale; L. M. Brown; Dr David Butler; Barry Day; David Evans, BBC Central Reference Library; William Garner; Donald Hickling; Sir David Hunt; M. R. Lewis; Frank Loxley; Malcolm Macdonald; Leonard Miall; Dr Jean-Claude Mougre; John G. Murray; Michael Grosvenor Meyer; John Julius Norwich; Michel Petheram, BBC Central Reference Library; Martin Walker; William J. Weatherby.

In addition, I should like to acknowledge and to thank all the authors and publishers of the works I have quoted.

NIGEL REES
London, 1988

ABBREVIATIONS USED TO IDENTIFY BOOKS CONSULTED

Bartlett	*Bartlett's Familiar Quotations* (15th ed.), 1980
Benham	*Benham's Book of Quotations*, 1948 (1960 revision)
Bible	The Authorised Version, 1611 (except where stated otherwise)
Brewer	*Brewer's Dictionary of Phrase and Fable*, 1975
Burnam	Tom Burnam, *The Dictionary of Misinformation*, 1975
Burnam 2	Tom Burnam, *More Misinformation*, 1980
CODP	*The Concise Oxford Dictionary of Proverbs*, 1982
DNB	*The Dictionary of National Biography*
D20CQ	Nigel Rees, *A Dictionary of Twentieth Century Quotations*, 1987
Flexner	Stuart Berg Flexner, *I Hear America Talking*, 1976
Flexner 2	Stuart Berg Flexner, *Listening to America*, 1982
Halliwell	Leslie Halliwell, *Halliwell's Film Guide* (6th ed.), 1987
Macquarie	*The Macquarie Dictionary*, 1981
Mencken	*H. L. Mencken's Dictionary of Quotations*, 1942
Morrises	William and Mary Morris, *Morris Dictionary of Word and Phrase Origins*, 1977
ODCIE	*The Oxford Dictionary of Current Idiomatic English* (2 vols), 1985
ODQ	*The Oxford Dictionary of Quotations* (3rd ed.), 1979
ODP	*The Oxford Dictionary of Proverbs* (3rd ed.), 1970

OED	*The Compact Edition of the Oxford English Dictionary*, 1987
OED Supp.	*A Supplement to the Oxford English Dictionary* (4 vols), 1972/86
Partridge/Catchphrases	Eric Partridge, *A Dictionary of Catch Phrases* (2nd ed., edited by Paul Beale), 1985
Partridge/Slang	Eric Partridge, *A Dictionary of Slang and Unconventional English* (8th ed., edited by Paul Beale), 1984
Polite Conversation	Jonathan Swift, *A Complete Collection of Genteel and Ingenious Conversation &c.*, 1738
Prayer Book	*The Book of Common Prayer* (1662)
Safire	William Safire, *Safire's Political Dictionary*, 1978
Sayings	Nigel Rees, *Sayings of the Century*, 1984
Shakespeare	The Arden Shakespeare (in the most recent editions available in 1987)

From each according to his ABILITY
See **each**.

Set Europe ABLAZE
This ringing call was one of the last Churchillisms to become publicly known. E. H. Cookridge wrote in *Inside S.O.E.* (1966): 'The Special Operations Executive was born on 19 July 1940 . . .' on the basis of a memo from Winston Churchill ' "to co-ordinate all action by way of subversion and sabotage against the enemy overseas". Or, as the Prime Minister later put it "to set Europe ablaze".' The title of the first chapter of Cookridge's book is 'Set Europe Ablaze'.

ACCIDENTS will happen in the best-regulated families
This proverbial expression is best remembered in the form delivered by Mr Micawber in Chapter 28 of *David Copperfield* (1850) by Charles Dickens: ' "Copperfield," said Mr Micawber, "accidents will occur in the best-regulated families; and in families not regulated by . . . the influence of Woman, in the lofty character of Wife, they must be expected with confidence, and must be borne with philosophy".'

However, the saying is not original to Dickens. Sir Walter Scott wrote in Chapter 49 of *Peveril of the Peak* (1823): 'Nay, my lady, . . . such things will befall in the best regulated families.'

The *CODP* finds 'P. Atall' writing in *Hermit in America* (1819), 'Accidents will happen in the best regulated families' and, even earlier, George Colman in *Deuce is in Him* (1763) with the more basic, 'Accidents will happen'.

J'ACCUSE
The Dreyfus Affair in France arose in 1894 when Captain Alfred Dreyfus, who had Jewish origins, was dismissed from the army

on trumped up charges of treason. Condemned to life imprison-
ment on Devil's Island, he was not reinstated until 1906. In the
meantime, the case had divided France. The writer Émile Zola
(1840-1902) came to the defence of Dreyfus with two open
letters addressed to the President of the French Republic and
printed in the paper *L'Aurore*. The first, under the banner
headline, '*J'accuse*' ('I accuse'), was published on 13 January
1898 – each paragraph began with the words; the second, more
moderate in tone, on 22 January.

   I Accuse was the title of a British film about the case, released in
1958 with José Ferrer as Dreyfus and Emlyn Williams as Zola.
An 'I accuse' is a term of limited use given to any kind of
crusading writing, especially in a newspaper. Graham Greene
entitled his short book on organized crime in the South of France
J'accuse: the dark side of Nice (1982).

   It is a small point, perhaps, but Georges Clemenceau (1841-
1929), who played a prominent part in the campaign with Zola,
claimed in a letter (19 June 1902) that: 'It was I who gave the
title "*J'accuse*" to Zola's letter.' He also said that he had written
most of the second letter.

   In 1919, Abel Gance made a film for Charles Pathé with the
title *J'Accuse*, but it was not about the Dreyfus Affair. In it, the
dead returned *en masse* from the First World War to accuse the
survivors. Another version of this film was made shortly before
the outbreak of the Second World War.

ACROSS the River and Into the Trees
The title of the novel (1950) by Ernest Hemingway alludes to the
last words of Stonewall Jackson, the Confederate general in the
American Civil War who was shot in error by his own troops in
May 1863. He said, 'Let us cross over the river, and rest under
[the shade of] the trees.'

   E. B. White's noted parody of Hemingway's style was called
Across the Street and Into the Bar.

ADOPT, Adapt, Improve
This is the motto of the National Association of Round Tables of
Great Britain and Ireland. The Round Table movement is a social
and charitable organization for young professional and business-
men under the age of 40 (after which age Rotary takes over). The
name 'round table' – although it may have some echoes of
Arthurian knights working together – and the motto, both derive

from a speech given in Birmingham in 1927 by the Prince of Wales (later Edward VIII). He told the British Industries Fair: 'The young business and professional men of this country must get together *round the table, adopt* methods that have proved so sound in the past, *adapt* them to the changing needs of the times and, whenever possible, *improve* them' (my italics).

It pays to ADVERTISE

This is a proverbial saying which almost certainly originated in the USA. Indeed, Mencken, in 1942, lists it simply as an 'American proverb'.

Bartlett (1980 edition) quotes the anonymous rhyme:

> The codfish lays ten thousand eggs,
> The homely hen lays one.
> The codfish never cackles
> To tell you what she's done.
> And so we scorn the codfish,
> While the humble hen we prize,
> Which only goes to show you
> That it pays to advertise.

I feel sure, though, that the rhyme came after the proverb or slogan was established.

It is possible to push back the dating of the phrase rather more positively. There was a play, co-written by Walter Hackett (1876-1944), which had it for a title in 1914, and this was turned into a film in 1931. Back even earlier, Cole Porter entitled one of his earliest songs 'It Pays to Advertise'. The song alludes to a number of advertising lines that were current when he was a student at Yale (*c.* 1912):

> I'd walk a mile for that schoolgirl complexion,
> Palmolive soap will do it every time.
> Oh cream, oh best cigar!
> Maxwell Motor Car!
> Do you have a baby vacuum in your home?
> Gum is good for you,
> Try our new shampoo,
> Flit will always free your home of flies.
> If you travel, travel, travel at all,
> You know, it pays to advertise.
>
> (included in *The Complete Lyrics of Cole Porter*,
> ed. Robert Kimball, 1983)

This suggests to me that the phrase, though not Porter's own, was not too much of a cliché by 1912. Ezra Pound wrote in a letter to his father in 1908 about the launch of his poems: 'Sound trumpet. Let rip the drum & swatt the big bassoon. It pays to advertise.'

We are probably looking for an origin in the 1870s/90s when advertising really took off in America (as in Britain). Indeed, Benham lists an 'American saying *c.* 1870' – 'The man who on his trade relies must either bust or advertise', and notes that 'Sir Thomas Lipton [*d.* 1931] is said to have derived inspiration and success through seeing this couplet in New York about 1875.'

Comfort the AFFLICTED, and afflict the comfortable
See **comfort.**

He who is not with us is AGAINST us
I have not been able to find a source for this quite frequently evoked view, as expressed by the Russian leader, Joseph Stalin (1879-1953). However, *Time* (11 August 1986) noted a corollary attributed to the Hungarian Communist Party leader, Janos Kadar, (*b.* 1912): 'He who is not against us is with us.'

In fact, of course, Stalin was quoting Jesus Christ who said, 'He that is not with me is against me' (Luke 11:23) and Kadar was also quoting Christ who provided the corollary: 'He that is not against us is for us' (Luke 9:50). It is not surprising that Stalin quoted scripture. He went from church school at Guri (1888-94) to the theological seminary at Tiflis (until expelled in 1899) to train for the Russian Orthodox priesthood.

One of our AIRCRAFT is missing
See **missing.**

The nation's AIRY navies grappling in the central blue
Sir John Colville's published diaries of his time as Winston Churchill's private secretary (*The Fringes of Power*, paperback editions 1986-87) reveal the wartime Prime Minister quoting 'Tennyson's prescient lines about aerial warfare' (19 March 1941) without saying what the lines are.

They are to be found in *Locksley Hall* (published 1842, probably written 1837-38). A rejected lover returns to his one-time home

by the sea and, among other things, complains of the modern
world of steamships and railways. He also makes an eerie
prediction of commerce and warfare being extended to the skies:

> . . . I dipt into the future far as human eye could see,
> Saw the Vision of the world, and all the wonder that would be;
>
> Saw the heavens fill with commerce, argosies of magic sails,
> Pilots of the purple twilight, dropping down with costly bales;
>
> Heard the heavens fill with shouting, and there rain'd a ghastly dew
> From the nation's airy navies grappling in the central blue.

ALL for one and one for all

This is no more and no less than the motto of the Three
Musketeers in the novel *Les Trois Mousquetiers* (1844-45) by
Alexandre Dumas – in French, '*Tous pour un, un pour tous*'.

Earlier, Shakespeare in his poem, *The Rape of Lucrece* (1594)
(lines 141-4) has:

> The aim of all is but to nurse the life
> With honour, wealth and ease, in waning age;
> And in this aim there is much thwarting strife
> That *one for all, or all for one* we gage[1].

More prosaically, 'Each for all and all for each' has been used in
Britain as a slogan for the Co-operative Wholesale Society.

ALL This and Heaven Too

The novel with this title by Rachel Field (1939, filmed 1940)
acknowledges its source. Matthew Henry (1662-1714) attributed
the saying to his father in the *Life of Philip Henry*.

There is no ALTERNATIVE

Mrs Thatcher's famously nannyish phrase provides a good
example of how it can be more difficult tracing the origins of
recent quotations than of older ones. By the early 1980s,
everyone in Britain knew the phrase, but how had it arisen?

If she had said it in the House of Commons it would have been
possible to search through *Hansard* (the electronic version
makes computer-searching deliciously simple). But she did not,
apparently. So one was faced with searching through newspapers

---

[1]pledge, wager, venture

for a mention of the phrase, except that most British newspapers were not being transferred on to computer databases until the mid-1980s.

Perhaps she had said it at one of her meetings with parliamentary lobby correspondents? But these occasions are never directly reported (hence the obscurity surrounding the coining of Harold Wilson's famous observation 'A *week* is a long time in politics', q.v.). And if she had, the political correspondents I consulted could not remember.

In 1984, Dr David Butler approached me regarding the phrase because he was revising his *British Political Facts*. I did some more asking around and made no progress. Patrick Cosgrave, an adviser to Mrs Thatcher before she became Prime Minister, suggested to me that, perhaps, it hadn't actually been coined by her, but simply picked up, in the way she has of seizing on ideas that she fancies.

David Butler wrote to Downing Street and received a letter from Mrs Thatcher's then political secretary espousing a similar view: 'I am not sure that the Prime Minister ever actually used the phrase . . . and my suspicion, shared by others, is that TINA was coined by those who were pressing for a change of policy.'

This only took us further away than ever from a satisfactory conclusion. Then, in 1986, and in the time-honoured fashion, I happened to stumble upon a report of a speech Mrs Thatcher made to the Conservative Women's conference, on 21 May 1980, marking the end of her first year in office. Describing the harsh economic measures already set in train by her government, she said: 'There is no easy popularity in that, but I believe people accept *there is no alternative*.'

So, there, she *had* said it, and publicly, too. I don't know whether this was the first time – in fact, I think she may well have said it at some stage in 1979 – but at last there was a reference.

The acronym 'TINA', said to have been coined by Young Conservatives, was flourishing by the time of the party conference in September 1981.

A correspondent suggests that I compare it to the old Hebrew catchphrase '*ain breira*' ('there is no choice').

An AMBASSADOR is . . . sent to lie abroad for . . . his country

Sir Henry Wotton (1568-1639) was England's envoy to Venice in

the reign of King James I. His punning view of the diplomat's
calling very nearly cost him his job. As Izaak Walton recounted in
his *Life* (1651), Wotton had managed to offend a Roman Catholic
controversialist called Gasper Scioppius. In 1611 Scioppius
produced a book called *Ecclesiasticus* which abused James I and
related an anecdote concerning Wotton. On his way out to Italy
in 1604, Wotton had stayed at Augsburg where a merchant,
Christopher Fleckmore, invited him to inscribe his name in an
album. Wotton wrote, *'Legatus est vir bonus peregre missus ad
mentiendum Reipublicae causa'* – 'which he would have been
content should have been thus Englished: An ambassador is an
honest man, sent to lie abroad for the good of his country.'
Scioppius, on the basis of this joke, accused James I of sending a
confessed liar to represent him abroad.

According to the *DNB*, 'Wotton's chances of preferment were
ruined by the king's discovery of the contemptuous definition of
an ambassador's function . . . James invited explanations of the
indiscreet jest. Wotton told the king that the affair was "a
merriment" but he was warned to take it seriously, and he
deemed it prudent to prepare two apologies.'

James said that one of these 'sufficiently commuted for a
greater offence', but the joke had done its damage, and, although
Wotton was later to be given further diplomatic work and
become Provost of Eton, he continued to suffer for it.

AND so to bed
See **bed.**

All ANIMALS are equal
See **equal.**

Queen ANNE is dead
See **queen.**

ANOTHER Country
Julian Mitchell's play (staged 1981, filmed 1984) showing how
the seeds of defection to Soviet Russia were sown in a group of
boys at an English public school does not take its title, as might at
first be thought, from the celebrated line in Christopher Marlowe's
The Jew of Malta (*c.* 1592):

> Fornication: but that was in another country;
> And besides the wench is dead.

But, rather, as Mitchell has confirmed to me, from the second verse of Sir Cecil Spring Rice's patriotic 'Last Poem' (1918), which begins, 'I vow to thee, my country':

> And there's another country, I've heard of long ago –
> Most dear to them that love her, most great to them that know.

In the original context, the 'other country' is Heaven, rather than the Soviet Union, of course.

ANOTHER Heart and Other Pulses

Curious title, curious book – Michael Foot's account of his unsuccessful leadership of the British Labour Party during the 1983 general election (published 1984). The title comes from a Keats sonnet 'Addressed to the Same' (i.e., Benjamin Robert Haydon):

> And other spirits there are standing apart
>   Upon the forehead of the age to come:
> These, these will give the world another heart,
>   And other pulses. Hear ye not the hum
> Of mighty workings?

My last APPEAL to reason

On Friday 19 July 1940, Adolf Hitler made a speech to the Reichstag. Following, as it did, the fall of France and the May blitz on London, it somewhat surprisingly appeared to contain an offer of peace to the British (though Hitler tried to draw a distinction between ordinary British folk and their warmongering leaders, principally Winston Churchill).

The speech and the peace proposal, although reported prominently in *The Times* next morning, were largely ignored and the Germans were much annoyed by the British rejection of the peace offer which followed, notably by Lord Halifax, the Foreign Secretary, within the next few days.

It was in an attempt to appeal to the British people, literally over the heads of the leadership, that copies of the speech were dropped over England by the Luftwaffe in a leaflet raid on the night of 1/2 August. The Imperial War Museum displays an actual copy of the tabloid-newspaper-sized leaflet dropped over Somerset. It is headed, 'A LAST APPEAL TO REASON/BY/ADOLF HITLER/ Speech before the Reichstag 19th July 1940', and makes very tedious reading.

A correspondent writes: 'I saw a copy myself at the time and tried to read it. Nearly half was taken up, I remember, by long lists of appointments, transfers and promotions in the German armed forces and civil administration . . . Needless to say, public opinion generally regarded the leaflet as beneath contempt. I remember hearing about an item on the subject in a cinema newsreel, which ended by showing a pair of hands cutting up the leaflet into small rectangles, threading a string through the corners, and hanging the bundle on a hook on a tiled wall. Very explicit for those prudish days: the audience, I was told, roared approval.'

Et in ARCADIA ego

Now, what does this mean? One finds the words associated with tombs, skulls and Arcadian shepherds in classical paintings, but not before the seventeenth century. Most notably the phrase occurs in two paintings by the French artist Nicolas Poussin, both of which depict shepherds reading the words carved on a tomb. One painted between 1626 and 1628 hangs in Chatsworth House, Derbyshire; the other, 'The Shepherds of Arcady' (1630-35), is in the Louvre. Just before this, however, the Italian artist Guercino had painted a painting known as '*Et in Arcadia ego*' which hangs in the Galleria Corsino, Rome. This was painted no later than 1623.

Is the inscription meant to suggest that, in death, the speaker is in Arcadia, the Greek name for a place of rural peace and calm taken from an actual area in the Peloponnese? Or is he saying he was formerly there? '*Et in Arcadia ego vixi*' ('I lived') or '*Et in Arcadia fui pastor*' ('I was a shepherd') are variants.

Or is it Death speaking – 'Even in Arcadia, I, Death, can not be avoided'?

As L. A. Moritz of University College, Cardiff pointed out in a letter to *The Times* (27 January 1982), 'The Latin cannot mean what Goethe and many others . . . took it to mean: "I too was in Arcadia." Its only possible meaning is "Even in Arcadia am I" . . . this association of the pastoral Arcadia with death goes back to Virgil's tenth *Eclogue*, which first placed idyllic shepherds in an Arcadian landscape.'

Erwin Panofsky pointed this out first in *Philosophy and History, Essays presented to E. Cassirer* (1936), in which he claimed that since the eighteenth century the English had had an instinct, not shared by Europeans, for making a special kind of sense out of the classical tag. ' "Even in Arcadia I, Death, hold sway" . . . while long forgotten on the Continent remained familiar' in England, he points out, and ultimately 'became part of what may be termed a specifically English or "insular" tradition – a tradition which tended to retain the idea of a *memento mori*.' Skulls juxtaposed with roses could be conventionally employed as an 'emblem of the omnipotence of Death, whose power is not finally to be excluded even from the sequestered "safe" world of pastoral.'

In German literature, the phrase first appeared in *Winterreise* (1769) by Johann Georg Jacobi: 'Whenever, in a beautiful landscape, I encounter a tomb with the inscription: "I too was in Arcadia", I point it out to my friends, we stop a moment, press each other's hands, and proceed.' The phrase was later used by Goethe as the motto of his *Travels in Italy* (1816).

In England, Sir Joshua Reynolds painted a picture in 1769 on which a tomb can be seen with the words inscribed. In Evelyn Waugh's *Brideshead Revisited* (1945), the narrator, while an undergraduate at Oxford, adorns his rooms with a 'human skull lately purchased from the School of Medicine which, resting in a bowl of roses, formed, at the moment, the chief decoration of my table. It bore the motto "*Et in Arcadia ego*" inscribed on its forehead.' (Book One of the novel is entitled '*Et in Arcadia Ego*'.)

ARREST several of these vicars
See **vicars.**

And when they ASK us how dangerous it was . . .
During the First World War, the following parody became famous. It was brought to a new audience in the stage show *Oh What a Lovely War* (1963, filmed 1969):

> And when they ask us, how dangerous it was,
> Oh, we'll never tell them, no, we'll never tell them:
> We spent our pay in some café
> And fought wild women night and day,
> 'Twas the cushiest job we ever had.
>
> And when they ask us, and they're certainly going to ask us,
> The reason why we didn't win the Croix de Guerre,
> Oh, we'll never tell them, oh, we'll never tell them
> There was a front, but damned if we knew where.

As such, it is a parody of the song 'They Didn't Believe Me' by Jerome Kern and Herbert Reynolds (M. E. Rourke) (1914), which goes:

And when I told them how beautiful you are
They didn't believe me, they didn't believe me.
Your lips, your arms, your cheeks, your hair,
Are in a class beyond compare,
You're the loveliest girl that one can see.

And when I tell them, and I'm certainly goin' to tell them,
That I'm the man whose wife one day you'll be
They'll never believe me, they'll never believe me,
That from this great big world you've chosen me.

The parody was thought to be anonymous until Robert Kimball, editor of the *Complete Lyrics of Cole Porter* (1983) was going through the composer's voluminous papers and came across the words in the 'oldest compilation Porter had preserved of his works, a set of typed miscellaneous lyrics'.

In fact, Porter's version is slightly different to the one given above – e.g., line 2 is 'We never will tell them, we never will tell them'; line 5, 'Twas the wonderfulest war you ever knew', etc. So, we don't have 100 per cent proof that Porter wrote the parody, but it is an intriguing possibility. Note how the words 'night and day', which he was to couple in his most famous song in 1932, make an early appearance together here.

The law is an ASS
See **law.**

ASTONISH me
See *étonne-moi.*

The ATHENS of the North
See **Edinburgh.**

Cheaper to lower the ATLANTIC
See **lower.**

A' BABBLED of green fields

One of the most pleasing touches to be found in all of Shakespeare may not have been his at all. In *King Henry V* (II.iii.17), the Hostess (formerly Mistress Quickly) is relating the death of Falstaff:

> A' parted ev'n just between twelve and one, ev'n at the turning o' th' tide: for after I saw him fumble with the sheets and play with flowers and smile upon his fingers' end, I knew there was but one way; for his nose was as sharp as a pen, and a'babbled of green fields.

The 1623 Folio of Shakespeare's plays renders the last phrase 'and a Table of green fields', which makes no sense, though some editors put 'as sharp as a pen, on a table of green field' (taking 'green field' to mean green cloth).

The generally accepted version was inserted by Lewis Theobald in his 1733 edition. As the 1954 Arden edition comments: '"Babbled of green fields" is surely more in character with the Falstaff who quoted the Scriptures . . . and who lost his voice hallooing of anthems. Now he is in the valley of the shadow, the "green pasture" of Psalm 23 might well be on his lips.'

Shakespeare may well have handwritten 'babld' and the printer read this as 'table' – a reminder that the text of the plays is far from carved in stone and a prey to mishaps in the printing process as are all books and newspapers.

Now BACH is decomposing
See **decomposing**.

BACK to the land

The cry 'Back to the land!' was first heard at the end of the nineteenth century when it was realized that the industrial revolution and the move of the population towards non-agricultural work had starved farming of labour. At about this time, a Wickham Market farmer wrote to Sir Henry Rider Haggard, who was making an inventory of the decline, published as *Rural England* (1902):

> The labourers 'back to the land'. That is the cry of the press and the fancy of the people. Well, I do not think that they will ever come back; certainly no legislation will ever bring them. Some of the rising generation may be induced to stay, but it will be by training them to the use of machinery and paying them higher wages. It should be remembered that the most intelligent men have gone: these will never come back, but the rising generation may stay as competition in the town increases, and the young men of the country are better paid.

The *OED Supp.* cites an 1894 formulation of the idea, from *The Times* (25 October): 'All present were interested in the common practice that it was desirable, if possible, to bring the people back to the land.' By 1905, the *Spectator* (23 December) was saying '"Back-to-the-land" is a cry full not only of pathos, but of cogency.'

In the 1980s, a British TV comedy series was called *Backs to the Land,* playing on the phrase to provide a *double entendre* about its heroines, Land Girls, members of the Women's Land Army conscripted to work on the land during the Second World War (though the WLA was first established in the First World War).

BALFOUR must go
See **go.**

BANZAI!
From a hundred war films and cheap comics we are familiar with the cry used by Japanese forces in the Second World War – '*Banzai!*' meaning '[May you live] ten thousand years!' During the war – and after it – this traditional cry came to mean 'Ten thousand years to the Emperor' or 'to Japan', but I have always thought it a rather curious thing for, say, a suicide pilot to come out with.

In a letter to me, M. R. Lewis observes that,

> The root of the problem is that a language written in the Chinese ideographic characters is often difficult to translate sensibly into a West European language, because it is often not apparent when the literal meaning is intended and when the figurative. '*Banzai*' literally

means no more than 'ten thousand years', but what it more usually means is 'for a long time'. So, a pen in Japanese is, when literally translated, a 'ten thousand year writing brush', which is gibberish in any language! What it actually means is 'a long-lasting writing instrument' . . .

For the suicide pilots, the ritual shout of *'Banzai!'* swept up many layers of meaning, of which the most immediate was undoubtedly *'Tenno heika banzai'* – 'Long live the Emperor', a phrase which goes back into the mists of Japanese history, despite its appropriation by the nationalist movements of the 1930s. The phrase is still in use on such occasions as the Emperor's birthday, as I can testify from recent experience. When he stepped out on to the balcony and the shouts rose around me, I began to feel that I was in the wrong movie!

As for the oddity of the phrase – if literally translated, is it really so different from: 'Zadok the priest, and Nathan the prophet, anointed Solomon king. And all the people rejoiced and said, God save the king. Long live the king, *may the king live for ever. Amen. Alleluia.'* – which has been sung at the coronation of almost every English sovereign since William of Normandy was crowned in Westminster Abbey on Christmas Day 1066?

Swift includes 'May you live a thousand years' among the conversational chestnuts in *Polite Conversation* (1738).

Now BARABBAS was a publisher . . .

The story has it that when John Murray, Byron's publisher, sent the poet a copy of the Bible in return for a favour, Byron sent it back with the words 'Now Barabbas was a robber' (John 18:40) altered to, 'Now Barabbas was a publisher . . .' This story was included in Kazlitt Arvine's *Cyclopedia of Anecdotes of Literature and the Fine Arts,* published in Boston, Mass. in 1851.

The present head of the firm, John G. Murray, told me in 1981 that those involved were, in fact, the poet Coleridge and *his* publishers, Longmans. But when I asked for evidence in 1988, he could only say that, 'I have satisfied myself that it was not Byron.' The copy of Byron's Bible which exists has no such comment in it. He also drew my attention to the fact that, in Byron's day, publishers were more usually called booksellers.

Mencken, on the other hand, gives Thomas Campbell (1777-1844) as the probable perpetrator, and so does Benham. Certainly, Campbell seemed to take the required attitude. At a literary dinner he once toasted Napoleon with the words, 'We must not forget that he once shot a bookseller.'

In 1978, Brian Masters wrote a biography of the novelist Marie

Corelli which, no doubt for very good reasons, he called *Now Barabbas was a Rotter* (the novel *Barabbas* was Corelli's first success).

The simple *Now Barabbas . . .* was used as the title of a film about prisoners (UK 1949), based on a play by William Douglas-Home, but it was also known as *Now Barabbas was a Robber*.

BASINGSTOKE

In the Gilbert and Sullivan opera *Ruddigore* (1887), the character Mad Margaret says:

> When I am lying awake at night, and the pale moonlight streams through the latticed casement, strange fancies crowd upon my poor mad brain, and I sometimes think that if we could hit upon some word for you to use whenever I am about to relapse – some word that teems with hidden meaning – like 'Basingstoke' – it might recall me to my saner self.

The mention of this place still raises a laugh, being one of those English names which, from sound alone, is irresistibly funny. Others would include Chipping Sodbury, Godalming, Scunthorpe, Wigan and Surbiton. More recently, Neasden has joined this select band.

However, I was first alerted by a correspondent to the modest Hampshire town having another claim upon the laughter of the original *Ruddigore* audience. He said he'd vaguely heard that the Tory party had recently held its annual conference there.

Ian Bradley in his *Annotated Gilbert and Sullivan: 2* (1984) makes no mention of this theory, however. He dismisses a suggestion that it was because Basingstoke had a well-known mental hospital, on the grounds that this had not been built in 1887. He relays another theory that W. S. Gilbert's father had featured the town in his novel *The Doctor of Beauvoir*, and that his father and sister lived in Salisbury which would have necessitated his passing through Basingstoke when paying visits.

A magazine called *Figaro*, reporting on rehearsals for *Ruddigore* in December 1886, made mention of a character called Mad Margaret 'with that blessed word Barnstaple' – which suggests that Basingstoke was not Gilbert's first choice.

Basingstoke had already rated a mention in Shakespeare (*The Second Part of King Henry IV*, II.i.169), but with rather less comic result.

We knocked the BASTARD off!

Sir Edmund Hillary (*b.* 1919), the New Zealand explorer and mountaineer, was, with his Sherpa guide Tenzing Norgay, the first person to reach the summit of Mount Everest in 1953. Various accounts have been given as to what his first words were on descending from the summit and rejoining his fellow climbers. Here is the version from his autobiography *Nothing Venture, Nothing Win* (1975):

> George [Lowe] met us with a mug of soup just above camp, and seeing his stalwart frame and cheerful face reminded me how fond of him I was. My comment was not specially prepared for public consumption but for George . . . 'Well, we knocked the bastard off!' I told him and he nodded with pleasure . . . 'Thought you must have!'

Every soldier has the BATON of a field-marshal in his knapsack

This is the anglicized form of saying usually attributed to Napoleon I (1769–1821). The earliest French version (E. Blaze, *La Vie Militaire sous l'Empire*) has it thus: '*Tout soldat français porte dans sa giberne le bâton de maréchal de France*', which was turned into English in 1840 as, 'Every French soldier carries in his cartridge-pouch the baton of a marshal of France'. The meaning is: 'Even the lowliest soldier may have leadership potential'.

Mencken ascribes it to Louis XVIII (1755-1824).

If you can't BEAT 'em, join 'em

A familiar saying, probably American in origin in the alternative form, 'If you can't lick 'em, join 'em'. The earliest citation in the *CODP* is from Quentin Reynolds, the American writer, in 1941. Mencken had it in his dictionary, however, by 1942.

William Safire in *Safire's Political Dictionary* (1978) calls it

> . . . a frequent bit of advice, origin obscure, given in areas dominated by one (political) party . . . The phrase, akin to the Scottish proverb 'Better bend than break', carries no connotation of surrender; it is used to indicate that the way to take over the opposition's strength is to adopt their positions and platform.

ODCIE (1985) takes in a broader view of the phrase's use: 'If a rival faction, political party, business firm, foreign power, etc. continues to be more successful than one's own, it is better to go over to their side and get what advantages one can from the alliance.'

The BEAT Generation

The *Guardian* for 4 April 1988 announced in an obituary: 'Although a novelist, poet and lecturer at many universities, John Clellon Holmes was chiefly known for giving the Beat Generation its name. The phrase first appeared in his 1952 novel *Go*.' The headline to the piece (by W. J. Weatherby) was, 'The naming of a generation'.

Well, this came as news to those of us who had believed until then that Jack Kerouac (1922-69) was not only the presiding genius of that phenomenon of the 1950s, but had really put the name to it. Indeed, in *The Origins of the Beat Generation*, Kerouac admitted to borrowing the phrase from a broken-down drug addict called Herbert Huncke.

Turning to Randy Nelson's *The Almanac of American Letters* (1981), we may discover a description of the moment of coinage. He reports Kerouac as saying:

> John Clellon Holmes . . . and I were sitting around trying to think up the meaning of the Lost Generation and the subsequent existentialism and I said, 'You know, this is really a beat generation': and he lept up and said, 'That's it, that's right'.

Holmes actually attributed the phrase directly to Kerouac in the *New York Times* magazine of 16 November 1952.

When I put these versions to William J. Weatherby in New York, he replied:

> I based my comment on what Holmes told me close to the end of his life. It's possible his memory was shadowed by then or he had oversimplified the past, but the majority view seems to be he fathered the phrase or at least it emerged in a conversation in which he was involved. I don't believe Kerouac himself thought it up or even cared much for it.

BECAUSE it's there

The mountaineer George Leigh Mallory (*b.* 1886) disappeared in 1924 on his last attempt to scale Mount Everest. The previous year, during a lecture tour of the USA, he had frequently been asked why he wanted to achieve this goal. On one such occasion, he replied: 'Because it's there.'

In 1911, at Cambridge, A. C. Benson had urged Mallory to read Carlyle's life of John Sterling – a book that achieved high quality simply 'by being *there*'. Perhaps that is how the construction entered Mallory's mind. On the other hand, Tom Holzel and

Audrey Salkeld in *The Mystery of Mallory and Irvine* (1986) suggest that 'the four most famous words in mountaineering' may have been invented for the climber by a reporter named Benson in the *New York Times* (18 March 1923). A report in the *Observer* (2 November 1986) notes that Howard Somervell, one of Mallory's climbing colleagues in the 1924 expedition, declared 40 years later that the 'much-quoted remark' had always given him a 'shiver down the spine – it doesn't smell of George Mallory one bit'. Mallory's niece, Mrs B. M. Newton Dunn, claimed in a letter to the *Daily Telegraph* (11 November 1986) that the mountaineer had once given the reply to his sister (Mrs Newton Dunn's mother) 'because a silly question deserves a silly answer'.

The saying has become a catchphrase in situations where the speaker wishes to dismiss an impossible question about motives and also to express his acceptance of a challenge that is in some way daunting or maybe foolish. In September 1962, President John F. Kennedy said:

> We choose to go to the moon in this decade, and do the other things, not because they are easy but because they are hard; because that goal will serve to organize and measure the best of our energies and skills . . . Many years ago the great British explorer George Mallory, who was to die on Mount Everest, was asked why did he want to climb it, and he said, 'Because it is there.' Well, space is there, and . . . the moon and the planets are there, and new hopes for knowledge and peace are there.

There have been many variations (and misattributions). Sir Edmund Hillary repeated it regarding his own attempt upon Everest in 1953. Richard Ingrams of *Private Eye* once invented for the Duke of Edinburgh a reply to the question why had he married Queen Elizabeth: 'Because she was there.'

And so to BED
Samuel Pepys's famous signing-off line for his diary entries occurs first on 15 January 1660. However, on that occasion, they are not quite his last words. He writes: 'I went to supper, and after that to make an end of this week's notes in this book, and so to bed.' Then he adds: 'It being a cold day and a great snow, my physic did not work so well as it should have done.'

Usually, the phrase is the last thing he writes, though sometimes he just puts, 'So to bed'. The fame of the phrase 'And so to bed' is in part due to its use as the title of a play by J. B.

Fagan (dating from the late 1920s) which was then turned into a musical.

Both Mencken and Bartlett give the date of its first appearance as 22 July 1660 (where the phrase in fact, is just 'So to bed'); the *ODQ* has 20 April 1660. The reason for this confusion is that these books may have been dealing with incomplete or inaccurate transcriptions of Pepys's shorthand which were superseded by the Latham/Matthews edition of 1970-83.

Indeed, the first time I read the diaries – in an old Dent's Everyman's Library edition (1906, revised 1953) – I was more than a little surprised that the full phrase 'And so to bed' was *nowhere* to be found. It couldn't have been excised on the grounds of taste, could it?

In Britain in 1988 there is a furnishing company which has taken the name And So To Bed.

It is perhaps the end of the BEGINNING
See **end.**

BELIEVE only half of what you see and nothing that you hear
I first heard this piece of advice from an Anglican clergyman (and former padre in the Western Desert) at a confirmation class in 1958.

Mencken finds a much earlier quotation in *A Woman's Thoughts* by Dinah Mulock Craik (1858), where it is already described as a 'cynical saying, and yet less bitter than at first appears'.

As such, it builds upon the simpler 'Don't believe all you hear' which *CODP* finds in some form before 1300, perhaps even as a proverb of King Alfred the Great.

BELL, Book and Candle
As in the title of John Van Druten's play (1950, filmed 1958) about a publisher who discovers his girlfriend is a witch, this refers to a solemn form of excommunication from the Roman Catholic Church. Bartlett says the ceremony has been current since the eighth century AD. There is a version dating from 1200 AD which goes, 'Do to the book [meaning, close it], quench the candle, ring the bell.' These actions symbolize the spiritual darkness the person is condemned to when denied further participation in the sacraments of the church.

Sir Thomas Malory in *Le Morte d'Arthur* (1485) has, 'I shall curse you with book and bell and candle.' Shakespeare has the modern configuration in *King John* (III.ii.22): 'Bell, book and candle shall not drive me back.'

Ich bin ein BERLINER

On 26 June 1963, President John F. Kennedy paid a visit to West Berlin and gave an address to a large and enthusiastic crowd outside the City Hall. He had rejected State Department drafts for his speech and found something better of his own to say: 'Two thousand years ago the proudest boast was *"Civis Romanus sum*[1]*"*. Today, in the world of freedom, the proudest boast is *Ich bin ein Berliner.'* He concluded: 'All free men, wherever they may live, are citizens of Berlin, and, therefore, as a free man, I take pride in the words *"Ich bin ein Berliner".'*

Stirring words, and it only detracts from them slightly to know that the President need only have said, '*Ich bin Berliner'* to convey the meaning, 'I am a Berliner'. It could be argued that the *'ein'* adds drama because he is saying not 'I was born and bred in Berlin' or 'I live in Berlin' but 'I am one of you'. But by saying what he did, he drew attention to the fact that in Germany *'ein Berliner'* is a doughnut!

In July 1978, when President Jimmy Carter was due to go to West Germany and wanted to come up with a slogan equally ringing, one of his aides (allegedly Gerald Rafshoon) impishly suggested he should perhaps go instead to Frankfurt and say . . .

Accidents will happen in the BEST-REGULATED families
See **accidents.**

He is no BETTER, he is much the same
See **electric.**

I would try to get BETWEEN them

During the First World War, the writer Lytton Strachey (1880-1932) appeared before a military tribunal to put his case as a conscientious objector. He was asked by the chairman what, in view of his beliefs, he would do if he saw a German soldier trying to violate his sister. With an air of noble virtue, the homosexual Strachey replied, 'I would try to get between them.'

---

[1]'I am a Roman citizen' – from Cicero's oration against Verres, *c.* 60 BC.

A correspondent suggests that it was much more likely that Strachey would have said something more grandiloquent – 'I would interpose my body', or some such – but the source for this anecdote is Robert Graves in *Goodbye To All That* (1929) and his version is the one given above.

To play BILLIARDS well is the sign of a misspent youth

Under Herbert Spencer (1820-1903), the *ODQ* has: 'It was remarked to me by the late Mr Charles Roupell . . . that to play billiards was the sign of an ill-spent youth.'

On the other hand, in the archives of the Savile Club in London it is recorded that Robert Louis Stevenson, who was a member from 1874 to 1894, propounded to Herbert Spencer that 'proficiency in this game [note: probably billiards, because it was said in the Savile billiards room] is a sign of a misspent youth' (mentioned in 'Words', *Observer*, 4 May 1986).

Other clubs also claim the honour. Other people would supply the word 'snooker' or 'bridge' instead of 'billiards'.

A keen billiards player, Herber Spencer was displeased when the saying kept being ascribed to him in newspapers. He had quoted it from someone else. Spencer dictated a denial to Dr David Duncan, who edited his *Life and Letters* (1908). Benham notes that a similar expression had earlier appeared in *Noctes Ambrosianae* in March 1827.

The BIRDS of the Air

This phrase – used, for example, by Alice Thomas Ellis as the title of a novel in 1980 – is essentially biblical: e.g., Matthew 8:20 ('the foxes have holes, and the birds of the air have nests'). However, it makes a later notable appearance in the rhyme 'Who Killed Cock Robin?' (first recorded in the eighteenth century):

> All the birds of the air
> Fell a-sighing and a-sobbing,
> When they heard the bell toll
> For poor Cock Robin.

A variant is 'fowl(s) of the air' (Genesis 1:26), though this appears much more commonly as 'fowls of the heavens' in (mostly) the Old Testament.

The 'fish(es) of the sea' occurs at least three times in the Old Testament (e.g., Genesis 1:26). 'All the beasts of the forest' is biblical, too (Psalms 104:20), though the much more common version is 'beasts of the field' (e.g., Psalms 8:7).

No BLADE of Grass

This was the title of a pretty forgettable film made in England during 1970, starrring Nigel Davenport and Jean Wallace, and directed by Ms Wallace's husband, none other than Cornel Wilde. The most to be said for the production is that it was quickly aboard the ecology band-wagon with a story of world-wide food shortages brought about by industrial pollution. I know all this because I played a small (uncredited) part in it as a television newscaster bringing word of fresh calamities.

I should have asked Cornel Wilde where he found the title at the time, as I've been wondering about it ever since. The film was based on a book by John Christoper called *The Death of Grass* (1956).

After many years' worrying, I came across this on the last page but one of Agatha Christie's *Autobiography* (1977, but written in 1965): 'There was no scrap of garden anywhere. All was asphalt. No blade of grass showed green – which seemed to confirm that the film title hadn't just been a one-off, would-be-poetic affair.

Of course, it is not a terribly exceptional thing to say. A former girlfriend of the critic, Ken Tynan, quoted in *The Life of Kenneth Tynan* by Kathleen Tynan (1987), states: 'I felt there was nothing about the country in Ken at all. Not a blade of grass . . .'.

The nearest the Bible gets is Isaiah 15:6: 'The grass faileth, there is no green thing.'

To date the only other precise use of the phrase I have found is in a 1902 citation of an old Turkish proverb in *ODP*: 'Where the hoof of the Turkish horse treads, no blade of grass ever grows.'

The BLAND leading the bland

'They be blind leaders of the blind. And if the blind lead the blind, both shall fall into the ditch' – Matthew 15:4. This famous observation from the gospels seems to cry out to be tampered with. And so it has been. I incorrectly believed that Kenneth Tynan (1927-80) had said about Sir Ralph Richardson that, in a certain play, he was guilty of being 'the bland leading the bland'. Not so, as I am reminded by Kathleen Tynan's *Life of Kenneth Tynan* (1987). Her husband had in fact been talking of the *New Yorker* magazine which he had been about to join as drama critic in 1958. He told a journalist before leaving England, 'They say the *New Yorker* is the bland leading the bland. I don't know if I'm bland enough.'

What Tynan did say about Ralph Richardson on one occasion

was, 'What is the word for that voice? Something between bland and grandiose: blandiose, perhaps' (in a review of *Flowering Cherry* in the *Observer*, 1957).

Come to think of it, the 'bland leading the bland' sounds just the sort of thing Dorothy Parker might have said about the *New Yorker* in her later years. Perhaps Tynan was quoting her. He had done so before. For example, it was she who first said 'Verlaine was always chasing Rimbauds . . .', which he purloined in his very early days as a (schoolboy) critic.

BLOOD, toil, tears and sweat

In his classic speech to the House of Commons on 13 May 1940, upon becoming Prime Minister, Winston Churchill said: 'I would say to the House, as I said to those who have joined this Government: I have nothing to offer but blood, toil, tears and sweat.'

In my *Sayings*, I looked at the echoes of Churchill's own and other people's speeches in this famous remark. Here, I would only draw attention to the difficulty people seem to have in getting the order of the words right. The natural inclination is to put 'blood', 'sweat' and 'tears' together, as did Byron in 1823 with 'blood, sweat and tear-wrung millions', and as did the Canadian/American rock group Blood Sweat and Tears in the late 1960s and 1970s.

Indeed, right from the word go people misremembered Churchill's precise order: Joan Wyndham in *Love Lessons – A Wartime Diary* (1985) concludes her entry for 13 May 1940 with, 'Later we listened to a very stirring speech by Churchill about "blood, toil, sweat and tears".' I have a slight suspicion that this diary may have been 'improved' somewhat in the editing, but not, obviously, to the point of imposing accuracy.

It's worse than a crime, it's a BLUNDER!

See **worse**.

Someone had BLUNDERED

The Charge of the Light Brigade at Balaclava, near Sebastopol, took place on 25 October 1854, during the Crimean War. Owing to a misunderstood order, 247 officers and men out of 637 were killed or wounded. Tennyson's famous poem about it was published in the *Examiner* newspaper on 9 December that same year. The second stanza ran:

> 'Forward the Light Brigade!'
> Was there a man dismay'd?
> Not tho' the soldier knew
> Someone had blundered.
> Their's not to make reply,
> Their's not to reason why,
> Their's but to do and die:
> Into the valley of Death
> Rode the six hundred.

According to Christopher Ricks's edition of the poems, Tennyson wrote it on 2 December 'in a few minutes, after reading . . . *The Times* in which occurred the phrase *someone had blundered*, and this was the origin of the metre of his poem.'

In fact, *The Times* had spoken rather (in a leader on 13 November) of 'some hideous blunder'. Advised to be careful because controversy would offend the War Office, Tennyson allowed the 'someone had blundered' line to be deleted when his next collection of poems was published (*Maud, and Other Poems*, 1855). When he heard that the Society for the Propagation of the Gospel intended to circulate this *revised* poem to the troops, he had copies of the uncut version printed and sent to the Crimea. A surviving copy of this rare edition of one thousand was sold privately for around £18,000 in 1987 (*source: Guardian* 24 June).

Of Human BONDAGE
See **human.**

BOOKS Do Furnish a Room
Books Do Furnish A Room is the title of the tenth volume in Anthony Powell's novel sequence, *A Dance to the Music of Time.* According to the blurb on the dust-jacket of the first edition in 1971,

> The scene is London during the two or three years after the second world war. The book's title is taken to some extent from the nickname of one of the characters, Books-do-furnish-a-room Bagshaw, all-purpose journalist and amateur of revolutionary theory, but the phrase also suggests an aspect of the rather bleak post-war period – London's literary world finding its feet again.

As with many nicknames, the reason for it is not precise. According to the novel:

> One asserted that, the worse for drink, trying to abstract a copy of *The Golden Treasury* from a large glass-fronted bookcase in order to verify a quotation required for a radio programme, Bagshaw overturned on himself this massive piece of furniture. As volume after volume descended on him, it was asserted he made the comment: 'Books do furnish a room.'

The other story was that Bagshaw had uttered these words, stark naked,

> . . . as he approached the sofa on which lay . . . the wife of a well-known dramatic critic . . . a clandestine meeting having reached emotional climax in her husband's book-lined study. Bagshaw was alleged to have spoken the words . . . a revolutionary's tribute to bourgeois values – as he rapidly advanced towards his prey.

The notion of books being looked upon as furniture – and the consequent taunt to people who regard them as such – is an old one, however. Lady Holland in her *Memoir* (1855) quotes the Revd Sidney Smith as joking, 'No furniture so charming as books'. And Edward Young (1683-1765) in the *Love of Fame: The Universal Passion* (Satire II, 57-66) (1725-28) has:

> With what, O Codrus! is thy fancy smit?
> The flow'r of learning, and the bloom of wit.
> Thy gaudy shelves with crimson bindings glow,
> And Epictetus is a perfect beau.
> How fit for thee, bound up in crimson too,
> Gilt, and like them, devoted to the view!
> Thy books are furniture. Methinks 'tis hard
> That science should be purchased by the yard,
> And Tonson, turned upholsterer, send home
> The gilded leather to fit up thy room.

A lie travels round the world while truth is putting on her BOOTS
See **lie.**

Lonely are the BRAVE
See **lonely.**

BRITONS never, never, never will be slaves
Of the several recordings of the famous patriotic song 'Rule, Britannia' few can match that by Cilla Black (on PCS 7103).

I suspect it was recorded when Swinging London was at its height and the Union Jack began to appear on everything from articles of clothing to tea-mugs. Anyway, what she is heard to sing is:

> Rule, Britannia,
> Britannia rules the waves;
> Britons never, never, never
> Shall be slaves.

Now, the words for what is now known as 'Rule, Britannia' were written by James Thomson (1700-48) for *Alfred: a Masque* (1740). (There was another author called Mallet, but Thomson is thought to have written this bit.) The music was by Dr Thomas Arne. Thomson's words, in their original form, are these (my italics):

> When Britain first, at Heaven's command,
> Arose from out the azure main,
> This was the charter of the land,
> And guardian angels sung this strain:
>   'Rule, Britannia, *rule* the waves;
>   Britons never *will* be slaves.'

Of course, Cilla Black is not alone in preferring to sing 'rules' and 'shall'. Annually, at the Last Night of the Proms, several hundred other people can be heard singing her version – and drowning out those who may feel like sticking to Thomson.

There is a difference, however, between a poetic exhortation – 'rule' – and a boastful assertion in – 'rules'. As for the difference between will/shall, life is really too short to allow one to go on about that at any length at all. But an interesting defence of the Cilla Black reading comes from Kingsley Amis and James Cochrane in *The Great British Songbook* (1986): 'When what a poet or lyric-writer wrote differs from what is habitually sung, we have generally preferred the latter . . . Britons never 'shall' be slaves here, not 'will' as James Thomson, a Scot following Scottish usage, naturally had them.'

Et tu, BRUTE?
See *et*.

Nasty, BRUTISH and short
Thomas Hobbes (1588-1679) wrote *Leviathan, or the Matter, Form, and Power of a Commonwealth, Ecclesiastical and Civil* in 1651. It is a treatise of political philosophy in which Hobbes sees man not as a social being but as a selfish creature. The state of nature

in which he resides is one in which there are, 'No arts; no letters; no society; and which is worst of all, continual fear and danger of violent death; and the life of man, solitary, poor, nasty, brutish, and short' (Chapter 13).

The last portion of this bleak view has almost become a cliché, as Philip Howard, literary editor of *The Times* noted on 15 August 1984. He warned of the danger that, 'We become so fond of hackneyed quotation that we trot it out, without thinking, at every opportunity.' He gave, as his example, 'the one about the life of man being "solitary, poor, nasty, brutish and short," just to let everybody know that I am an intellectual sort of chap who reads Hobbes in the bath.'

Curiously, later that year, on 1 November, when *The Times* came to give a first leader on the assassination of Mrs Indira Gandhi, it began by observing that world leaders know all too sickeningly well 'the continual fear and danger of violent death' that Thomas Hobbes identified as a condition of man. And added: 'With that awful daily awareness, now goes for some a reminder of his definition of life as nasty, brutish and short.'

Just fancy that.

They BURIED him among the kings
The 'Unknown Warrior' was buried in Westminster Abbey on Armistice Day 1920. On the tombstone, set into the floor of the nave, is an inscription, written by Dean Ryle, concluding with the words, 'They buried him among the kings because he had done good toward God and toward his house.'

This is based on 2 Chronicles 24:16 (concerning Jehoida, a 130-year-old man): 'And they buried him in the city of David among the kings, because he had done good in Israel, both toward God, and toward his house.'

The idea of such a burial first came to a chaplain at the front in 1916 after he had seen a grave in a back garden in Armentières, at the head of which was a rough wooden cross and the pencilled words, 'An unknown British Soldier'.

The American 'Unknown Soldier' was buried on 11 November 1921 at Arlington National Cemetry and lies under the inscription: 'Here Rests in Honored Glory an American Soldier Known But to God'.

Over the graves of most of the unknown dead, in Europe, had been put the simple inscription: 'A Soldier of the Great War Known unto God'.

CABBAGES and Kings

In 1979, I had to find a title for a television version of my radio quiz *Quote . . . Unquote*. It was felt that a new title was needed to distinguish it from the original, and the ITV company in question, Granada, did not wish to be seen adopting yet another idea which had originated in BBC Radio.

Somewhere near the bottom of my list of suggestions was 'Cabbages and Kings', and that, inevitably, was the one chosen. Its virtue was that it could mean that the programme was about everything or nothing. As such it was a clear reference to the passage in Lewis Carroll's 'Walrus and the Carpenter' episode in Chapter 4 of *Through the Looking Glass and What Alice Found There* (1871):

> 'The time has come,' the Walrus said,
>   'To talk of many thing:
> Of shoes – and ships – and sealing-wax –
>   Of cabbages and kings . . .'

By the end of the fourth series, the quiz which had started off being about quotations seemed to have lived up to its new title only too well and was now about any old thing.

This is how the phrase 'cabbages and kings' is occasionally used in other contexts. Apart from which it makes a handy title. Earlier than mine, there was a children's TV series with the title. The American writer O. Henry also took it for his first collection of short stories published in 1904. And there is a book *Of Kennedys and Kings: Making Sense of the Sixties* by Harris Wofford (1980).

The words of the original verse – the most quoted of the whole poem – are typical Carrollian nonsense but the last two lines gain direction through alliteration. But I wonder if there was more to the bringing together of 'cabbages' and 'kings' than that?

For me, the passage echoes Shakespeare's *King Richard II* (III.ii.145) in which the about-to-be-deposed king says:

> Let's talk of graves, of worms, and epitaphs . . .
> Let's choose executors and talk of wills . . .
> For God's sake let us sit upon the ground
> And tell sad stories of the death of kings.

However, the conjunction of 'cabbages' and 'kings' pre-dates Carroll. In Hesketh Pearson's *Smith of Smiths,* a biography of the Revd Sydney Smith (1771-1845), he quotes Smith as saying about a certain Mrs George Groce: 'She had innumerable hobbies, among them horticulture and democracy, defined by Sydney as "the most approved methods of growing cabbages and destroying kings".'

Could the Revd C. L. Dodgson (Lewis Carroll) have encountered this comment by his fellow clergyman? Were they both alluding to some other source which escapes me? Whatever the case, it may be observed that both cabbages and kings do, of course, tend to get their heads cut off.

She sits among the CABBAGES and peas
See **peas.**

CAESAR's wife must be above suspicion
See **wife.**

Let them eat CAKE
This remark is commonly ascribed to Marie-Antoinette (1755-93), an Austrian disliked by the French people, after she had arrived in France to marry King Louis XVI in 1770. More specifically, she is supposed to have said it during the bread shortage of 1789, although no evidence exists.

The saying is to be found in Book Six of Rousseau's *Confessions,* published posthumously (1781-88) but written during the 1760s. Rousseau's version, referring to an incident in Grenoble about 1740, goes: 'At length I recollected the thoughtless saying of a great princess who, on being informed that the country people had no bread, replied, "Let them eat cake".' (*'Qu'ils mangent de la brioche.'*)

ODQ notes that Louis XVIII in his *Relation d'un Voyage à Bruxelles et à Coblentz en 1791* (published 1823) attributes to Marie-Thérèse

(1638-83), wife of Louis XIV, 'Why don't they eat pastry?' ('*Que ne mangent-ils de la croûte de pâté?*')

Burnam adds that Alphone Karr, writing in 1843, recorded that a Duchess of Tuscany had said it in 1760 or before. Later, it was circulated to discredit Marie-Antoinette.

Similar remarks are said to date back to the thirteenth century, so if Marie-Antoinette did ever say it, she was quoting.

CAKES and Ale
'Life isn't all cakes and ale', or so goes the expression, rather as one might say it isn't all 'beer and skittles'. 'Cakes and ale' becomes a synonym for enjoyment. However, when W. Somerset Maugham called his 1930 novel *Cakes and Ale* he was more likely to be alluding to Sir Toby Belch's famous remark to Malvolio in *Twelfth Night*: 'Does thou think, because thou art virtuous, there shall be no more cakes and ale?' (II.iii.114). Maugham's novel is about a barmaid once married to a man who has since turned into the Grand Old Man of English letters.

The Arden edition of *Twelfth Night* comments that cakes and ale were 'traditionally associated with festivity, and disliked by Puritans both on this account and because of their association with weddings, saints' days, and holy-days'. (The only other occasion Shakespeare links the two is in *King Henry VIII*, as 'ale and cakes').

One of my laws of quotation is that however sure you are that you have attributed a quotation correctly, an earlier source will be pointed out to you. I once had a letter telling me that the phrase 'cakes and ale' occurs in a papyrus dated *c.* 1,000-90 BC: 'Grant ye cakes and ale and oxen and feathered fowl to Osiris.' I rather suspect Maugham was unaware of this, though you can't go much further back than that.

Oh! CALCUTTA!
See **oh!**

CAST a cold eye on death
See **death.**

First CATCH your hare
See **first.**

Things fall apart; the CENTRE cannot hold
Of all the quotations used by and about politicians, the most commonly used by far in recent years in Britain has to be the lines from 'The Second Coming' (1921) by W. B. Yeats:

> Things fall apart; the centre cannot hold;
> Mere anarchy is loosed upon the world . . .
> The best lack all conviction, while the worst
> Are full of passionate intensity.

The trend was probably started by Roy Jenkins in his Dimbleby Lecture of 23 November 1979 (which pointed towards the setting up of the centrist Social Democratic Party). In the *Listener* of 14 December 1979, Professor Bernard Crick threatened to horse-whip the next politician who quoted the poem. On the very next page, Neil Kinnock (later to become Labour Party leader) could be found doing so. The threat has had no lasting effect, either.

CHARIOTS of Fire
The title of the film (1981) about the inner drives of two athletes in the 1924 Olympics presumably derives from William Blake's poem 'Milton' (more usually called 'Jerusalem'):

> Bring me my bow of burning gold,
> Bring me my arrows of desire
> Bring me my spear! Oh, clouds unfold
> Bring me my chariot of fire.

Note the singular form. 'Chariots of fire' in the plural does occur in 2 Kings 6:17.

CHEER up! The worst is yet to come
See **worst.**

Underneath the spreading CHESTNUT tree
See **underneath.**

Give us a CHILD until it is seven, and it is ours for life
See **give.**

CHILDE Roland to the Dark Tower came
Who wrote this? Well, working backwards, Robert Browning wrote a poem with this title which concludes with the lines:

> Dauntless the slug-horn to my lips I set,
> And blew. *'Childe Roland to the Dark Tower came.'*

He was no doubt aware that Edgar in Shakespeare's *King Lear* (III.iv.179), mouthing snatches of verse in his assumed madness, says:

> Child Rowland to the dark tower came,
> His word was still *Fie, foh, and fum,*
> I smell the blood of a British man.

So, even Shakespeare was quoting a line from an older ballad (a 'child' was a candidate for knighthood). In certain Scottish ballads of uncertain date, Childe Roland is the son of King Arthur who rescues his sister from a castle to which she has been abducted by fairies. In the *Chanson de Roland* (French, twelfth century) and other tellings of the legend, he is the nephew of Charlemagne.

Shakespeare probably combined material from two completely different sources – the first line from a ballad about Roland, the second two from the old story of Jack the Giant-killer.

CHILDREN of a Lesser God

The title of Marc Medoff's play about the relationship between a deaf girl and a speech therapist (produced on Broadway 1979, filmed 1986) has puzzled many people. It alludes to, rather than quotes, a passage from Tennyson's *Idylls of the King* (1859-85):

> For why is all around us here
> As if some lesser god had made the world,
> But had not force to shape it as he would.
> 'The Passing of Arthur' (lines 13-15)

Medoff's suggestion, presumably, is that people with a disability like deafness could be said to be the work of a 'lesser god'.

Never work with CHILDREN or animals

This is a well-known piece of show business lore, from American vaudeville originally, I should think. Phyllis Hartnoll, in *Plays and Players* (1985), has, 'W. C. Fields is quoted as saying, "Never act with animals or children".' Although this line reflects his known views, I suspect the attribution may result from confusion with 'Any man who hates dogs and babies can't be all bad' (which he didn't say either: it was said by Leo Rosten *about* him at a dinner in 1939).

Another version of the saying is contained in Noel Coward's remark about the child actress Bonnie Langford who appeared along with a horse in a West End musical version of *Gone With the Wind* in 1972. Inevitably, there came the moment when the horse messed up the stage. Coward said: 'If they'd stuffed the child's head up the horse's arse, they would have solved two problems at once.'

The CHURCH of England is the Tory party at prayer

This is a description often attributed to Benjamin Disraeli. However, Robert Blake, the historian and author of *Disraeli* (1966) told the *Observer* (14 April 1985) that he could not say who said it, and that correspondence in *The Times* some years before had failed to find an answer.

According to Robert Stewart's *Dictionary of Political Quotations*, Agnes Maude Royden (1876-1956), the social reformer and preacher, said in an address at the City Temple, London, in 1917: 'The Church should no longer be satisfied to represent only the Conservative Party at prayer.'

This sounds rather as though it is alluding to an already-established image, but it is the best we can do so far.

In 1986, Kingsley Amis remarked in a radio programme that, 'People talk about the Church of England being the Tory Party at prayer; the *Daily Telegraph* is often the Tory Party half-asleep.'

A woman is only a woman, but a good CIGAR is a Smoke

See **woman.**

We have not here a lasting CITY

I had a request from a listener in Ireland wanting to know the 'author of the following quotation and the title of the book or poem, if any, in which it appeared'. The quote was, 'We have not here a lasting city.'

At first glance it was not a very notable saying, but that has never stopped one from appealing to somebody somewhere. The solution, however, is interesting, if only because it reminds us that there are more translations of the Bible than we may care to think, and more ways of expressing the simplest thought than we might think possible.

It was soon spotted that it was probably a version of Hebrew 13:14, which goes (in the Authorized Version), 'For here have we no continuing city, but we seek one to come [i.e., heaven].'

The Revised Version says, 'For we have not here an abiding city'; the Good News Bible says, 'For there is no permanent city for us here on earth'; the Jerusalem has, 'For there is no eternal city for us in this life'; the New English Bible, 'For we have no permanent home.'

For good measure, I looked it up in the New International Bible, kindly placed by my hotel bed. Its version was, 'For here we do not have an enduring city, but we are looking for the city that is to come.'

Relaying this bundle of information back to the original questioner, I soon heard from him that he had now found *his* version in the Douai-Rheims Bible (1609): 'For we have not here a lasting city, but we seek one that is to come.' ('Lasting city' also occurs in the Revised Standard Version.)

Next day I happened to be reading Chapter 3 of Churchill's *History of the English-Speaking Peoples* (Vol. 1) in which he quoted the verse, in the Authorized Version, of course. In T. S. Eliot's *Murder in the Cathedral* (1937) we find the line: 'Here is no continuing city, here is no abiding stay.'

A shining CITY on a hill

Ronald Reagan often used the image of a shining city on a hill to describe America as a land of security and success. A writer in the *Observer* (8 March 1987) recalled him using it as early as 1976 when he had just lost the Republican nomination to Gerald Ford. He told his supporters he would be back, they would win in the end, and once again America would be a 'shining city on a hill'.

He used it particularly during his bid for re-election as President in 1984. At the Democratic Convention, New York Governor Mario Cuomo remarked that a shining city might be what Reagan saw 'from the veranda of his ranch' but he failed to see despair in the slums. 'There is despair, Mr President, in the faces that you don't see, in the places that you don't visit in your shining city . . . This nation is more a tale of two cities than it is just a shining city on a hill.'

Reagan, in so far as he ever 'quoted' anybody, was quoting Governor Winthrop of the Massachussetts Bay Colony. Talking to new settlers in 1630, Winthrop said: 'We shall be as a city upon a hill, the eyes of all people are upon us.' It was meant as a warning as much as a promise. He didn't use the word 'shining'.

If anything, the image is biblical. Matthew 5:14 has 'A city that is set on a hill cannot be hid . . . Let your light so shine before men that they may see your good works'; the 'holy hill' of Zion is a 'sunny mountain' according to one etymology; New Jerusalem was the jewelled city lit by the glory of God, in Revelation (information from a letter to the *Observer* from Alan MacColl, University of Aberdeen, 15 March 1987).

The Sound of Two Hands CLAPPING

A collection of Kenneth Tynan's critical writings was published with this title in 1975. It derives from a Zen koan: 'We know the sound of two hands clapping. But what is the sound of one hand clapping?'

This koan (a riddle used in Zen to teach the inadequacy of logical reasoning) is said to appear as the epigraph to J. D. Salinger's *For Esmé – with Love and Squalor* (1953), though not in my edition.

Too CLEVER by half

To say that someone is 'too clever by half' is to show that you think they are more clever than wise, and are overreaching themselves. As such, this is a fairly common idiom. However, the most notable political use of the phrase was by the fifth Marquess of Salisbury (1893-1972), a prominent British Conservative, about another such, Iain Macleod. In a speech to the House of Lords in 1961, he said:

> The present Colonial Secretary has been too clever by half. I believe he is a very fine bridge player. It is not considered immoral, or even bad form to outwit one's opponents at bridge. It almost seems to me as if the Colonial Secretary, when he abandoned the sphere of bridge for the sphere of politics, brought his bridge technique with him.

The third Marquess of Salisbury anticipated him in a debate on the Irish Church Resolutions in the House of Commons on 30 March 1868, when he said of his leader, Disraeli's, amendment: 'I know that with a certain number of Gentlemen on this side of the House this Amendment is popular. I have heard it spoken of as being very clever. It is clever, Sir; it is too clever by half.'

Rodney Ackland's version of an Alexander Ostrovsky play was presented as *Too Clever by Half* at the Old Vic, London, in 1988. Previously, the Russian title had been translated as *The Diary of a Scoundrel* and *Even the Wise Can Err, Even a Wise Man Stumbles* and *Enough Stupidity in Every Wise Man.*

Of Dr Jonathan Miller, the polymath, in the mid-1970s, it was said, 'He's too clever by three-quarters.'

Forever poised between a CLICHÉ and an indiscretion

I don't know whether this is an old expression or not. The first use I have come across is by Harold Macmillan. He was quoted in *Newsweek* (30 April 1956) as saying that his life as Foreign Secretary was 'forever poised between a cliché and an indiscretion'.

It surfaced again in 1981 when Robert Runcie, Archbishop of Canterbury, was quoted in *The Times* (14 July 1981) on discussions he had had with the Prince and Princess of Wales prior to marrying them. 'My advice', he said, 'was delicately poised between the cliché and the indiscretion.'

CLOSE your eyes and think of England

The source that Partridge/Catchphrases gives for this saying – in the sense of advice to women when confronted with the inevitability of sexual intercourse, or jocularly about doing almost anything unpalatable – is the *Journal* (1912) of Alice, Lady Hillingdon: 'I am happy now that Charles calls on my bedchamber less frequently than of old. As it is, I now endure but two calls a week and when I hear his steps outside my door I lie down on my bed, close my eyes, open my legs and think of England.'

There *was* an Alice, Lady Hillingdon (1857-1940). She married the second baron in 1886. He was Conservative MP for West Kent (1885-92) and, according to *Who's Who* owned 'about 4,500 acres' when he died (in 1919). A portrait of Lady Hillingdon was painted by Sir Frank Dicksee PRA in 1904. I believe a rose may have been named after her.

But where her journals are, if they were ever indeed published, I have not been able to discover.

Salome Dear, Not With a Porcupine (ed. Arthur Marshall, 1982) has it instead that the newly wedded Mrs Stanley Baldwin is supposed to have declared: 'I shut my eyes tight and thought of the Empire.' I think we may discount Bob Chieger's assumption in *Was It Good for You, Too?* (1983) that 'Close your eyes and think of England' was advice given to Queen Victoria on her wedding night.

I went to New Zealand but it was CLOSED
see **New Zealand.**

A damn CLOSE-RUN thing

As with most of the first Duke of Wellington's alleged remarks, this wasn't quite what he said, but it is how it is remembered.

What he told the memoirist Thomas Creevey (on 18 June 1815) about the outcome of the Battle of Waterloo, was: 'It has been a damned serious business. Blucher and I have lost 30,000 men. It has been a damned nice thing – the nearest run thing you ever saw in your life.'

The *Creevey Papers*, in which this account appears, were not published until 1903. Somehow, out of this description, a conflated version arose, with someone else presumably supplying the 'close-run'.

COLLAPSE of stout party

This is a catchphrase that one might use as the tag line to a story about the humbling of a pompous person. It has long been associated with the magazine *Punch* and was thought to have occurred in those wordy captions that used to be given to the cartoons. But, as Ronald Pearsall explains in his book called *Collapse of Stout Party* (1975): 'To many people Victorian wit and humour is summed up by *Punch* when every joke is supposed to end with "Collapse of Stout Party", though this phrase tends to be as elusive as "Elementary, my dear Watson" in the Sherlock Holmes sagas.'

At least the *OED Supp.* has managed to find a reference to a 'stout party' in the caption to a cartoon in the edition of *Punch* dated 25 August 1855.

COMFORT the afflicted, and afflict the comfortable

This is a good example of a quotation formula which can be applied to more than one subject, to the extent that it is difficult to say that it was originally applied to.

However, Mencken (1942) has 'Anon.' saying, 'The duty of a newspaper is to comfort the afflicted and afflict the comfortable' – and I think that newspapers were the original subject of the remark.

In the film *Inherit the Wind* (1960), Gene Kelly gets to say to Fredric March: 'Mr Brady, it's the duty of a newspaper to comfort the afflicted and to flick the comfortable.'

To Michael Ramsey, the former Archbishop of Canterbury, I have heard *this* version attributed: 'The duty of the church is to comfort the disturbed and to disturb the comfortable.'

COMIN' in on a Wing and a Prayer

A popular American song of the Second World War (published in 1943) took its title from an alleged remark by a pilot who was coming in to land with a badly damaged plane. Harold Adamson's lyrics included the lines:

> Tho' there's one motor gone, we can still carry on
> Comin' In On A Wing And A Pray'r.

So rapidly had the phrase gained hold that by 1944 an American film about life on an aircraft carrier could be called simply *Wing and a Prayer*.

The COMMANDING heights of the economy

In a speech to the Labour Party conference in November 1959, Aneurin Bevan said: 'Yesterday, Barbara [Castle] quoted from a speech which I made some years ago, and she said that I believed that Socialism in the context of modern society meant the conquest of the commanding heights of the economy . . .'.

Hugh Gaitskell, the party leader, quoted the same phrase, apparently, but no one has been able to find Bevan's original coinage, least of all his most recent biographer, John Campbell.

Alan Watkins, in a throwaway line in his *Observer* column (28 September 1987), said 'the phrase was originally Lenin's'.

A COMMITTEE should consist of three men, two of whom are absent

Committees have come in for a good deal of ribbing from the phrase-makers. The above remark is attributed to Lord Mancroft (*d.* 1987) in some anthologies, but I notice in Hesketh Pearson's 1956 life of Sir Herbert Beerbohm Tree that he attributes it to the great actor-manager. The *Treasury of Humorous Quotations* (1951) has E. V. Lucas (1868-1938) saying, 'The best committee is a committee of two when one is absent.' *A Treasury of Humorous Quotations* (1969) has Hendrik Van Loon saying, 'Nothing is ever accomplished by a committee unless it consists of three members, one of whom happens to be sick and the other absent.' All of which just goes to show how hard it is keeping a good joke out of other people's mouths.

To J. B. Hughes is attributed the remark, 'If Moses had been a committee the Israelites would still be in Egypt'. (Or, 'never would have got across the Red Sea' in a remark attributed [1965] to the late General Booth, founder of the Salvation Army.)

The anonymous observation, 'A camel is a horse designed by a committee' (quoted, for example, in American *Vogue*, 1958) bears an interesting resemblance, surely to Lichtenburger's 'A donkey is a horse translated into Dutch.'

John Le Carré included in his *Tinker, Tailor, Soldier, Spy* (1974), the observation, 'A committee is an animal with four back legs.' Anon. said: 'A committee of one gets things done.'

If you don't become a COMMUNIST by the time you're twenty . . .

A number of people have asked me if I know of a saying to the effect, 'If you don't vote Socialist/Communist before you're twenty, you have no heart; if you do vote Socialist/Communist after you're twenty, you have no head.' Winston Churchill, inevitably, was put forward as a probable source.

The nearest I have come is to find Will Durant, the American teacher, philosopher, historian (*b.* 1885) saying, 'There is nothing in Socialism that a little age or a little money will not cure.' And Bennett Cerf in *Try and Stop Me* (1944) attributes this to Georges Clemenceau, on hearing his son had joined the Communist Party: 'My son is twenty-two years old. If he had not become a Communist at twenty-two, I would have disowned him. If he is still a Communist at thirty, I will do it then.'

Clemenceau, like Churchill, has had many remarks fathered on him that he didn't make, but this is probably the best source we are likely to get.

England and America, two COUNTRIES separated by a common language

This is a saying that interests a lot of people. Was it Shaw or Wilde who said it, they ask? Well, in Wilde's *The Canterville Ghost* (1887) he wrote: 'We have really everything in common with America nowadays except, of course, language.'

The 1951 *Treasury of Humorous Quotations* (Esar & Bentley), however, quotes Shaw as saying, 'England and America are two countries separated by the same language', without giving a source. Where in all Shaw's vast outpourings is one going to find out whether he said it or not? Or, like so much else, has it just been fathered upon him?

A radio talk prepared by Dylan Thomas shortly before his death (and published after it in the *Listener*, April 1954), contained an observation about European writers and scholars in America 'up against the barrier of a common language'.

Another COUNTRY
See **another.**

COUNTRY matters
A much-praised TV drama series dating from 1972 used this umbrella title over an anthology of stories by H. E. Bates and A. E. Coppard, linked only by their setting in the English countryside. I assume the producers knew what they were doing using a phrase from *Hamlet* in this way. At III.ii.115, we find the following:

> HAMLET: Lady, shall I lie in your lap?
> OPHELIA: No, my lord.
> HAMLET: I mean, my head upon your lap.
> OPHELIA: Ay, my lord.
> HAMLET: Do you think I meant country matters?
> OPHELIA: I think nothing, my lord.
> HAMLET: That's a fair thought to lie between maids' legs.

Shakespeare's bawdy is sometimes obscure, but few can miss that 'country matters' means physical love-making, or fail to note the pun in the first syllable.

Crucify mankind upon a CROSS of gold
See **gold.**

CROWN Imperial
Sir William Walton's march 'Crown Imperial' was composed for the coronation of King George VI in 1936, his march 'Orb and Sceptre' for that of Queen Elizabeth II in 1953. I heard him say in a television interview that if he lived to write a march for a third coronation it would be called 'Sword and Mace'. The key to these titles lies in a passage from Shakespeare's *King Henry V* (IV.i.266). The king says, ''Tis not the balm, the sceptre and the ball,/ The sword, the mace, the crown imperial/ . . . That beats upon the high shore of this world.'

Oddly enough, the orchestral parts of 'Crown Imperial' bear a different quotation: 'In beauty bearing the crown imperial' – William Dunbar.

The CUP that cheers

This usually means tea, in preference to alcohol. In William Cowper's *The Task* (1783), it's in the plural:

> Now stir the fire, and close the shutters fast,
> Let fall the curtains, wheel the sofa round,
> And, while the bubbling and loud-hissing urn
> Throws up a steamy column, and the cups,
> That cheer but not inebriate, wait on each,
> So let us welcome peaceful ev'ning in.
> 　　　　　　　　　　　　　　'The Winter Evening'

Partridge lists 'cups that cheer but not inebriate' as a cliché in his dictionary of same, and notes that in *Siris* (1744), Bishop Berkeley had earlier said of tar water that it had a nature 'so mild and benign and proportioned to the human constitution, as to warm without heating, to cheer but not inebriate'.

Took some CURDS to show you the whey

One of my most treasured moments from the radio is when a foreign correspondent, referring to the Kurdish autonomy movement in northern Iran, *c.* 1980, said, 'There is the danger of civil war if the Kurds don't get their way.'

This only goes to confirm one theory about the roots of humour, that people don't make up jokes, the jokes are there in the English language waiting to be let out. Ronald Pearsall, in his survey of Victorian humour, *Collapse of Stout Party* (1975), relates that the joke was alive and well a hundred years ago:

> In New College common room Walter Thursby, don and explorer, related how he had scaled Mount Ararat. The snow was not so bad as expected, he explained, but because of marauding tribes a guard of Kurdish soldiers had been provided. Later Arthur Riding went up to him and commented: 'I understand you took some Curds with you to show the whey'.

Ring down the CURTAIN, the farce is over

The last words of Ruggiero Leoncavallo's opera *I Pagliacci* ('The Clowns') (1892) are, famously, '*La commedia è finita*' – 'the comedy is finished'.

According to Motteux's life of François Rabelais (*c.* 1494-1547), the writer's alleged last words were, '*Tirez le rideau, la farce est jouée*' – 'Ring down the curtain, the farce is played'. This has been disputed on the grounds that there is no contemporary evidence of him having said it. However, Motteux lived from 1660 to 1718 which, if nothing else, predates Leoncavallo.

A host of golden DAFFODILS

In her journal for 15 April 1802, Dorothy Wordsworth described a windy walk she had taken from Eusemere with her brother, the poet William. They encountered a huge number of daffodils. She wrote:

> We saw that there was a long belt of them along the shore, about the breadth of a country turnpike road. I never saw daffodils so beautiful. They grew among the mossy stones about and about them; some rested their heads upon these stones as on a pillow for weariness; and the rest tossed and reeled and danced, and seemed as if they verily laughed with the wind, that blew upon them over the lake; they looked so gay, ever glancing, ever changing.

It is interesting that William's poem 'The Daffodils' makes direct use of phrases from this description, though always enhancing them. Dorothy's 'a long belt of them' becomes 'a crowd, a host'; her 'tossed and reeled and danced' becomes 'tossing their heads in sprightly dance'.

This is not to suggest that William in any way 'stole' his ideas from Dorothy's diary. She jotted down descriptions which he used more than once as a reminder of experiences he wrote about in his poetry. Colette Clark, in her comparison of the poems with the journal in *Home at Grasmere* (1960), asks:

> Was it Dorothy or William who first spoke the phrases which seem so spontaneous in the Journal and then reappear in the poems? Sometimes we know it to be Dorothy . . . Such a lively chronicle close at hand would have been irresistible to any poet, and William seems to have used it again and again. It was not until two years later after that heavenly walk from Eusemere that he wrote 'The Daffodils', but there is no doubt that he first re-read Dorothy's account, and tried to recapture the joy and delight of her description in his own poem.

A DANCE to the Music of Time

This is the title of Anthony Powell's novel sequence (published 1951-75) giving a panoramic view of post-war Britain. In the first novel, *A Question of Upbringing*, the narrator, Nicolas Jenkins, looking at workmen round a bucket of coke in falling snow, is put in mind of the painting with this title by Nicolas Poussin (1594-1665) which hangs in the Wallace Collection in London:

> For some reason, the sight of snow descending on fire always makes me think of the ancient world . . . and something in the physical attitudes of the men themselves as they turned from the fire, suddenly suggested Poussin's scene in which the Seasons, hand in hand and facing outwards, tread in rhythm to the notes of the lyre that the winged and naked greybeard plays. The image of Time brought thoughts of mortality: of human beings, facing outward like the Seasons, moving hand in hand in intricate measure: stepping slowly, methodically, sometimes a trifle awkwardly, in evolutions that take recognizable shape: or breaking into seemingly meaningless gyrations, while partners disappear only to reappear again, once more giving pattern to the spectacle; unable to control the melody, unable perhaps, to control the steps of the dance.

A perfect image to provide a title for a twelve-novel sequence. One is never quite sure, though, whether a painter himself has given a title to a work or whether it has been applied subsequently. Powell uses the title as at the Wallace Collection but in books on Poussin it is sometimes given, less interestingly, as merely 'The Dance of Human Life' or, as in Italian, *'Ballo della vita humana'*.

Thirty is a DANGEROUS Age, Cynthia
See **thirty**.

And when they ask us how DANGEROUS it was
See **ask**.

It was a DARK and stormy night

As a scene-setting, opening phrase, this appears to have been irresistible to more than one story-teller and has now become a joke. It was used in all seriousness by the English novelist Edward Bulwer-Lytton (1803-73) at the start of *Paul Clifford* (1830):

> It was a dark and stormy night, the rain falling in torrents – except at occasional intervals, when it was checked by a violent gust of wind which swept up the streets and then (for it is in London that our scene lies), rattling along the housetops, and fiercely agitating the scanty flames of the lamps that struggled against the darkness.

Stephen Leacock, the Canadian humorist (1869-1944), went for something similar to start his *Gertrude the Governess* (1911): 'It was a wild and stormy night on the West Coast of Scotland. This, however, is immaterial to the present story as the scene is not laid in the West of Scotland.'

At some stage, the phrase became part of a children's joke game – 'The tale without an end'. Iona and Peter Opie in *The Lore and Language of Schoolchildren* (1959) describe the workings thus:

> The tale usually begins: 'It was a dark and stormy night, and the Captain said to the Bo'sun, "Bo'sun, tell us a story," so the Bo'sun began . . .'. Or it may be: 'It was a dark and stormy night, the rain came down in torrents, there were brigands on the mountains, and thieves, and the chief said unto Antonio: "Antonio, tell us a story." And Antonio, in fear and dread of the mighty chief, began his story: "It was a dark and stormy night, the rain came down in torrents, there were brigands on the mountains, and thieves . . .' ". And such is any child's readiness to hear a good story that the tale may be told three times round before the listeners appreciate that they are being diddled.

The Opies noted that each of these variations was also current in the USA, 'except that in the first tale American children say: "It was a dark and stormy night, some Indians were sitting around the camp fire when their chief rose and said . . .'.

Presumably with knowledge of this game – if not of Bulwer-Lytton's mighty line – Charles M. Schultz (*b.* 1922), the creator of the Peanuts syndicated cartoon, gave the line to Snoopy in his doomed attempts to write the Great American Novel. Consequently, the dog is acclaimed as author of the world's greatest one-line novel. Schultz's own book *It Was a Dark and Stormy Night* was a bestseller.

The culmination of all this has been the annual Bulwer-Lytton Fiction Contest, founded by Dr Scott Rice, a professor of English literature at San Jose State University, California. Contestants are asked to compose truly atrocious opening sentences to hypothetical bad novels. Rice was quoted in *Time* (21 February 1983) as saying, 'We want the kind of writing that makes readers say, "Don't go on".' Some of the entries have now been published in book form – with the authors given every inducement not to keep on writing . . .

The opening words of Agatha Christie's thriller *Murder on the Links* are: 'I believe that a well-known anecdote exists to the effect that a young writer, determined to make the commencement of his story forcible and original enough to catch the attention of the most blasé of editors, penned the first sentence: "'Hell!' said the Duchess".'

DARK night of the soul

The phrase *'La Noche oscura del alma'* was used as the title of a work in Spanish by St John of the Cross (1542-91). This was a treatise based on his poem 'Songs of the Soul Which Rejoices at Having Reached Union with God by the Road of Spiritual Negation' (*c.* 1578).

By the twentieth century, the phrase, defined by the *OED Supp.* as 'a period of spiritual aridity suffered by a mystic' has come to mean, almost ironically, a period of mental and spiritual suffering prior to some big step. In *The Crack-up* (1936), F. Scott Fitzgerald wrote: 'In a real dark night of the soul it is always three o'clock in the morning, day after day.'

The DARLING of the Halls

Sir George Robey, the British music hall comedian, was often known as 'the Darling of the Halls'. This appellation derived from the possibly apocryphal exchange between the lawyer F. E. Smith (1872-1930) (later Lord Birkenhead) and a judge. In the way judges have of affecting to be ignorant of popular culture ('And who are the Beatles?' is a more modern equivalent), the judge asked who George Robey was and Smith replied: 'Mr George Robey is the Darling of the Music Halls, m'lud.' This gains added sense when you know that the judge was Mr Justice Darling.

Hold Back the DAWN

See **hold.**

Go ahead, make my DAY

Almost a catchphrase of the mid-1980s. In March 1985, President Ronald Reagan told the American Business Conference, 'I have my veto pen drawn and ready for any tax increase that Congress might even think of sending up. And I have only one thing to say to the tax increasers. Go ahead – make my day.'

For once, he was not quoting from one of his own film roles, or old Hollywood. The laconicism was originally spoken by Clint Eastwood, himself brandishing a .44 Magnum, to a gunman he was holding at bay in *Sudden Impact* (1983). At the end of the film he says (to another villain, similarly armed), 'Come on, make my day.' In neither case does he add 'punk', as is sometimes supposed.

The phrase may have been eased into Reagan's speech by having appeared in a parody of the New York *Post* in the autumn of 1984, put together by editors, many of them anti-Reagan. He was shown starting a nuclear war by throwing down this dare to the Kremlin (information from *Time*, 25 March 1985).

Our DAY will come

This is the English translation of the Provisional IRA slogan, in Gaelic *'Tiocfaidh Ar La'*. Relatives of those accused of trying to blow up the British Prime Minister at Brighton in 1984 shouted it out as the defendants were being sentenced in court on 23 June 1986.

That the English translation was the title of a song performed by the American vocal group Ruby and the Romantics in 1963 may only be coincidence. This is not to be confused with the older song, 'We Shall Overcome', which carries similar sentiment.

DEAD! . . . and never called me mother!

This line is recalled as typical of the three-volume sentimental Victorian novel, yet nowhere does it appear in Mrs Henry Wood's *East Lynne* (1861) where it is supposed to have originated. Nevertheless, it was inserted in one of the numerous stage versions of the novel (that by T. A. Palmer in 1874) which were made between publication and the end of the century. Mrs Wood's obituary writer noted in 1887:

> At present, there are three dramatic versions of *East Lynne* nightly presented in various parts of the world. Had the author been granted even a small percentage of the returns she would have been a rich woman . . . The adapters of *East Lynne* grew rich and Mrs Henry Wood was kept out of their calculations.

Thus did *East Lynne* become 'a synonym for bad theatrical melodrama' (Colin Shindler, *Listener*, 23-30 December 1982).

The line arises in a scene when an errant but penitent mother, who has returned to East Lynne, her former home, in the guise of a governess, has to watch the slow death of her eight-year-old-son (Little Willie) unable to reveal her true identity. Whether the line was carried through to any of the various film versions of the tale, I do not know, but expect so.

DEAD as a doornail

In the Middle Ages doors were strengthened and decorated with iron nails, so if anyone was looking for a suitable metaphor for 'totally lifeless', 'dead as a doornail' (given the alliteration) would be a logical choice (Robert L. Shook, *The Book of Why*, 1983). Or, the door-nail was the knob on which the knocker struck: 'As this is frequently knocked on the head, it cannot be supposed to have much life in it' (Brewer).

The phrase occurs as early as 1350, then in 1362 in Langland's *Piers Plowman* ('And ded as a door-nayl'). Shakespeare uses it a couple of times, in the usual form and, as in *The Second Part of King Henry IV* (V.iii.117):

> FALSTAFF: What, is the old king dead!
> PISTOL: As nail in door!

Dickens uses the phrase in *A Christmas Carol* (Stave i), 'Old Marley was as dead as a door-nail.'

He being DEAD yet speaketh

The Revd Francis Kilvert (1840-79) was an Anglican curate at Langley Burrell in Wiltshire, then at Clyro near the Welsh border. He was then vicar of Saint Harmon and moved to Bredwardine two years before his early death.

As such he would now be completely forgotten but for the diary which he kept from 1870 to his death. First, having been well pruned by his widow (he died a month or so after their marriage), selections from the diary were published in 1938-40. They are exceptionally well written, and a classic of their kind.

How appropriate, therefore, that the inscription on his grave at Bredwardine (chosen, presumably, by his widow, not knowing how apt it was to be for a posthumously published diarist) is: 'He being dead yet speaketh', from Hebrews 11:4.

Cast a cold eye on DEATH

The epitaph on the grave of W. B. Yeats in Drumcliff churchyard, Co. Sligo, Ireland, is:

> Cast a cold Eye
>   On Life, on Death.
> Horseman, pass by!
>
> W. B. YEATS
> June 13th 1865
> January 28th 1939

The inscription was chosen by Yeats himself. It, and his place of burial, were described in his poem, 'Under Ben Bulben', written on 4 September 1939, a year before his death. (Ben Bulben is the mountain above Drumcliff.)

> Under bare Ben Bulben's head
> In Drumcliff churchyard Yeats is laid . . .
> On limestone quarried near the spot
> By his command these words are cut:
>
> *Cast a cold eye, etc.*

In fact, Yeats died in France and his remains were not brought back for burial at the designated spot until 1948.

DEATH is nothing at all

The following passage by Henry Scott Holland is often read at funerals and, judging by the number of people who have asked me for copies of it, the words have a message of valued comfort for many who are bereaved:

> Death is nothing at all. I have only slipped away into the next room. I am I and you are you. Whatever we were to each other, that we are still. Call me by my old familiar name, speak to me in the easy way which you always used. Put no difference into your tone; wear no forced air of solemnity or sorrow. Laugh as we always laughed at the little jokes we enjoyed together. Play, smile, think of me, pray for me. Let my name be ever the household word that it always was. Let it be spoken without effect, without the ghost of a shadow on it. Life means all that it ever meant. It is the same as it ever was; there is absolutely unbroken continuity. What is this death but a negligible accident? Why should I be out of mind because I am out of sight? I am but waiting for you, for an interval, somewhere very near, just around the corner. All is well.

Scott Holland (1847-1918) was an editor of the magazines *Commonwealth* and *Miracles,* a canon of St Paul's Cathedral, noted for his sermons (some of which were published), and Regius Professor of Divinity at Oxford. I have not been able to find out how the words have come to be used at so many funerals, nor in what part of Scott Holland's writings they are to be found. One suggestion is that they come from a letter he directed to be read after his own death.

As far as I know, the version given above is the complete one; certainly there is no more in the illustrated text published by Souvenir Press in 1987.

Now Bach is DECOMPOSING

In the archaeology of humour one is never really going to know who first cracked a joke. Nevertheless, as one can date it, why not allow W. S. Gilbert to claim credit for originating this famous exchange? On a visit to the United States with Arthur Sullivan in 1879-80, Gilbert was told by a matron at a dinner party, 'Your friend Mr Sullivan's music is really too delightful. It reminds me so much of dear Baytch [Bach]. Do tell me: what is Baytch doing just now? Is he still composing?'

'Well, no, madam,' Gilbert returned, 'Just now, as a matter of fact, dear Baytch is by way of decomposing.'

This, at any rate, is how the joke appears in *Gilbert and Sullivan* by Hesketh Pearson (1947).

DECUS et tutamen

When the British pound note began to be replaced with a pound coin (from 21 April 1983), users noticed at once that on the rim was the inscription *'Decus et tutamen'*. The same inscription, suggested by John Evelyn the diarist had occurred on the rim of a Charles II crown of 1662-3 – the purpose then was as a safeguard against clipping.

In 1983, the inscription was translated as 'an ornament and a safeguard' – which is fair enough, though it was pointed out that the original line of Virgil from which it was taken, went: *Decus et tutamen in armis'*. The object so described in the *Aeneid* (Book 5) was a coat of mail which Aeneas gave to one of his ships' captains for coming second in a race. This has been translated as 'a glory and defence in war' – suitable no doubt for a coat of mail, but hardly for a coin. But then it was explained that the inscription itself, rather than the coin, was the 'ornament and the safeguard', if it prevented clipping and looked well. And so it does, and so it is.

No good DEED goes unpunished
See **good.**

So DEEP is the night

For those like myself who are permanently alert to the use of quotations wherever they occur, the titles of romantic and historical fiction – and some non-fiction, too – are a perpetual torment. Often, though not always, the would-be poetry of the title is not the quotation it pretends to be.

I am thinking of songs like 'So Deep is the Night' which, despite being based on Chopin's 'Etude in E Major', Op. 10, No. 3, has a title that appears to be the creation of the lyric-writer Sonny Miller. His song was first featured in the 1940 film *Hear My Song,* though originally Mario Melfi's setting appears to have had French words.

Then again, there are novels like *On a Far Wild Shore* (1987) (whose title I am assured by Malcolm Macdonald, the writer in question, is all his own work) and TV serials like the one about the English Civil War *By the Sword Divided* (1983-85). That is not a quotation either, so far as I can tell.

See elsewhere in this book about: '**Across** the River and Into the Trees'; '**All** This and Heaven Too'; '**Another** heart and Other Pulses'; '**England,** my England'; 'Tell **England';** 'The True **Glory';** 'The **Heart** is a Lonely Hunter'; '**Hold** Back the Dawn'; 'A **Horseman** Riding By'; 'Of **Human** Bondage'; '**Journey's** End'; 'I **Know** Where I'm Going'; '**Lonely** are the Brave'; 'The **Longest** Pleasure'; '**Love** Is a Many-Splendoured Thing'; 'The **Moon** and Sixpence'; 'Nor the **Moon** By Night'; 'There Shall be No **Night';** 'The **Night** Has a Thousand Eyes'; '**None** But the Lonely Heart'; '**Random** Harvest'; 'The **Razor's** Edge'; '**Reap** the Wild Wind'; 'One More **River';** 'To **Serve** Them All My Days'; 'One Brief **Shining** Moment'; 'The **Singer** Not the Song'; 'The **Stars** Look Down'; 'Not as a **Stranger';** 'The **Sun** Also Rises'; **Tender** is the Night'; 'Now **Voyager';** 'The **Way** to the Stars'.

We are not interested in the possibility of DEFEAT

During one week of the South African war in December 1899 – 'Black Week', as it came to be called – British forces suffered a series of setbacks in their fight against the Boers. Queen Victoria 'braced the nation in words which have become justly famous' (W. S. Churchill, *A History of the English-Speaking Peoples,* Vol. 4). 'Please understand', she told A. J. Balfour, who was in charge of the Foreign Office, 'that there is no one depressed in *this* house. We are not interested in the possibilities of defeat. They do not exist.'

Margaret Thatcher quoted these words in her first television interview during the Falklands campaign (5 April 1982). 'Do you remember what Queen Victoria once said? "Failure – the possibilities do not exist". That is the way we must look at it. I'm not talking about failure. I am talking about supreme confidence in the British fleet, superlative troops, excellent equipment.' So she was reported in *Time* (19 April 1982), though she might have been surprised to find the quote being attributed directly to her by *Time* in December of that year.

Quiet calm DELIBERATION disentangles every knot
See **quiet.**

Après nous le DÉLUGE
The Marquise de Pomadour's celebrated remark to Louis XV was made on 5 November 1757 after Frederick the Great had defeated the French and Austrian armies at the Battle of Rossbach. Bartlett notes that this 'reputed reply' by Louis XV's mistress was recorded by three authorities, though a fourth gives it to the king himself. Bartlett then claims the saying was not original anyway, but 'an old French proverb'. I have no confirmation of this.

However, the *ODP* has as an English proverb, 'After us the deluge', deriving from Mme de Pompadour. Its only citation is Burnaby's 1876 *Ride to Khiva:* 'Our rulers did not trouble their heads much about the matter. "India will last my time . . . and after me the Deluge".'

Make the DESERTS bloom
The modern state of Israel has made this injunction come true, but it 'dates from Bible times', according to Daniel J. Boorstin in *The Image* (1960). Adlai Stevenson also alluded to the phrase in a speech at Hartford, Connecticut (18 September 1952): 'Man has wrested from nature the power to make the world a desert or to make the deserts bloom.'

The exact phrase does not appear in the Authorized Version, though Isaiah 35:1 has, 'The desert shall rejoice, and blossom as the rose', and 51:3 has, 'For the Lord shall comfort Zion . . . and he will make . . . her desert like the garden of the Lord'.

Cruden's *Concordance* (1737) points out: 'In the Bible this word [desert] means a deserted place, wilderness, not desert in the modern usage of the term.'

DESPERATE diseases require desperate remedies
Commonly ascribed to Guy Fawkes on 6 November 1605 (on his arrest the day after attempting to blow up the Houses of Parliament), 'A desperate disease requires a dangerous remedy' *(DNB)* was apparently said by him to King James I, one of his

intended victims. King James asked if he did not regret his proposed attack on the royal family. Fawkes replied that one of his objects was to blow the royal family back to Scotland. He was subsequently tried and put to death.

What he said, however, appears to have been a version of an established proverbial saying. In the form, 'Strong disease requireth a strong medicine', *ODP* traces it to 1539. In *Romeo and Juliet* (IV.i.68) *(c.* 1595), there is: 'I do spy a kind of hope,/ Which craves as desperate an execution/ As that which we would prevent' – and Shakespeare also alludes to the saying on two other occasions.

Why must the DEVIL have all the best tunes?

According to E. W. Broome's biography of the Revd Rowland Hill (1744-1833), what he said was, 'I do not see any good reason why the devil should have all the good tunes.' He was referring to Charles Wesley's defence of the practice of setting hymns to the music of popular songs. The phrase is now used generally to rebut the necessity for the virtuous and worthy to be dull and dreary. (This Revd Hill is not to be confused with the Sir Rowland Hill, originator of the English penny postage system.)

A perhaps better known, but later, use of the phrase concerns General Booth, the founder of the Salvation Army. It was his practice to use established tunes to accompany religious lyrics. In this way, over 80 music hall songs acquired religious lyrics. 'Champagne Charlie is My Name', for example, became, 'Bless His Name He Sets Me Free'. When Booth was challenged on the suitability of such a process, he was doubtful at first, but then exclaimed, 'Why should the Devil have all the best tunes!'

DIAMONDS are a Girl's Best Friend

In this form, the remark derives from the title of the Jule Styne and Leo Robin song in the film *Gentlemen Prefer Blondes* (1953). In Anita Loo's novel (1925), upon which the film is based, Lorelei Lee merely says, 'Kissing your hand may make you feel very, very good but a diamond and sapphire bracelet lasts forever.'

We who are about to DIE salute you

'Morituri te salutant' (literally, 'those who . . .) were the words addressed to the emperor by gladiators in ancient Rome on entering the arena. This practice seems to have been first mentioned in Suetonius, *Claudius (c.* 140). In time, the phrase was extended to anyone facing difficulty, and then ironically so.

The DIGNITY of labour

This phrase goes curiously unrecorded in most UK reference books. The *Collins English Dictionary* (1979), gives as an example of the word 'dignity' (meaning 'the stage or quality of being worthy of honour'): *'the dignity of manual labour'*. At the moment, all the Oxford dictionaries ignore it.

Booker T. Washington, the American negro writer, alludes to the idea in *Up from Slavery* (1901): 'No race can prosper till it learns that there is as much dignity in tilling a field as in writing a poem.'

You DIRTY rat!

Although impersonators of James Cagney (1899-1986) always have him saying, 'You dirty rat!' it may be that he never said it like that himself. Not wishing to split hairs, however, I should say that in *Blonde Crazy* (1931) he calls someone a 'dirty, double-crossing rat'.

In Joan Wyndham's war-time diaries *(Love Lessons,* 1985) her entry for 1 October 1940 begins: 'Double bill at the Forum with Rupert. *Elizabeth and Essex,* and a gangster film where somebody actually *did* say "Stool on me would ya, ya doity rat!"'

What film could this have been? Note her surprise that the line was uttered at all. A strange double bill to be watching.

DO what you will
See **fay.**

Mairzy DOATS and dozy doats
See **mairzy.**

If a man bites a DOG, that's news . . .

As a definition of news, this has been variously ascribed. Chiefly, in the form, 'When a dog bites a man, that is not news, because it happens so often. But if a man bites a dog, that is news,' to John B. Bogart, city editor of the New York *Sun,* 1873-90. To Charles A. Dana, the editor of the same paper from 1868 to 1897, it is ascribed in the form, 'If a dog bites a man, it's a story; if a man bites a dog, it's a good story.'

She DONE Him Wrong

When Mae West's play *Diamond Lil* was transferred to the screen in 1933, it was renamed *She Done Him Wrong*. This title must surely allude to the refrain of the famous anonymous American ballad 'Frankie and Johnny' (which Mencken dates *c.* 1875). There are numerous versions (200 is one estimate) and it may be of Negro origin. 'Frankie and Johnnie were lovers' (or husband and wife) but he (Johnnie) does her wrong by going off with other women – 'He was her man, but he done her wrong.' So, to equal the score, Frankie shoots him, and has to be punished for it (in some versions in the electric chair):

> Frankie walked up to the scaffold, as calm as a girl
>   could be,
> She turned her eyes to Heaven and said, 'Good Lord,
>   I'm coming to Thee;
> He was my man, but I done him wrong.'

Bartlett draws a comparison with Shakespeare, *The Rape of Lucrece* (line 1462): 'Lucrece swears he did her wrong.'

So little DONE, so much to do

The gist of what the colonial financier and statesman Cecil Rhodes said before he breathed his last on 26 March 1902 is 'So little done, so much to do', though this is sometimes quoted with the phrases reversed. It was a theme that had obviously preoccupied him towards the end of his life. He said to Lord Rosebery: 'Everything in the world is too short. Life and fame and achievement, everything is too short.'

Tennyson had already anticipated him. *In Memoriam* (1850) has these lines in section lxxiii:

> So many worlds, so much to do,
>   So little done, such things to be.

Compare also Charles Dickens, *Nicholas Nickleby* (1838-9) (Chapter 5):

> There was so much to be done, and so little time to do it in.

The actual last words of Rhodes were much more prosaic: 'Turn me over, Jack.'

Lions led by DONKEYS
See **lions.**

The DOORS of perception
In William Blake's *The Marriage of Heaven and Hell* (*c.* 1790) occurs the thought: 'If the doors of perception [i.e., the senses] were

cleansed, every thing would appear to man as it is, infinite.' This was seized on by proponents of drug culture in the 1960s and from it was derived the name of the US vocal/instrumental group The Doors. Before this, Aldous Huxley had called his 1954 book about his own experiments with mescalin and LSD, *The Doors of Perception*.

If in DOUBT, strike it out

A piece of journalists' lore is 'If in doubt, strike it out' – meaning, if you're not sure of a fact or about the wisdom of including an item of information or opinion, leave it out. It may be that the advice was more specific originally. Mark Twain in *Pudd'nhead Wilson* (1894) says: 'As to the adjective, when in doubt strike it out.'

Compare this with the advice Samuel Johnson quoted from a college tutor (30 April 1773): 'Read over your compositions, and where ever you meet with a passage which you think is particularly fine, strike it out.' Which might be recommended to journalists also.

Another little DRINK wouldn't do us any harm

This boozer's jocular justification of another snort is rather more than a catchphrase. I first became aware of the phrase through the allusion to it made in Edith Sitwell's bizarre lyrics for 'Scotch Rhapsody' in *Façade* (1922):

> There is a hotel at Ostend
> Cold as the wind, without an end,
> Haunted by ghostly poor relations . . .
> And 'Another little drink wouldn't do us any harm,'
> Pierces through the sabbatical calm.

The actual origin is in a song with the title written by Clifford Grey to music by Nat D. Ayer and sung by George Robey in *The Bing Boys Are Here* (1916). This includes a reference to the famous fact that Prime Minister Asquith was at times the worse for drink when on the treasury bench:

> Mr Asquith says in a manner sweet and calm:
> 'And another little drink wouldn't do us any harm.'

The DUSTBIN of history

This is Trotsky's phrase, but quite where he wrote it I have not been able to establish. Was it with reference to the fate of the decrees emanating from Kerensky's provincial government in the Winter Palace in 1917? Or was it about the fate of his opponents (as suggested by E. H. Carr in his *Socialism in One Country* (1958)?

In a similar coinage, Charles Dickens reflected on Sir Robert Peel's death in 1850: 'He was a man of merit who could ill be spared from the Great Dust Heap down at Westminster.' Augustine Birrell, politician and writer (1850-1933), wrote of 'that great dust-heap called "history"' in his essay on Carlyle.

I am DYING, as I have lived, beyond my means

So said Oscar Wilde as he called for champagne when he was approaching death in 1900, but they were not his 'dying words'. He lived for another month. Similarly, his remark about the furnishings in his room, 'This wall paper'll be the death of me – one of us'll have to go' was indeed said by Wilde, but not *in extremis*.

From EACH according to his ability, to each according to his needs

Usually attributed to Karl Marx, but not from *Das Kapital* or *The Communist Manifesto*. The slogan appears in his *Critique of the Gotha Programme* (1875), in which he says that after the workers have taken power, capitalist thinking must first disappear. Only then will the day come when society can 'inscribe on its banners: from each according to his ability, to each according to his needs'.

John Kenneth Galbraith commented in *The Age of Uncertainty* (1977): 'It is possible that these ... twelve words enlisted for Marx more followers than all the hundreds of thousands in the three volumes of *Capital* combined.'

There is some doubt as to whether Marx originated the slogan or whether he was quoting either Louis Blanc, Morelly or M. Bakunin. The latter wrote: 'From each according to his faculties, to each according to his needs' (declaration, 1870, by anarchists on trial after the failure of their uprising in Lyons).

Also, Saint-Simon, the French reformer, had earlier said: 'The task of each be according to his capacity, the wealth of each be according to his works.' And, much earlier, Acts 4:34-35 had: 'Neither was there any among them that lacked: for as many as were possessors of lands or houses sold them, and brought the prices of things that were sold, and laid them down at the apostles' feet: and distribution was made unto every man according as he had need.'

The EAGLE Has Landed

In an author's note at the beginning of his thriller *The Eagle Has*

Landed (1975), Jack Higgins suggests that Heinrich Himmler was informed on 6 November 1943 that, 'the eagle has landed' – meaning that a small force of German paratroopers has safely landed in England in order to kidnap Winston Churchill. Higgins then claims that 'fifty per cent of [this exploit] is documented historical fact. The reader must decide for himself how much of the rest is a matter of speculation, or fiction . . . '.

Well, yes, that's as may be. What I have always doubted is the wisdom of applying to a book 'about' the Second World War a phrase that was well known in a very different sphere. In July 1969, when the lunar module bearing Neil Armstrong touched down for the first ever moon visit, he declared, 'Tranquillity Base here – the Eagle has landed'. ('Eagle' was the name of the craft, referring to the American national symbol.)

He has Van Gogh's EAR for music
See **Van.**

You are what you EAT
This neat encapsulation of a sensible attitude to diet was used as the title of an 'alternative' US film that was first shown in Britain in 1969. Of its content, *Films and Filming* (April 1969) noted: '"You are what you eat," says an old hermit in a fairy-tale-painted wood; a band of blissfully beautiful people hopefully munch flowers in the park.' The BFI's *Monthly Film Bulletin* described the film as, 'A disjointed psychedelic picture of America's hippy revolution . . . The moralising note struck by the title is echoed nowhere else in the film.' In other words, a load of 1960s tosh.

The idea behind the phrase has been around for many a year. Compare Brillat-Savarin in *La Physiologie du goût*: 'Tell me what you eat and I will tell you what you are', and L. A. Feuerbach: 'Man is what he eats (*Der Mensch ist, was er ißt*)' – in a review of Moleschott's *Lehre der Nahrungsmittel für das Volk* (1850). The German film chronicle *Heimat* (1984) included the version, '*Wie der Mensch ißt, so ist er*' ('As a man eats, so he is').

His death has ECLIPSED the gaiety of nations
One of the finest obituary tributes ever penned was Samuel Johnson's lament for his friend, the actor David Garrick who died

in 1779. In his 'Life of Edmund Smith', one of the *Lives of the English Poets* (published the same year), Johnson wrote:

> At this man's table I enjoyed many cheerful and instructive hours . . . with David Garrick, whom I hoped to have gratified with this character of our common friend; but what are the hopes of man! I am disappointed by that stroke of death, which has eclipsed the gaiety of nations, and impoverished the public stock of harmless pleasure.

John Wilkes wasn't so sure and made an 'attack' on the phrase about eclipsing the gaiety of nations. Boswell relayed this to Johnson, who replied: 'I could not have said more nor less, for 'tis truth; "eclipsed," not "extinguished," and his death did eclipse; 'twas like a storm.'

'But why *nations*?' Boswell continued. 'Did his gaiety extend farther than his own nation?' Johnson deftly tossed in the Scots ('if we allow the Scotch to be a nation, and to have gaiety'), but Boswell pressed on, 'Is not *harmless pleasure* very tame?'

To which Johnson replied: 'Nay, Sir, harmless pleasure is the highest praise. Pleasure is a word of dubious import; pleasure is in general dangerous, and pernicious to virtue; to be able therefore to furnish pleasure that is harmless, pleasure pure and unalloyed, is as great a power as men can possess.'

Boswell's initial account of this exchange appears in his journal for 24 April 1779 and appears substantially the same in the *Life of Johnson*.

When Charles Dickens died in 1870, Thomas Carlyle wrote, 'It is an event world-wide, a *unique* of talents suddenly extinct, and has "eclipsed" (we too may say) "the gaiety of nations".'

ECONOMICAL with the truth

In *Why Do We Say . . . ?* I examined Sir Robert Armstrong's famous use of this phrase when, in November 1986, he was being cross-examined, as British Cabinet Secretary, in the Supreme Court of New South Wales. I pointed out that he had made no claim for originality when making the remark and had prefaced it with, 'As one person said . . . '.

In March 1988, (by now) Lord Armstrong said in a TV interview that he had no regrets about using the phrase. And he said again it was not his own, but Edmund Burke's.

To add to the citations, including Burke, Mark Twain and Sir William Strang, mentioned in my earlier book, here are two more:

Arnold Bennet in *These Twain* (1915), Chapter 17:

> The boy was undoubtedly crafty; he could conceal subtle designs under a simple exterior; he was also undoubtedly secretive. The recent changes in his disposition had put Edwin and Hilda on their guard, and every time young George displayed cunning, or economized the truth, or lied, the fear visited them.

Samuel Pepys used the precise phrase in his evidence before the Brooke House Committee in its examination of the Navy Board in 1669-70 (Pepysian MSS. 2874, ff. 388-90).

The commanding heights of the ECONOMY
See **commanding**.

EDINBURGH, the Athens of the North
In one of Tom Stoppard's plays, a character muses on this sobriquet. How would the Athenians feel, he wonders, about being said to live in 'the Edinburgh of the South'?

Calling the Scottish capital either 'Athens of the North' or 'Modern Athens' seems always to have occasioned some slight unease. James Hannay writing 'On Edinburgh' (*c.* 1860), said:

> Pompous the boast, and yet a truth it speaks:
> A Modern Athens – fit for modern Greeks.

The nickname was presumably earned by Edinburgh as a seat of learning, with many long-established educational institutions and a university founded in 1583. When the 'New Town' was constructed in the early 1800s, the city took on a fine classical aspect. As such it might remind spectators of the Greek capital with its ancient reputation for scholastic and artistic achievement.

Brewer notes that Belfast has been called the 'Athens of Ireland', Boston, Mass. the 'Athens of the New World', Cordoba, in Spain, the 'Athens of the West'.

EIGHTY in the shade
This is no more than a catchphrase used to express extreme temperature. However, one notes that it is alluded to comically with regard to age rather than temperature in Gilbert and Sullivan's *The Mikado* (1885). Ko-Ko asks Katisha:

> Are you old enough to marry, do you think?
> Won't you wait till you are eighty in the shade?

There is also a song 'Charming Weather' in *The Arcadians* (1908) with the lines:

> Very, very warm for May
> Eighty in the shade they say,
> Just fancy!

Eighty in the Shade was the title of a play by Clemence Dane (published 1959).

Across the wires the ELECTRIC message came: 'He is no better, he is much the same'

Often quoted as an example of bathos, and of a poet laureate writing to order at his worst, this needs some qualification. No one seems terribly sure that it was ever written. Sir Philip Magnus, in his life of Edward VII (1964), has a slightly different version, anyway. His begins, 'Flash'd from his bed, the electric tidings came . . .' but he suggests it referred to the future king's illness, when still Prince of Wales, in 1871.

If so, this was before Alfred Austin, the supposed author, took up the laureateship in 1896. Rather more likely is it that Austin (who died in 1913) wrote something akin to the lines before becoming laureate and later had them suppressed.

D. B. Wyndham Lewis and Charles Lee, in their noted selection of bad verse, *The Stuffed Owl* (1930), interestingly include the lines as at the top of this entry, but ascribe them to a 'university poet unknown'.

Queen ELIZABETH slept here
See **queen**.

It is perhaps the END of the beginning

In a speech at the Mansion House on 10 November 1942, Winston Churchill spoke of the Battle of Egypt in these terms: 'This is not the end. It is not even the beginning of the end. But it is, perhaps, the end of the beginning.'

This formula seems to have a particular appeal to people, judging by the number of times it has been recalled. One occasion that comes to mind is when Ian Smith, the Rhodesian leader, broadcast a speech containing —or so it seemed at the time – a commitment to majority rule, after Dr Henry Kissinger's shuttle diplomacy in the autumn of 1976.

Note that Talleyrand went only half-way when he said, 'It is the beginning of the end (*Voilà le commencement de la fin*)' either after Napoleon's defeat at Borodino (1812) or during the Hundred Days (20 March-28 June, 1815).

With friends like that who needs ENEMIES?
See **friends.**

My friend's friend is my ENEMY
See **friend.**

The ENEMY within
This phrase – used to describe an internal rather than external threat – has been used in an unusual range of situations. In 1980 Julian Mitchell used it as the title of a play about anorexia, although he tells me he considered it 'an old phrase' then. Indeed, *ODCIE*'s entry suggests that it is a shortened version of 'the enemy/traitor within the gate(s)' – 'one who acts, or is thought to act, against the interests of the family, group, society etc of which he is a member'.

On 22 January 1983, *The Economist* wrote of the industrial relations scene in Britain: 'The government may be trusting that public outrage will increasingly be its ally. Fresh from the Falklands, Mrs Thatcher may even relish a punch-up with the enemy within to enhance her "resolute approach" further.'

Seven months later, Mrs Thatcher was using exactly the same phrase and context regarding the British miners' strike. She 'told Tory MPs that her government had fought the enemy without in the Falklands conflict and now had to face an enemy within . . . she declared that the docks and pit strikers posed as great a threat to democracy as General Galtieri, the deposed Argentine leader' (*Guardian*, 20 July 1984).

The phrase does not appear to have been used, as such, in films and TV – though we have had *The Enemy Below* (1957) and *The Enemy at the Door* (1978). It does not occur in the Bible or Shakespeare.

Close your eyes and think of ENGLAND
See **close.**

Tell ENGLAND
This film (UK 1931) was about Gallipoli, the title being an

apparent concoction. It was based on Ernest Raymond's 1922 novel.

ENGLAND expects that every man will do his duty

At 11.30 a.m. on 21 October 1805, the British fleet approached Napoleon's combined French and Spanish fleets before the Battle of Trafalgar. Admiral Horatio, Lord Nelson told one of his captains, 'I will now amuse the fleet with a signal.' At first, it was to be, 'Nelson confides that every man will do his duty.' But it was suggested that 'England' would be better than 'Nelson'. Flag Lieutenant Pasco then pointed out that the word 'expects' was common enough to be in the signal book, whereas 'confides' would have to be spelt out letter by letter and would require seven flags, not one.

When Admiral Lord Collingwood saw the signal coming from HMS *Victory*, he remarked, 'I wish Nelson would stop signalling, as we all know well enough what we have to do.'

Mencken found an American saying from 1917 – during the First World War – 'England expects every American to do his duty.' In Britain, at about the same time, there was a recruiting slogan: 'England Expects that Every Man will Do His Duty and Join the Army Today'.

The things I've done for ENGLAND

In Sir Alexander Korda's film *The Private Life of Henry VIII* (1933), Charles Laughton as the king is just about to get into bed with one of his many wives when, alluding to her ugliness, he sighs: 'The things I've done for England.' The original screenplay was written by Lajos Biro and Arthur Wimperis.

This became a catchphrase, to be used ironically when confronted with any unpleasant task. In 1979, Prince Charles on a visit to Hong Kong sampled curried snake meat and, with a polite nod towards his ancestor, exclaimed, 'Boy, the things I do for England . . . '.

ENGLAND home and beauty
See **home.**

ENGLAND, my England

When a book of short stories by D. H. Lawrence is known by this title (1922), and A. G. MacDonell's satire on country life is called *England, Their England* (1933), and a book of George Orwell's essays is called *England, Your England* (1953), someone is obviously alluding to something. It is to a poem by W. E. Henley (1849-1903), called 'For England's Sake' (1892):

> What have I done for you,
> England, my England?
> What is there I would not do,
> England, my own?

ENGLISH as she is spoke

This phrase – now a way of referring to the way the language might be spoken by foreigners or the illiterate – comes from an actual 'guide of the conversation in Portuguese and English' published last century. The guilty author was P. Carolino, according to Mencken; A. W. Tuer (1838-1900), according to the *Penguin Dictionary of Quotations* (1960); Andrew White Tuer, according to *A Dictionary of Famous Quotations* (1973).

In *Baldness Be My Friend*, Richard Boston dug out the story. Originally, there was a French-Portuguese phrase-book, *O Novo Guia da Conversacão em frances e portuguez* by José da Fonseca, published in Paris in 1836. The text was in parallel columns. Then, in 1865, a third column, carrying English translations, was added by one Pedro Carolino.

To give you an idea of his excellence as a translator it will only be necessary to quote from a section he cleverly but unwittingly called 'Idiotisms and Proverbs'. It included:

> In the country of blinds, the one-eyed men are kings.
> To do a wink to some body.
> The stone as roll not, heap up not foam.
> After the paunch comes the dance.
> To craunch the marmoset.
> To come back to their muttons.
> He sin in trouble water.

By 1883, the awfulness of this non-joke had become known in London. Publishers Field and Tuer brought out a selection under the title *English as she is Spoke* (a phrase taken from the chapter on 'Familiar Dialogues'). The same year, Mark Twain introduced an edition of the complete work in the USA. That is how we come to have the expression.

All animals are EQUAL

'. . . but some are more equal than others.' George Orwell's slogan from *Animal Farm* (1945), his satire on communist excesses, develops the basic idea of 'all men are equal' in a cynical way. 'All men are created equal and independent,' wrote Thomas Jefferson in the Preamble to the American Declaration of Independence (1776).

Orwell, of course, was not the first to cast doubt on this proposition. According to Hesketh Pearson's biography of Sir Henry Beerbohm Tree, the actor wished to have inserted into a play called *Nero*, produced in 1906, his epigram: 'All men are equal – except myself.'

First among EQUALS
See **first.**

ET tu, Brute?
Julius Caesar's supposed dying words to Brutus, one of his assassins in 44 BC were made famous through Shakespeare's use of the Latin in the form, '*Et tu, Brute?* – Then fall Caesar!'

The Latin words are not found in any classical writer but occur in English drama just before Shakespeare. *The True Tragedie of Richard Duke of Yorke* (printed in 1595) has the line, '*Et tu, Brute,* wilt thou stab Caesar too?'

The origin of the phrase lies probably in Suetonius's account of the assassination, in which Caesar is made to say in *Greek,* 'And thou, my son.' The 'son' has been taken literally – as, according to Suetonius, Caesar had had an intrigue with Brutus's mother and looked upon Brutus as his likely son.

ÉTONNE-moi!
Serge Diaghilev, the Russian ballet impresario, said it to Jean Cocteau, the French writer and designer, in Paris in 1912. Cocteau had complained to Diaghilev that he was not getting enough encouragement and the Russian exhorted him with the words, 'Astound me! I'll wait for you to astound me.'

In Cocteau's journals he comments, 'I was at the absurd age when one thinks oneself a poet, and I sensed in Diaghilev a polite resistance.' When he received the command he felt it was one he could, and should, obey. In due course, he may be said to have done so.

Set EUROPE ablaze
See **ablaze.**

The EVIL Empire
Towards the end of his presidency, Ronald Reagan took a much more accommodating attitude towards the Soviet Union than had ever been predicted of the arch-anti-Soviet. In a speech to the National Association of Evangelicals at Orlando, Florida, on 8 March 1983, he said: 'In your discussions of the nuclear freeze proposals, I urge you to beware the temptation of pride – the temptation blithely to declare yourselves above it all and label both sides equally at fault, to ignore the facts of history and the aggressive impulses of an *evil empire . . .* '

The reason for this startling turn of phrase was made later the same month (23 March) when he first propounded his 'Star Wars' proposal as part of a campaign to win support for his defence budget and arms-control project. The proposal (more properly known by its initials, SDI, for Strategic Defence Initiative) was to extend the nuclear battleground into space.

The President did not use the term 'Star Wars' but it was an inevitable tag to be applied by the media, given his own fondness for adapting lines from the movies. The film *Star Wars* and the sequel *The Empire Strikes Back* had been released in 1977 and 1980, respectively.

As for his view of the Soviet Union, it remained constant until the final shift. In 1964, he had said it was, 'The most evil enemy mankind has ever known in his long climb from the swamp to the stars.'

During his visit to Moscow in June 1988, President Reagan was asked about his 'evil empire' phrase. He replied: 'I was talking about another time, another era.'

Hear no EVIL, see no evil, speak no evil
This well-known phrase is remarkably little documented. Bartlett describes it as a legend related to the Three Wise Monkeys carved over the door of the Sacred Stable, Nikko, Japan in the seventeenth century. The monkeys are represented as having their paws over, respectively, ears, eyes and mouth.

The motto of Yorkshiremen is said to be:

> Hear all, see all, say nowt,
> Aight all, sup all, pay nowt
> And if ever tha does owt for nowt
> Do it for thisen.

Whether this is real folk-poetry, I know not. A Noel Gay song written in 1938 for Sandy Powell, the Yorkshire comedian, has the title, 'Hear all, See all, Say nowt'.

EVIL Under the Sun

The provenance of the title of Agatha Christie's thriller about murder in a holiday hotel (1941, filmed 1982) is not explained in the text, although Hercule Poirot, the detective, remarks before any evil has been committed: 'The sun shines. The sea is blue . . . but there is evil everywhere under the sun.' Shortly afterwards, another character remarks, 'I was interested, M. Poirot, in something you said just now . . . It was almost a quotation from Ecclesiastes . . . "Yea, also the heart of the sons of men is full of evil, and madness is in their heart while they live".'

But Ecclesiastes (which finds everything 'under the sun') gets nearer than that: 'There is a sore evil which I have seen under the sun, namely, riches kept for the owners thereof to their hurt' (5:13); 'There is an evil which I have seen under the sun' (6:1, 10:1).

Were it not for the clue about Ecclesiastes, one might be tempted to think that Christie had once more turned to an old English rhyme for one of her titles. In this one, the phrase appears exactly:

> For every evil under the sun,
> There is a remedy or there is none;
> If there be one, try and find it;
> If there be none, never mind it.

The only thing necessary for the triumph of EVIL
See **nothing.**

Made an EXCURSION to hell and came back glorious

The notion of war being like hell is probably as old as war itself. General Sherman warned, in a speech at Columbus, Ohio (11 August 1880): 'There is many a boy here today who looks on war as all glory, but, boys, it is all hell.'

The notion of going to war/hell and coming back again was most notably summed up in the title *To Hell and Back*, given to the war memoirs of Audie Murphy — 'America's most decorated infantryman' – and the subsequent film (1955).

I recall seeing a cartoon of a couple buying tickets for this film at the cinema box office. The caption was, '. . . And a single for the wife.'

In a 'Postscript to the News' on BBC Radio, 5 June 1940, J. B. Priestley had said of the 'little holiday steamers' used in the evacuation from Dunkirk, '[They] made an excursion to hell and came back glorious.'

My FAIR Lady

I suppose it was understandable that when Lerner and Loewe wished to make a musical out of Shaw's *Pygmalion* they should seek a new title. After all, not even in Shaw's preface (only in his Afterword) does he allude to the relevance of the Greek legend to his story of a Covent Garden flower-girl who was raised up and taught to 'speak proper' just like a Mayfair lady.

Lerner and Loewe turned, it seems, to the refrain of the nursery rhyme (first recorded in the eighteenth century):

> London Bridge is broken down,
> Broken down, broken down,
> London Bridge is broken down,
> My fair lady.

It has also been suggested that they were drawn to the title because 'my fair lady' is how a Cockney flower-seller would pronounce the phrase 'Mayfair lady'.

Accidents will happen in the best-regulated FAMILIES
See **accidents**.

To see you, Mr Shaw, one would think there was a FAMINE in the land

'. . . And looking at you, Mr Chesterton, one would know who to blame.' This celebrated fat man/thin man exchange was the subject of a letter to the *Guardian* from a Mr Robert Turpin of Plymouth (14 May 1985): 'I first heard the story from a great-uncle of mine who knew both Shaw and Chesterton and actually attended the meeting at which the exchange took place.' (If so, the great-uncle was privileged to be one of those rare people to have been present at the cracking of an immortal joke.)

Caution immediately sets in, however – especially as the paper also carried a letter from Peter Black, the journalist, saying he'd first enountered the story in Australia involving the portly Prime Minister, Sir Robert Menzies. The *Penguin Dictionary of Modern Quotations,* meanwhile, had cast Lord Northcliffe, the portly press baron, in the Chesterton role.

I myself would rely on the version that appears in *Thirty Years with GBS* by Blanche Patch, Shaw's secretary, published in 1951: 'One look at you, Mr Shaw, and I know there's famine in the land.'

One look at you, *Mr Hitchcock,* and I know who caused it.'

It is a FAR, far better thing that I do

'. . . than I have ever done; it is a far, far better rest that I go to, than I have ever known.' These words, appearing at the end of *A Tale of Two Cities* (1859) by Charles Dickens are sometimes said to be Sydney Carton's last words as he ascends the scaffold to be guillotined. But he does not actually speak them. They are prefaced with: 'If he had given any utterance to his [last thoughts], and they were prophetic, they would have been these . . .'

One editor refers to this as, 'a complicated excursus into the pluperfect subjunctive'. In dramatizations, however, Carton has often got to say the lines – as did Sir John Martin-Harvey in the play, *The Only Way.*

Ring down the curtain, the FARCE is over
See **curtain.**

Who's your FAT friend?

There was a play by Charles Laurence, presented in the West End in 1972, called *My Fat Friend* which turned upon a fat girl's changed fortunes when she lost weight. It was originally going to be called *The Fat Dress.* I couldn't help but detect in the final title a slight nod towards Beau Brummell's famous question to Lord Alvanley about the Prince Regent. Brummell (1778-1840), a dandy almost by profession, had fallen out with the Prince of Wales and when they met in London in July 1813, the prince cut him and greeted his companion. As the prince walked off, Brummell asked in ringing tones, 'Tell me, Alvanley, who is your fat friend?'

The prince's reaction is, unfortunately, not recorded.

Women's FAULTS are many

The observation regarding quotations – or jokes – that there is always an earlier example if only you can find it, is particularly true of graffiti. The rash of feminist graffiti of the 1970s (spreading in time to T-shirts, buttons, etc.) produced this popular verse:

> Women's faults are many
> Men have only two:
> Everything they say
> And everything they do.

How ironic, therefore, that there is a well-documented rhyme from the eighteenth century that goes – and note the change of gender:

> We men have many faults:
> Poor women have but two –
> There's nothing good they say,
> There's nothing good they do.

> Anon.: 'On Women's Faults', 1727

FAVOURITES of the Moon

A film with this title was released in the English-language market in 1984. It was a quirky, wry French piece about various crooks, petty and otherwise, in Paris, whose activities overlap one way and another. The English title hardly seems relevant to this subject, and isn't. The original French title was *Les Favoris de la Lune*.

As a caption at the beginning makes clear, this is a French translation of a Shakespeare quotation: in *The First Part of King Henry IV* (I.ii.25), Falstaff says to Prince Hal: 'Let not us that are squires of the night's body be called thieves of the day's beauty: let us be Diana's foresters, gentlemen of the shade, minions of the moon.'

Not, of course, that 'Minions of the Moon' would have made a more graspable title for anyone.

FAY *ce que vouldras*

– or *'fais ce que vouldras'*, meaning 'do what you will', 'do as you please' – an appealing motto and one that has been snapped up by more than one free-living soul.

It appears first in Book 1 of *Gargantua and Pantagruel* (1532) by Rabelais. Then, in the eighteenth century it was the motto of the

Monks of Medmenham, better known as the Hell Fire Club. Sir Francis Dashwood founded a mock Franciscan order at Medmenham Abbey in Buckinghamshire in 1745 and the members of the club were said to get up to all sorts of disgraceful activities, orgies, black masses and the like. The politician John Wilkes was of their number. The motto was written up over the ruined door of the abbey.

Aleister Crowley (*c.* 1876-1947), the satanist, who experimented in necromancy and the black arts, sex and drugs, also picked up the motto. Newspapers called him the 'Wickedest Man in the World' though he fell short of proving the claim. Of his 'misunderstood commandment', Germaine Greer comments in *The Female Eunuch (1970)*: '*Do as thou wilt* is a warning not to delude yourself that you can do otherwise, and to take full responsibility for what you do. When one has genuinely chosen a course for oneself it cannot be possible to hold another responsible for it.'

FEASTING with Panthers

At the 1981 Chichester Festival there was a play with this title, devised and directed by Peter Coe, about the trials of Oscar Wilde. The phrase comes from Wilde's *De Profundis*, in a passage about his life before he was sent to Reading gaol for homosexual offences:

> People thought it dreadful of me to have entertained at dinner the evil things of life, and to have found pleasure in their company. But then, from the point of view through which I, as an artist in life, approach them they were delightfully suggestive and stimulating. It was like feasting with panthers; the danger was half the excitement.

Never in the field of human conflict was so much owed by so many to so FEW

In my *Sayings* I have already noted how Winston Churchill's classic tribute to the Royal Air Force on 20 August 1940 was made well before the Battle of Britain had reached its peak. I also noted the circumstances of its composition and its echo of Shakespeare's line 'We few, we happy few, we band of brothers' in *King Henry V*. Benham quotes Sir John Moore (1761-1809) after the fall of Calpi (where Nelson lost an eye): 'Never was so much work done by so few men'.

Another pre-echo may be found in Vol. 2 of Churchill's own *A History of the English-Speaking Peoples* (1956, but largely written pre-war). In describing a Scottish incursion in the run-up to the English Civil War in 1640, he writes: 'All the Scots cannon fired and all the English army fled. A contemporary wrote that "Never so many ran from so few with less ado". The English soldiers explained volubly that their flight was not due to fear of the Scots, but to their own discontents.'

The immediate impact of Churchill's phrase is evidenced by a letter to him of 10 September from Lady Violet Bonham Carter (from the Churchill papers, quoted by Martin Gilbert in Vol. 6 of his biography):

> Your sentence about the Air-war – 'Never in the history [sic] of human conflict has [sic] so much been owed by so many to so few' – will live as long as words are spoken and remembered. Nothing so simple, so majestic & so true has been said in so great a moment of human history. You have beaten your old enemies 'the Classics' into a cocked hat! Even my Father [H. H. Asquith] would have admitted that. How *he* would have loved it!

By 22 September, Churchill's daughter, Mary, was uttering a *bon mot* in his hearing about the collapse of the France through weak leadership: 'Never before has so much been betrayed for so many by so few' (recorded by John Colville, *The Fringes of Power*, Vol. 1, 1986).

FIDDLER on the Roof

This expression became known to a wide audience as a result of the musical, so-entitled, first produced on Broadway in 1964 and filmed in 1971, with book by Joseph Stein and lyrics by Sheldon Harnick. It tells of Tevye, a Jewish milkman in pre-revolutionary Russia, who cheerfully survives family and political problems before emigrating to America, and was based on Sholom Aleichem's stories collected under the title *Tevye and His Daughters*.

Not having heard the story told in any of these versions, I can only assume that the title is used allusively to describe the easy-going nature of the hero. The title song of the musical is not very helpful. It merely asks the question, why is the fiddler playing up on the roof all day and in all weathers? It concludes, 'It might not mean a thing/ But then again it might!' The meaning of the expression would seem to be: 'an opportunist, one who takes life easy, one who does what he pleases, a happy-go-lucky person'.

I note, however, that 'fiddling on the roof' is one of the proverbial expressions portrayed (literally) in the painting known as 'The Proverbs' by David Teniers the Younger (1610-90) which hangs in Belvoir Castle. In the key to these Flemish proverbs, 'fiddling on the roof' is compared to 'eat, drink and be merry'. I am not sure at what date the English key was provided, but it is odd that the saying does not seem to have taken a hold in the language, although there is the nautical expression 'Fiddler's Green', defined in *OED* as 'a sailor's elysium, in which wine, women and song figure prominently'. From the nineteenth-century citations given, it appears that non-sailors also aspired to it. There is also the English proverb, 'In the house of the fiddler, all fiddle.'

Every soldier has the baton of a FIELD-MARSHAL in his knapsack
See **baton.**

Where do we FIND such men?
See **men.**

FIRST among equals
As *primus inter pares* this is an anonymous old Latin saying. It has been used about the position of politicians in a number of countries. It can also be extended. *ODCIE* defines it as an idiom meaning, 'the one of a group who leads or takes special responsibility but who neither feels himself, nor is held by others to be, their superior'. The Round Table in Arthurian legend was meant to show not only that there was no precedence among the knights who sat at it, but also that King Arthur was no more than first among equals.

Used specifically regarding the British Prime Minister within cabinet, the phrase cannot pre-date Sir Robert Walpole (in power 1721-42) who is traditionally the first to have held that position. (The name 'Prime Minister' was originally applied to him mockingly by his opponents.)

Lord Morley (1838-1923) may have been the first to use the phrase in this context in his life of Walpole (1889) where he says:

> Although in Cabinet all its members stand on an equal footing, speak with equal voice, and, on the rare occasions when a division is taken, are counted on the fraternal principle of one vote, yet the head of the Cabinet is *primus inter pares,* and occupies a position which, so long as it lasts, is one of exceptional and peculiar authority.

However, Morley may have been anticipated by Sir William Blackstone (1723-80), the legal writer, or by Walter Bagehot in *The English Constitution* (1867).

FIRST catch your hare

In the proverbial sense this means, 'You can't begin to do something until you have acquired a certain necessary agreement (which may be difficult to acquire).' *CODP* finds the equivalent thought in *c.* 1300, in Latin: 'It is commonly said that one must first catch the deer, and afterwards, when he has been caught, skin him.'

For a long time, however, the saying was taken to be a piece of practical, blunt good sense to be found in Mrs Beeton's *Book of Household Management* (1851), but it does not appear there. In Mrs Hannah Glasse's *The Art of Cookery made plain and easy* (1747), there is the similar, 'Take your hare when it is cased' (skinned).

It was known in the familiar form by 1855 when it appeared in Thackeray's *The Rose and the Ring*. Similar proverbs include: 'Catch your bear before you sell its skin', 'Never spend your money before you have it' and 'Don't count your chickens before they are hatched'.

The FIRST Hundred Thousand

This was the title of a war novel by Ian Hay (1876-1952), published in 1915. Subtitled 'Adventures of a typical regiment in Kitchener's army', the book begins with a poem – 'We're off a hundred thousand strong./ And some of us will not come back.'

A. J. P. Taylor in his *English History 1914-45*, describing a period of 'patriotic frenzy' in the First World War, says that the 'spirit of 1915 was best expressed by Ian Hay, a writer of light fiction, in *The First Hundred Thousand* – a book which treated soldiering as a joke, reviving "the best days of our lives" at some imaginary public school.'

The FIRSTEST with the mostest

To describe anything as 'the mostest' might seem an exclusively American activity. However, the *OED* finds English dialect use in the 1880s and Partridge recognizes its use as a jocular superlative without restricting it to the USA. As such, it is a consciously ungrammatical way of expressing extreme degree.

Whether this was consciously the case with the Confederate general, Nathan B. Forrest (1821-77) is very much in doubt. He could hardly read or write but he managed to say that the way to win battles was to be 'Firstest with the mostest', or that you needed to 'Git thar fustest with the mostest'. Bartlett gives this last as the usual rendering of the more formally reported words, 'Get there first with the most men'.

In Irving Berlin's musical *Call Me Madam* (1950) there is a song with the title 'The Hostess with the Mostes' on the Ball'. One assumes that Berlin's use, like any evocation of 'the mostest' nowadays, refers back to Forrest's remark.

FLOREAT Etona
The motto of Eton College is also the last remark of the villain, Captain Hook, before being eaten by a crocodile in J. M. Barrie's play *Peter Pan* (1904). In the 'novelization', as it would now be called, that Barrie prepared in 1911, the playwright appears to have had second thoughts. '"Bad form", he cried jeeringly, and went content to the crocodile.'

FOLD their tents like the Arabs
At the conclusion of his case for the defence in the Jeremy Thorpe trial (1979), Mr George Carman QC said to the jury: 'I end by saying in the words of the Bible: "Let this prosecution fold up its tent and quietly creep away".'

Bong! His client should not have got off after that. The words are not from the Bible, but from Longfellow's 'The Day is Done':

> And the night shall be filled with music
> And the cares that infest the day
> Shall fold their tents, like Arabs,
> And as silently steal away.

Only FOOLS and Horses
The BBC Television comedy with this title, written by John Sullivan, has been on the air since 1981 and concerns itself with a pair of wide boy brothers sparring together in London. The title must have puzzled many people. Although unrecorded in reference books, it apparently comes from an old Cockney expression, 'Only fools and horses *work.*'

One FOOT in the grave
To have one foot in the grave means to be near death. Swift uses the phrase of the Struldbruggs of Laputa in *Gulliver's Travels* (1726). The earliest citation in the *OED* is from 1632. Mencken

quotes William George Smith as tracing 'One of his feet is already in the grave' to 1566. Bartlett provides a translation of Plutarch's *Morals: Of the Training of Children* which goes, 'An old doting fool, with one foot already in the grave.'

Proof that the phrase was well known by the eighteenth century can be found in a punning inscription upon the grave of one Samuel Foote in Westminster Abbey. Foote (1720-77) was an actor and dramatist, famous for his mimicry and for making Samuel Johnson laugh against his will. He was buried by torchlight in an unmarked grave but his inscription reads: 'Here lies one Foote, whose death may thousands save,/ For death has now one foot within the grave.'

What is that man FOR?

'It was an anonymous little girl who, on first catching sight of Charles James Fox, is supposed to have asked her mother: what is that gentleman for?' – Alan Watkins, *Observer*, 20 May 1988.

'I am reminded of the small boy who once pointed at Hermione Gingold and asked, "Mummy, what's that lady for?"' – Michael Billington, *Guardian*, 21 July 1988.

Hold the FORT, for I am coming

One might say 'Hold the fort' to mean 'Look after this place while I'm away', but in the sense of the longer phrase, meaning 'Hang on, relief is at hand', there is a specific origin. In the American Civil War, General William T. Sherman signalled words to this effect to General John M. Corse at the Battle of Allatoona, Georgia on 5 October 1864. What he actually semaphored from Keneshaw Mountain was: 'Sherman says hold fast. We are coming' (Mencken), or 'Hold out. Relief is coming' (Bartlett).

The phrase became popularized in its present form as the first line of a hymn/gospel song written by Philip Paul Bliss in *c.* 1870 ('Ho, My Comrades, See the Signal!' in *The Charm*). This was introduced to Britain by Moody and Sankey during their evangelical tour of the British Isles in 1873, though not written by them:

> 'Hold the fort, for I am coming,'
> Jesus signals still;
> Wave the answer back to heaven,
> 'By the grace we will.'

More recently, perhaps thanks to a pun on 'union' (as in the

American Civil War and Trade Union), the song has been adapted
as a trade union song in Britain:

> 'Hold the fort, for we are coming
> Union men be strong.
> Side by side keep pressing onward.
> Victory will come.'

FOUR score and seven years ago

The Federal victory at the Battle of Gettysburg in the American
Civil War forshadowed the ultimate defeat of the Confederacy.
But what immortalized the battle was President Abraham
Lincoln's address at the dedication of the cemetery on 19
November 1863. Few recitations get beyond the first sentence, so
here it is in full:

> Four score and seven years ago our fathers brought forth on this
> continent a new nation, conceived in Liberty, and dedicated to the
> proposition that all men are created equal.
>
> Now we are engaged in a great civil war, testing whether that
> nation, or any nation so conceived and so dedicated, can long endure.
> We are met on a great battlefield of that war. We have come to
> dedicate a portion of that field, as a final resting-place of those who
> here gave their lives that the nation might live. It is altogether fitting
> and proper that we should do this.
>
> But, in a larger sense, we can not dedicate, we can not consecrate,
> we can not hallow this ground. The brave men, living and dead, who
> struggled here, have consecrated it, far above our poor power to add
> or detract. The world will little note, nor long remember what we say
> here, but it can never forget what they did here. It is for us, the living,
> rather to be dedicated here to the unfinished work which they who
> fought here have thus far so nobly advanced. It is rather for us to be
> here dedicated to the great task remaining before us, that from these
> honoured dead we take increased devotion to that cause for which
> they gave the last full measure of devotion; that we here highly
> resolve that these dead shall not have died in vain, that this nation,
> under God, shall have a new birth of freedom; and that government of
> the people, by the people, and for the people, shall not perish from the
> earth.

Lincoln's prophecy that the world would 'little note or long
remember' what he said seemed likely to be true, judging by
initial reaction to the speech. One American paper spoke of the
President's 'silly remarks'. *The Times* of London (as did many
American papers) ignored the speech in its report of the ceremony.

Later it was to say: 'Anything more dull and commonplace it wouldn't be easy to reproduce.' The *Chicago Tribune* wrote, however, that the words would, 'Live among the annals of man.'

There is a legend that Lincoln jotted down the Gettysburg Address on the back of an envelope on a train going to the battlefield, but the structure is so tight that this seems unlikely and Burnam 2 suggests that there were some five drafts of the speech. Also, the Associated Press was given an advance copy.

FOUR thousand holes in Blackburn, Lancashire
See **holes.**

Prayer of St FRANCIS
See **where.**

Tomorrow to FRESH fields and pastures new
This should read, 'Tomorrow to fresh *woods* and pastures new' whether or not one is aware that Milton's *Lycidas* (1637) is being quoted. The misquotation probably gained hold because of the alliteration – always a lure in phrase-making.

My FRIEND'S friend is my enemy
I think I first heard this expression at the time of the Suez crisis (1956). It might have been President Nasser of Egypt referring to the United States (the friend) and Israel (the friend's friend).

There seem to be many precedents. Mencken lists a legal maxim, 'The companion of my companion is not my companion *(socii mei socius meus socius non est)'*, but compare the French proverb, 'The enemy of my enemy is my friend', and the Flemish proverb, 'The friends of my friends are my friends'.

God Protect Me from my FRIENDS
This was the title of a book (1956) by Gavin Maxwell about Salvatore Giuliano (*d.* 1950), the Sicilian bandit. The full expression is 'I can look after my enemies, but God protect me from my friends.' *CODP* traces it to 1477 in the forms 'God keep/ save/defend us from our friends' and says it is now often used in the abbreviated form, 'Save us from our friends.' It appears to be common to many languages.

The Morrises confuse this saying with the next one, but find a quotation from Maréchal Villars who, on leaving Louis XIV, said: 'Defend me from my friends; I can defend myself from my enemies.'

With FRIENDS like that who needs enemies?

– said in desperation after one has been betrayed by a friend. The earliest note I made of this was Richard Crossman talking about some Labour MPs in 1969, but it is of much older provenance. Charlotte Brontë said it, in a letter, concerning a patronizing reviewer of one of her books. Partridge/Slang compares it to the proverb, 'With a Hungarian for a friend, who needs an enemy.' George Canning, the British politician, wrote a verse ending, 'Save, save, Oh, save me from the candid friend.'

FUNNY without being vulgar

A Quaker singer, David Bispham, noted in his *Recollections* (1920) that he had heard W. S. Gilbert say to Sir Henry Beerbohm Tree on the stage of the Haymarket Theatre, London, after the first performance of the actor's Hamlet: 'My dear fellow, I never saw anything so funny in my life, and yet it was not in the least vulgar.'

At the time, the line quickly went round in its abbreviated form, and apparently Tree put up a brave show of not being offended. He wrote to Gilbert on 25 March 1893:

> By the bye, my wife told me that you were under the impression that I might have been offended at some witticism of yours about my Hamlet. Let me assure you it was not so. On the contrary, it was I believe *I* who circulated the story. There could be no harm, as I knew you had not seen me act the part, and moreover, while I am a great admirer of your wit, I have also too high an opinion of my work to be hurt by it.

Hesketh Pearson, in his biography of Tree, seems to think this letter shows the actor claiming not only to have circulated the story against himself but to have *invented* it. I do not see this. On the other hand, Pearson, in his biography of Gilbert and Sullivan, does report that Shaw told him that Gilbert complained shortly before his death (1911) of the way ill-natured witticisms had been fathered on him. He instanced the description of Tree. There seems little doubt, though, that he did say it.

Shaw himself had used the phrase in a review of pantomime in *London Music* on 23 January 1897: 'Pray understand that I do not want the pantomime artists to be "funny without being vulgar". That is the mere snobbery of criticism. Every comedian should have vulgarity at his fingers' ends.'

   J. B. Booth in *Old Pink 'Un Days* (1924) recalls an exchange in a
London theatre after Pavlova's successes when a large lady from
Oldham or Wigan was attempting to pass herself off as a Russian
dancer. 'What do you think of her?' asked one. Came the reply,
'Funny without being Volga.'

The GAIETY of nations
See **death.**

GETTING there is half the fun
This expression sloganizes Robert Louis Stevenson's views, 'I travel not to go anywhere, but to go' and 'To travel hopefully is a better thing than to arrive.' It also reflects 'the journey not the arrival matters' (an expression used as the title of an autobiographical volume by Leonard Woolf, 1969). I understand that, as a slogan, it was used to promote Cunard steamships in the 1920s and 1930s. It was also used to promote the Peter Sellers film *Being There* (1980) in the form, 'Getting there is half the fun. Being there is all of it.'

GETTYSBURG Address
See **four.**

To GILD the lily
– i.e. to attempt to improve something that is already attractive and risk spoiling it. In quoting Shakespeare's *King John* (IV.ii.11) this should be 'To gild refined gold, to paint the lily':

> *Salisbury:*
>
> Therefore, to be possess'd with double pomp,
> To guard a title that was rich before,
> To gild refined gold, to paint the lily,
> To throw a perfume on the violet,
> To smooth the ice, or add another hue
> Unto the rainbow, or with taper-light
> To seek the beauteous eye of heaven to garnish,
> Is wasteful and ridiculous excess.

Arden notes that 'to gild gold' was a common expression in Shakespeare's time.

GIVE us a child until it is seven, and it is ours for life
I believe the above to be a saying of the Jesuits, founded in 1534
by St Ignatius Loyala. And another version, sourceless, is 'Give us
the child, and we will give you the man.'

Lenin had his own version. To the Commissars of Education in
Moscow (1923) he said, 'Give us the child for eight years and it
will be a Bolshevik for ever.' Muriel Spark in her novel *The Prime
of Miss Jean Brodie* (1962) had her heroine, a teacher, say: 'Give
me a girl at an impressionable age and she is mine for life.'

GLAD, I tell you, glad, glad, glad
In the 1940 film version of W. Somerset Maugham's *The Letter*,
Bette Davis plays a woman who has killed a man in what seems
to have been self-defence. According to Leslie Halliwell in his
Filmgoer's Book of Quotes (1978), she utters the memorable line:
'Yes, I killed him. And I'm glad, I tell you. Glad, glad, glad!'

The only thing is, whenever I have seen the film she has not
said it. Could someone have doctored the film for TV showing?
Might the line have been used on posters rather than in the film?
Indeed, Halliwell notes in his book, 'They even used the line as a
catch-phrase on the posters.'

The line does not appear in Maugham's play.

All that GLITTERS is not gold
– i.e., appearances may be deceptive. When quoting Shakespeare's
The Merchant of Venice (II.vii.65) this should be, 'All that *glisters* is
not gold,/ Often have you heard that told.' The proverb was
common by Shakespeare's time. *CODP* quotes a Latin version –
'*Non omne quod nitet aurum est*' ('not all that shines is gold') and
also an English one in Chaucer.

The now obsolete word 'glisters' rather than 'glitters' or
'glistens' was commonly used in the saying from the seventeenth
century onwards, although in poetic use, Thomas Gray, for
example, used 'glisters' in his 'Ode on the Death of A Favourite
Cat drowned in a tub of Gold Fishe' (1748).

Sic transit GLORIA mundi
see *sic*.

The True GLORY
The title of the documentary (UK/USA 1945) about the end of
the Second World War must refer back to the dispatch from Sir

Francis Drake to Sir Francis Walsingham before the Battle of Cadiz (1587): 'There must be a beginning of any great matter, but the continuing unto the end until it be thoroughly finished yields the true glory.'

This is clearly a favourite quotation of Margaret Thatcher. To a Conservative Women's conference on 21 May 1980 (in the same speech in which she said, 'There is no alternative', and which marked the start of her government's second year in office), she said: 'When we endeavour any great matter it is not the beginning but the continuing of the same until it be thoroughly finished which yieldeth the true glory.'

In an address to the 1922 committee of backbench MPs on 19 July 1984,

> After reminding them of their success in the recent Euro-elections, and pointing out that few people during last year's general election could have foreseen a 19-week pit strike, she declared that it was not the beginning of the struggle that mattered. It was the continuation of the fight until it was truly concluded (*Guardian,* 20 July).

Balfour must GO

A slogan incorporating the cry that he 'must go' is liable to pursue any prominent politician who falls seriously out of favour. To date, A. J. Balfour, British Prime Minister (1902-6) is the first example I have found. In his case, the cry was sometimes abbreviated to 'BMG'. After losing the 1906 election, Balfour lingered on as leader of his party. Leo Maxse, editor of the *National Review* wrote an article in the September 1911 edition in the course of which, demonstrating that the Conservative party needed a new leader, he invented the slogan, 'Balfour must go'. And he went in November.

'Eden must go' arose during Sir Anthony Eden's inept premiership (1955-57) when he instigated the disastrous landings in Egypt to 'protect' the Suez Canal. On the evening of 4 November 1956, while he met with his cabinet ministers in 10 Downing Street, he could hear roars of 'Eden must go!' from an angry mass meeting in Trafalgar Square. He went under the guise of illness early the following year.

The most notable such campaign in British politics was directed at Ernest Marples, an energetic Minister of Transport (1959-64). The slogan arose in October 1962 when he intervened in the build-up of opposition to sweeping cuts in the railway service (announced the following year in the Beeching Report). However, it was because of motoring matters that the slogan was taken up at a more popular level. He introduced various unpopular measures including, in the summer of 1963, a 50 m.p.h. speed limit at peak summer weekends in an effort to reduce the number of road accidents. It was this measure that produced a rash of car stickers bearing the cry. It appeared daubed on a bridge over the M1 motorway in August (and remained visible for many years).

'The saloon must go' was the slogan of the Anti-Saloon League in the United States (organized 18 December 1895).

Let my people GO!
See **let.**

GO ahead, make my day
See **day.**

GO, go, go, said the bird
An ITV documentary programme with this title was shown on 26 October 1966 when 'go-go' and 'birds' were all the rage in the Swinging Sixties. Clever choice, really, as the line comes in fact from 'Burnt Norton' in T. S. Eliot's *Four Quartets* (1935): 'Go, go, go, said the bird; human kind/ Cannot bear very much reality.'

GO now, pay later
Daniel Boorstin in *The Image* (1962) makes oblique reference to travel advertisements using the line, 'Go now, pay later'. Was hire purchase ever promoted with 'Buy now, pay later'? It seems likely. These lines – in the USA and UK – seem to be the starting point for a construction much used and adapted since.

Live Now Pay Later was the title of Jack Trevor Story's 1962 screenplay based on the novel *All on the Never Never* by Jack Lindsay. As a simple graffito, the same line was recorded in Los Angeles (1970) in *The Encyclopedia of Graffiti* (1974).

The same book records a New York subway graffito on a funeral parlour ad: 'Our layway plan – die now, pay later'.

'Book now, pay later' was used in ad in the programme of the Royal Opera House, Covent Garden, in 1977.

GOD protect me from my friends
See **friends.**

Whom the GODS love, die young

Thus said Lord Byron in *Don Juan* (1819), adding that it was 'said of yore'. Indeed, Menander the Greek and Plautus said it in times BC.

Related to this saying is what Euripides and other classical authors said: 'Whom the Gods wish to destroy, they first make mad'. Sophocles in *Antigone* (*c.* 450 BC) quotes as a proverb, 'Whom Jupiter would destroy, he first makes mad.'

Cyril Connolly in *The Unquiet Grave* (1944) added, '. . . they first call promising'.

I Know Where I'm GOING
See **know.**

Crucify mankind upon a cross of GOLD

One of the most notable examples of American oratory, but little known in Britain, is William Jennings Bryan's speech to the Democratic convention in July 1896. It contained an impassioned attack on supporters of the gold standard. 'You shall not press down upon the brow of labour this crown of thorns. You shall not crucify mankind upon a cross of gold.'

Bryan (1860-1925) had said virtually the same in a speech to the House of Representatives on 22 December 1894. Now, he won the nomination and fought the presidential election against William J. McKinley who supported the gold standard. He lost.

There's GOLD in them thar hills

Presumably this phrase was established in US gold-mining by the end of the nineteenth century. It seems to have had a resurgence in the 1930s and 1940s, probably through use in Western films. A Laurel and Hardy short called *Them Thar Hills* appeared in 1934. The melodrama *Gold in the Hills,* by J. Frank Davis, has been performed every season since 1936 by the Vicksburg Theatre Guild in Mississippi.

The phrase now has a jokey application to any enterprise containing a hint of promise.

There ain't GONNA be no war

As Foreign Secretary to Anthony Eden, Harold Macmillan attended a four-power summit conference at Geneva where the chief topic for discussion was German reunification. Nothing much was achieved but the 'Geneva spirit' was optimistic and on his return to London he breezily told a press conference on 24 July 1955, 'There ain't gonna be no war.'

Why this conscious Americanism? One, rather good, suggestion was that he was alluding to Mark Twain's *Tom Sawyer Abroad*, Chapter 1 (1894): 'There's plenty of boys that will come hankering . . . when you've got an apple . . . but when they've got one . . . they . . . say thank you 'most to death, but there ain't a-going to be no core.' This situation may also have appeared as a *Punch* cartoon *c.* 1908.

But it is almost certainly a direct quote from the *c.* 1910 music hall song which was sung in a raucous Cockney accent by a certain Mr Pélissier (1879-1913) who had a show called 'Pélissier's Follies' during the reign of King Edward VII:

> There ain't going to be no waar
> So long as we've a king like Good King Edward.
> 'E won't 'ave it, 'cos 'e 'ates that sort of fing.
> Muvvers, don't worry,
> Not wiv a king like Good King Edward.
> Peace wiv honour is 'is motter [*snort*] –
> Gawd save the King!

Although Macmillan was born the year *Tom Sawyer Abroad* was published, it is presumably to this song of his youth that he was referring. And yet why did he say 'gonna'? Cockney pronunciation maybe, but some time before December 1941 an American called Frankl did write a song called, precisely, 'There Ain't Gonna Be No War', which had a brief vogue:

> Rock-a-bye, my baby
> There ain't gonna be no war over here
> . . . It's all on the other side.
> We ain't goin' to need no ride of Paul Revere.
>
> We're going to have peace and quiet
> And if they start a riot
> We'll just sit back and keep score.
> The only place you'll go marching to
> Will be the corner grocery store.
> So rock-a-bye, my baby
> There ain't gonna be no war

Sir David Hunt confirmed to me (1988) that it was the Pélissier song that Macmillan had in mind. In fact, he (Hunt) sang it to him on one occasion.

I will be GOOD
These pious words were not said by Queen Victoria on her accession to the throne in 1837, but six years earlier when she was a mere twelve years of age.

No GOOD deed goes unpunished
This is a consciously ironic rewriting of the older expression 'No *bad* deed goes unpunished.' Joe Orton recorded it in his diary for 13 June 1967: 'Very good line George (Greeves) came out with at dinner: "No good deed ever goes unpunished".'
 I have also heard it attributed to Oscar Wilde.

No Blade of GRASS
See **blade.**

The roar of the GREASEPAINT, the smell of the crowd
A conscious inversion of 'the smell of the greasepaint, the roar of the crowd' – a description of the lure of show business. Used as the title of a musical by Leslie Bricusse and Anthony Newley in 1964.

A'babbled of GREEN fields
See **a'babbled.**

GREEN Grow the Rushes O!
One of the most-quoted-from folk songs is also one of the most impenetrable. As a pamphlet from the English Folk Dance and Song Society (*c.* 1985) remarks, 'This song has appeared in many forms in ancient and modern languages from Hebrew onwards, and it purports in almost all cases to be theological.' Here, line by line, is what it *may* be about:

> I'll sing you one oh,
> Green grow the rushes oh,
> One is one and all alone and ever more shall be so.

(Refers to God Almighty.)

> Two, two for the lilywhite boys,
> Clothed all in green oh.

(Christ and St John the Baptist as children, although what the green refers to is not clear. Cf. the title of Christopher Logue's 1950s play *The Lily-White Boys*.)

> Three, three for the rivals

(The Trinity? The Three Wise Men?)

> Four for the Gospel makers

(Matthew, Mark, Luke and John?)

> Five for the symbol at your door

(The pentagram or five-pointed star inscribed on the threshold to drive away the evil one.)

> Six for the six proud walkers

(The six *waterpots* used in the miracle of Cana of Galilee. Cf. the title of Donald Wilson's detective series on BBC TV [1954, 1964], *The Six Proud Walkers*.)

> Seven for the seven stars in the sky

(The group of Ursa Major called Charley's Wain; or the seven days of the week; or Revelation 1, 10:16: 'And he had in his right hand seven stars and out of his mouth went a two-edged sword'.)

> Eight for the eight bold rainers/rangers/archangels

(Bold rainers = angels? But why eight? There are only four archangels, so why double? A 1625 version refers to the people in Noah's Ark who might well be described as 'bold rangers'.)

> Nine for the nine bright shiners

(The nine choirs of angels? The nine months before birth?)

> Ten for the ten commandments

(Obvious, this one.)

> Eleven for the eleven that went up to heaven

(The Apostles without Judas Iscariot.)

> Twelve for the twelve apostles.

(Or the tribes of Israel.)

HAMLET, Revenge!

is the title of a detective novel (1937) by Michael Innes which is set in a stately home during a private performance of *Hamlet*. But does the line 'Hamlet, revenge!' occur in Shakespeare's play? Well, no it doesn't. It comes from an earlier play on the same subject which is now lost to us. One Thomas Lodge saw it in 1596 and noted the pale-faced ghost of Hamlet's father 'which cried so miserably at the theatre, like an oyster-wife, *Hamlet, revenge*'.

It seems that this appearance was a notorious feature of the production and the cry seems to have been something of a catchphrase of the time.

The HAPPIEST Days of Your Life

The traditional platitude intoned by those who give away prizes at school speech days is that his listeners must agree that schooldays are 'the happiest days of your life'. I'm sure the expression of this sentiment pre-dates its use as the title of a famous play by John Dighton (produced in London in 1948, filmed 1950). However, the schoolchildren in the work may have had special cause to believe this – the plot hinges on wartime confusion in which a boys' school and a girls' school are lodged under the same roof.

The Best Years of Our Lives is the title of an American film (1946) about what happens to a group of ex-servicemen when they return from the war – presumably having 'given the best years of their lives' to their country. 'The best *days* of our lives' is also an expression used in this kind of context.

HAPPY Birthday to You

is the most frequently sung song in English, according to *The Guinness Book of Records 1985* (which also lists 'For He's a Jolly

Good Fellow' and 'Auld Lang Syne' as the top songs of all time). It started out as 'Good Morning to All' with words by Patty Smith Hill (1868-1946) and music by Mildred J. Hill (1859-1916) in *Song Stories for the Kindergarten* (1893):

> Good morning to you;
> Good morning to you;
> Good morning, dear children;
> Good morning to you.

'Happy Birthday to You' is the first line of the second stanza, but was not promoted to the title-line until 1935.

The song has had a chequered legal history, chiefly due to the widely held belief that it is in the public domain. In fact, following the American practice of renewing copyrights, the song will be controlled until 2010. In 1988, the copyright of the song was put up for sale and was reckoned to be worth £750,000 a year. The figure represents but a proportion of what could be its revenue if all performances were paid for. In recent times 'Happy Birthday' has been sung in the films *10, The Great Santini, Oh God* and *Fame*. On 8 March 1969, it was sung by the Apollo IX astronauts as they orbited the moon.

A HARD Day's Night
The title of the Beatles' first feature film (1964) was apparently decided towards the end of filming when Ringo Starr used the phrase to describe a 'heavy' night (Ray Coleman, *John Lennon*, 1984). What, in fact, Ringo must have done was to use the title of the Lennon and McCartney song (presumably already written if it was towards the end of filming) in a conversational way. Indeed, Hunter Davies in *The Beatles* (1968) noted 'Ringo Starr came out with the phrase, though John *had used it earlier in a poem.*' It certainly sounds like a Lennonism.

It may have had some limited general use subsequently as a catchphrase meaning that one has had 'a very tiring time'.

HARD-FACED men who had done well out of the war
The men were members of the House of Commons who had been returned after the 1918 general election. They were so described by a 'Conservative politician', according to John Maynard Keynes, the economist, in *The Economic Consequences of Peace* (1919). Stanley Baldwin, a future Conservative Prime Minister, was the one who said it. In the biography of Baldwin by Keith

Middlemas, he is also quoted as having noted privately on 12 February 1918: 'We have started with the new House of Commons. They look much as usual – not so young as I had expected. The prevailing type is a rather successful-looking business kind which is not very attractive.'

On *Quote . . . Unquote* in 1988, Julian Mitchell described the current crop of Conservative MPs as 'hard-faced men who have done well out of the peace'.

First catch your HARE
See **first.**

HARK the herald angels sing, Mrs Simpson's pinched our king
Great historical events can produce a whole subculture of jokes, and none more so this century than the crisis which led to the abdication of King Edward VIII in December 1936. His affair with the American divorcee, Mrs Wallis Simpson, was kept from the British public through newspaper self-censorship until 25 November. The king had gone by 11 December.

Given the general tight-lipped attitude then of (what would now be called) the media, it is hardly surprising that popular jokes and comments on the affair were not published or broadcast at the time as they probably would be now (judging by the jokes that surfaced at the time of the Jeremy Thorpe trial in 1979).

I recall my parents telling me an abdication joke in the 1950s: 'Why does King Edward leave the lavatory doors open at Buckingham Palace?' – 'It's the only way he'll ever see Mrs Simpson on the throne.'

Rather more well known is the rhyme above. Iona and Peter Opie in *The Lore and Language of Schoolchildren* (1959) recall how it was on juvenile lips all over the country and how at a school party in Swansea just before Christmas 1936 children had to be restrained from singing the words when the music to the carol was played. 'Word of mouth' had been very busy in the three or so weeks since the rhyme had been thought up by God knows whom.

The future Prime Minister Clement Attlee wrote in a letter on 26 December (printed in Kenneth Harris's biography): 'Felicity [his daughter] produced a ribald verse which was new to me: 'Hark the herald . . . &c.'

Where there is HATRED
See **where.**

Men wanted for HAZARDOUS journey
Nominated by Julian L. Watkins in his book *The 100 Greatest Advertisements* (Chicago, 1949-59) for the simplicity and 'deadly frankness' of its copy, is this small ad, said to have appeared in London newspapers in 1900:

> Men wanted for hazardous journey. Small wages, bitter cold, long months of complete darkness, constant danger, safe return doubtful. Honour and recognition in case of success – Ernest Shackleton.

Watkins quoted Shackleton as saying of the ad: 'It seemed as though all the men in Great Britain were determined to accompany me, the response was so overwhelming.'

Sir Ernest Shackleton (1874-1922), the explorer, led three expeditions to the Antarctic in 1907-9, 1914-17, 1921-22. His biographer, Roland Huntford, suggests that the advertisement would have been published before the 1914 expedition but casts doubt on it ever appearing. Shackleton had no need to advertise for companions, he says.

Another HEART and Other Pulses
See **another.**

The HEART and stomach of a king
See **stomach.**

The HEART is a Lonely Hunter
This was the title of a novel by Carson McCullers (1940, filmed 1968). From the poem 'The Lonely Hunter' by William Sharp (Fiona Macleod) (1855-1905): 'My heart is a lonely hunter that hunts on a lonely hill'.

All This and HEAVEN Too
See **all.**

HEAVEN'S Gate
Michael Cimino's 1980 film with this title is famous for having lost more money than any other film to date – about £34 million. In it, 'Heaven's Gate' is the name of a roller-skating rink used by settlers and immigrants in Wyoming in 1891. Conceivably, the

name is meant to be taken as an ironic one for the rough situation many of the characters find themselves in as they arrive to start a new life.

The idea of a 'gate to heaven' goes back to the Bible. For example, Genesis 28:17 has: 'This is none other but the house of God, and this is the gate of heaven.' Psalm 78:23 has: 'He commanded the clouds from above, and opened the doors of heaven.'

Shakespeare twice uses the phrases. In *Cymbeline* (II.iii.20), there is the song, 'Hark, hark, the lark at heaven's gate sings', and Sonnet 29 has, 'Like to the lark at break of day arising/ From sullen earth sings hymns at heaven's gate.'

Steven Bach in his book *Final Cut* (1985), about the making of the film, cites two more possible sources. William Blake in *Jerusalem* (1820) wrote:

> I give you the end of a golden string;
> Only wind it into a ball,
> It will lead you in at Heaven's gate,
> Built in Jerusalem's wall.

Browning uses the phrase and there is a poem by Wallace Stevens with the title, 'The Worms at Heaven's Gate'.

Made an excursion to HELL and came back glorious
See **excursion**.

All HELL broke loose
This popular descriptive phrase is actually a quotation, though you might never have thought so. In Milton's *Paradise Lost* (1667), the Archangel Gabriel speaks to Satan the lines, 'Wherefore with thee/Came not all hell broke loose' (Book 4, line 917).

As an idiomatic phrase it was already established by 1738 when Swift compiled his *Polite Conversation*. When there is 'A great Noise below', Lady Smart exclaims: 'Hey, what a clattering is there; one would think Hell was broke loose.'

HOIST with his own petard
I wonder how many people hearing the expression about being 'hoist with one's own petard' meaning 'to be caught in one's own trap' think it has something to do with being stabbed with one's own knife, or hung with one's own rope? The context in which Hamlet uses it in Shakespeare's play (III.iv.209) makes the source

clear: 'For 'tis the sport to have the engineer/ Hoist with his own petard.'

A petard was a newly invented device in Shakespeare's day, used for blowing up walls, etc., with gunpowder. Thus the image is of the operator being blown up into the air by his own device.

In modern times an exactly similar expression has been acquired from football. In Northern Ireland, for a terrorist to suffer an 'own goal' means that he has blown himself up with his own bomb.

HOLD Back the Dawn
This is, apparently, an original title for the US film (1941) – as also is *Hold Back the Night* (USA, 1956) and *Hold Back Tomorrow* (USA, 1956).

HOLD the fort, for I am coming
See **fort.**

Four thousand HOLES in Blackburn, Lancashire

> I heard the news today oh boy
> Four thousand holes in Blackburn, Lancashire
> And though the holes were rather small
> They had to count them all
> Now they know how many holes it takes
> To fill the Albert Hall

from the Lennon and McCartney lyrics of 'A Day in the Life' on the *Sergeant Pepper* album (1967).

The inspiration for these odd lines – nothing to do with drug needle-marks or anything like that – can be traced directly to the *Daily Mail* of 17 January 1967. John Lennon had the newspaper propped up on his piano. The original brief story, topping the 'Far & Near' column stated:

> There are 4,000 holes in the road in Blackburn, Lancashire, or one twenty-sixth of a hole per person, according to a council survey.
>
> If Blackburn is typical there are two million holes in Britain's roads and 300,000 in London.

England HOME and beauty
Home and Beauty, the play by W. Somerset Maugham (1919), concerns itself with the complications of a First World War 'widow' who remarries and then has her original husband turn

up (in the USA the play was known as *Too Many Husbands*).

Clearly, Maugham was alluding to the longer phrase, 'England, Home and Beauty' which occurs in a song 'Nelson', in *The Americans* by John Braham (1774-1856). Sometimes also called 'The Death of Nelson', this song is described in *The Oxford Companion to Music* as 'at one time known to every patriotic Briton'. Here is that part of the lyrics which provides the context for the phrase:

> 'Twas in Trafalgar bay,
> We saw the Frenchmen lay,
> Each heart was bounding then,
> We scorn'd the foreign yoke
> For our ships were British Oak,
> And hearts of Oak our men.
>
> Our Nelson mark'd them on the wave,
> Three cheers our gallant Seamen gave,
> Nor thought of home or beauty (*rpt.*)
> Along the line this signal ran,
> 'England expects that every man
> This day will do his duty!' (*rpt.*)

Charles Dickens has Captain Cuttle quote, 'Though lost to sight, to memory dear, and England, Home, and Beauty!' in *Dombey and Son* (1844-46) (Chapter 48) – though these words do not appear in the text that I have.

Braham was not alone in perceiving the rhyming delights of 'duty' and 'beauty'. In Gilbert and Sullivan's *Trial by Jury* (1875), 'Time may do his duty' is rhymed with 'Winter hath a beauty' – at which point, Ian Bradley, in his annotated edition, remarks: 'This is the first of no fewer than fifteen occasions, exclusive of repetitions, when the words "duty" and "beauty" are rhymed in the Savoy Operas . . . *HMS Pinafore* holds the record with four separate songs in which the words are rhymed.'

HOME is the sailor, home from the sea

In Robert Louis Stevenson's poem 'Requiem' (1887) it is very definitely 'home from sea' – without the definite article. Alas, when they decided to quote from the poem on Stevenson's grave in Somoa, this is what they put:

> 1850 ROBERT LOUIS STEVENSON 1894
> Under the wide and starry sky
> Dig the grave and let me lie.

Glad did I live and gladly die,
And I laid me down with a will.

This be the verse you grave for me:
Here he lies where he longed to be;
Home is the sailor, home from the sea
And the hunter home from the hill.

Can one hear him turning in his grave, I wonder?

HONORIFICABILITUDINITATIBUS

The longest word in Shakespeare occurs in *Love's Labour's Lost* (V.i.37) and appears to be a schoolmasterly joke, not original to him. The context allows it no meaning, just length, though it has something to do with being honourable. The *OED* does not list it as a headword, preferring 'honorificabilitudinity'. Samuel Johnson noted that it was 'often mentioned as the longest word known'. At 27 letters it was overtaken, in time by 'floccipaucinihilipilification', with 29, meaning, 'the action of estimating as worthless' which was first used in 1741, and is the longest word actually in the *OED*. Scientific words of 47 and 52 letters have also been invented, but don't really count.

Those seeking to prove that Francis Bacon wrote Shakespeare's plays claimed that the 27 letter word was, in fact, an anagram – '*Hi ludi, F Baconis nati, tuiti orbi*' ('These plays, born of F. Bacon, are preserved for the world') – which surely deserves some sort of prize for ingenuity, if nothing else.

There is nothing better for the inside of a man than the outside of a HORSE

When *Time* quoted President Reagan as saying this (28 December 1987), it received many letters from readers saying such things as: 'This quotation bears a striking resemblance to a remark made by the California educator and prep school founder Sherman Thacher: "There's something about the outside of a horse that's good for the inside of a boy"'; and, 'Rear Admiral Grayson, President Woodrow Wilson's personal physician put it . . . "The outside of a horse is good for the inside of a man"'; and 'Lord Palmerston said it'.

Time sensibly replied (19 January 1988): 'Everyone is right. The origin of the saying is unknown. It is one of the President's favorite expressions.'

A HORSE! a horse! My kingdom for a horse!
The actual King Richard III's last words when he met Henry
Tudor at the Battle of Bosworth on 23 August 1485 were, 'I will
die King of England. I will not budge a foot . . . Treason! treason!'
That was how it was reported by John Rowe who presumably
picked it up from someone who had actually been at the battle,
for he was not. Evidently, the king then rushed on the future
Henry VII and was killed.

Shakespeare's memorable, twice-repeated cry (*King Richard III*,
V.iv.7/13) may have been inspired by lines in other plays written
about the time he wrote his (*c.* 1591). The only indication that
Richard III might have had a similar concern at the actual battle is
contained in the book of Edward Hall's chronicle called '*The
tragical doynges of Kyng Richard the thirde*' (1548) where it states,
'When the loss of the battle was imminent and apparent, they
brought to him a swift and light horse to convey him away.'

A HORSEMAN Riding By
This is the title of a novel (1966) by R. F. Delderfield. Just possibly
an allusion to Yeats (see 'Cast a cold eye on *death*', above), but
given Delderfield's talent for creating titles that sound tantalizingly
like quotations, but which are not, probably not.

As long as you don't frighten the HORSES
A celebrated saying of the actress, Mrs Patrick Campbell (1865-
1940), is to the effect that 'It doesn't matter what you do, so long
as you don't frighten the horses.' (Ted Morgan's biography of
W. Somerset Maugham actually attributes this to Kind Edward
VII on the subject of the double standard of sexual morality.)

But what gave rise to that remark? Another version, as in *ODQ*,
is: 'I don't mind where people *make love*, so long as they don't do
it in the street and frighten the horses . . . '. Bartlett has, 'My dear,
I don't care what they do, so long as they don't do it in the street
and frighten the horses.'

Margot Peters in her painstakingly footnoted biography *Mrs Pat*
(1984) nevertheless doesn't give any reason for her belief that it
was 'when told of a homosexual affair between actors' that she
uttered, 'I don't care what people do, as long as they don't do it in
the street and frighten the horses.'

I am reminded of the joke about the preacher who demanded
that 'murder, rape and robbery be cleared from our streets . . .
and brought back into our homes — where they really belong!'

Some Like It HOT

The 1959 US film *Some Like It Hot* is a comedy about two unemployed musicians who are accidental witnesses of the St Valentine's Day Massacre and flee to Miami disguised as members of an all-girls jazz band. So the 'hotness' may come from the jazz or the position they find themselves in.

There had, however, been a completely different US film with the same title in 1939 (starring Bob Hope). So where does the phrase come from? All I can suggest is the nursery rhyme 'Pease porridge hot' which dates (in Britain) from about 1750. The second verse goes:

> Some like it hot
> Some like it cold
> Some like it in the pot
> Nine days old.

This is such nonsense that it is sometimes ended with a riddle, 'Spell me that without a P' ('that' being quite easy to spell without a P).

Ring Lardner's story 'Some Like Them Cold' (1935) contains a song, referring to women:

> Some like them hot, some like them cold
> Some like them fat, some like them lean (etc.)

A HOUSE is a machine for living in

Some feel that the French architect Le Corbusier's description of the purpose of a house (*'La maison est une machine à habiter'*) is a rather chilling one. The phrase first appeared in *Vers une Architecture* (1923), but in the context of his expanded use of the phrase, it is not so bad. He wrote in *Almanach de l'Architecture* (1925):

> The house has two aims. First it's a machine for living in, that is, a machine destined to serve as a useful aid for rapidity and precision in our work, a tireless and thoughtful machine to satisfy the needs of the body: comfort. But it is, secondly, a place intended for meditation and thirdly a place whose beauty exists and brings to the soul that calm which is indispensible.

Of HUMAN Bondage

The novel (1915) by W. Somerset Maugham is named after one of the books in Spinoza's *Ethics* (1677).

Somebody's HUSBAND, Somebody's Son

See **somebody's.**

On ILKLA Moor Bah t'at

The most famous – and impenetrable – of Yorkshire songs comes in two versions. The older, said to have been written by Thomas Clark to the hymn tune 'Cranbrook' in 1805, was sung in a spirited way:

1 Wheear baht thee bahn when I been gone? [*repeated three times*]
   Wheear baht?
   On Ilkla Moor bah t'at [repeated twice]
   Bah t'at, bah t'at.

2 Then thou wilt catch a cold and dee
   In Lonnenfuit bah t'buit [repeated twice]
   Bah t'buit, bah t'buit.

3 Then we shall cum and bury thee
   Inn Saltruble Docks bah t'socks [repeated twice]
   Bah t'socks, bah t'socks.

4 Then worms'll cum and eat up thee
   On Ilkla Moor bah t'at [etc.]

5 Then doocks'll cum and eat them worms
   In Lonnenfuit bah t'buit [etc.]

6 Then we shall cum and eat them doocks
   In Saltruble Docks bah t'socks [etc.]

7 Then we shall catch th'auld cold and dee
   On Ilkla Moor bah t'at [etc.]

(Salter Hebble Docks and Luddenden Foot are canal points on the Hebble and Calder rivers near Halifax.)

A later (and now more popular) version, is sung more dolefully. It has a second verse, beginning 'I've been a courting Mary Jane', and a final verse sung thus:

Then we shall all 'av 'etten thee
That's how we get our owen back
This is the moral of this tale,
Doan't go a-courtin Mary Jane.

This one was reputedly composed on an outing to Ilkley Moor
by the choir of Ebenezer Chapel, Halifax, in 1886. The meaning
of the old saga is roughly this: 'You've been on Ilkley Moor
without a hat, courting Mary Jane. You'll catch your death of
cold, and we shall have to bury you. The worms will eat you up,
and the ducks will eat up the worms. Then we shall eat the ducks,
so we shall have eaten you.'

Jolly lot, Yorkshire folk.

Our true INTENT is all for your delight
These words were written over the entrance to the first Butlin's
holiday camp to be opened, at Skegness, in 1936. One wonders
how many of the campers who passed under it recognized it as a
great 'unspoken' quotation from Shakespeare? When Quince
reads the prologue of the play-within-a-play in *A Midsummer
Night's Dream* (V.i.113), he mispunctuates: 'We do not come, as
minding to content you,/ Our true intent is. All for your delight,/
We are not here . . .'

It is also a motto that has popped up on the programmes of
countless repertory theatres.

An IRON hand in a velvet glove
Napoleon I is supposed to have said, 'Men must be led by an iron
hand in a velvet glove' but this expression is hard to pin down as
a quotation. The Emperor Charles V may have said it earlier.
Sometimes an iron 'fist' rather than 'hand' is evoked. Either way,
the image evoked is of unbending ruthlessness or firmness
covered by a veneer of courtesy and gentle manners.

The ISLAND race
The characterization of Britain as an 'island race' understandably
reached its apogee in the Second World War, but at big patriotic
moments there has always been a tendency to draw attention to
the fact of Britain being an island, from John of Gaunt's 'sceptr'd
isle' in Shakespeare's *King Richard II* onwards.

Winston Churchill said, 'We shall defend our island, whatever
the cost may be' in his 'We shall fight on the beaches' speech of
4 June 1940. The flag-waving film *In Which We Serve* (1942) refers

specifically to the 'island race'. Churchill used the phrase as the title of Book 1, Vol. 1 of his *History of the English-Speaking Peoples* (1956). In his *History of the Second World War* (vol. 5, 1952) he also quotes the 'island *story*' phrase from Tennyson's 'Ode on the Death of the Duke of Wellington' (1852):

> Not once or twice in our rough island story
> The path of duty was the way to glory.

The first prominent appearance of 'island race', however, appears to have been as the title of a poem by Sir Henry Newbolt in 1898.

ITALIA . . .

A thorough inspection of the dying words of monarchs and emperors, especially those dying in exile, reveals that the correct form is to expire with the name of one's country on one's lips. I would cite (some in translation):

Napoleon I died on St Helena in 1821 saying: *'Mon Dieu! La nation Française. Tête d'armée.'* ('My God! The French nation. Head of the army.') Or: *'France – armée – tête d'armée – Joséphine.'* (Tristan de Montholon, who reported the second version, heard Napoleon say it twice.)

King Alfonso XIII of Spain died in exile in Rome in 1941, having said: 'Spain, my God!' (He was reburied in Spain in 1980.)

The Duke of Windsor, formerly King Edward VIII, died in Paris in 1972, saying, 'England . . . the waste . . . the waste.'

Ex-King Umberto II of Italy, denied the opportunity of dying in his fatherland, died in exile on 18 March 1983, saying: 'Italia . . .'.

I should die in JERUSALEM

The last words of King Henry IV of England (*d.* 1413), according to Raphael Holinshed's *The Chronicles of England, Scotland and Ireland* (1587), are supposed to have been: 'Lauds be given to the Father of heaven, for now I know that I shall die here in this chamber, according to the prophecy of me declared, that I should depart this life in Jerusalem.' He had just been told that the chamber he was lying in was the Jerusalem Chamber of Westminster Abbey. He had been preparing for an expedition to the Holy Land and was visiting the abbey on the eve of his departure when he was taken ill.

Shakespeare in *The Second Part of King Henry IV* takes this situation almost word for word from the chronicle (IV.v.232):

> KING: Doth any name particular belong
>   Unto the lodging where I first did swoon?
> WARWICK: 'Tis called Jersualem, my noble lord.
> KING: Laud be to God! Even there my life must end.
>   It hath been prophesied to me, many years,
>   I should not die but in Jerusalem,
>   Which vainly I suppos'd the Holy Land.
>   But bear me to that chamber; there I'll lie;
>   In that Jerusalem shall Harry die.

The Jerusalem Chamber became the meeting place of the dean and chapter after the dissolution of the abbey. Its name derives from mention of Jersualem in inscriptions round the fireplace or from the original tapestry hangings.

Next year in JERUSALEM

In the Diaspora of the Jews, the eternal hope – expressed particularly at the Feast of the Passover in a toast – was that they should all be reunited ... 'next year in Jerusalem'. Passover originally celebrated the exodus of the Jews from Egypt and their deliverance from enslavement some 3,200 years ago. In the centuries of the Diaspora, the central Jewish dream was of being reunited in the land of Israel. In June 1967, following the Six Day War, when the modern state of Israel encompassed once more the old city of Jerusalem, every Jew could, if he was able, end his exile.

The JEWEL in the Crown

In the space of a single day – 2 March 1988 – I read in the *Guardian,* 'Poor David Steel. He's bound for Southport on Saturday for a regional conference in what ought to be one of the precious few jewels in the Liberals' dented crown'; in *Harpers & Queen* I read, 'Annecy is considered to be the jewel in the Savoyard crown'; and in Michael Powell's book *A Life in Movies* (published two years before), 'Sir Thomas Beecham, Bart., conducting the "Ballet of the Red Shoes" would be the final jewel in our crown.'

It would be reasonable to suppose that the 1984 television adaptation of Paul Scott's 'Raj Quartet' of novels had something to do with the popularity of this phrase. The first of the novels (published in 1966) is called *The Jewel in the Crown* and gave its name to the TV series. 'The Jewel in *Her* Crown' (my italics) is the title of a 'semi-historical, semi-allegorical' picture referred to early on in the book. It showed Queen Victoria,

> ... surrounded by representative figures of her Indian Empire: princes, landowners, merchants, money-lenders, sepoys, farmers, servants, children, mothers, and remarkably clean and tidy beggars ... An Indian prince, attended by native servants, was approaching the throne bearing a velvet cushion on which he offered a large and sparkling gem.

(In fact, Victoria, like Disraeli, who is also portrayed, never set foot in India.)

Children at the school where the picture was displayed had to be told that, 'the gem was simply representative of tribute, and that the jewel of the title was India herself'. The picture had been painted *after* 1877, the year in which Victoria became Empress of India.

I imagine this was an actual picture, no doubt much reproduced, but I have no idea who painted it.

The *OED Supp.* refers only to the 'jewels of the crown' as a rhetorical phrase for the colonies of the British Empire and has a citation from 1901. The specifying of India as *the* jewel is understandable. The Kohinoor, a very large oval diamond of 108.8 carats, from India, had been part of the British crown jewels since 1849. In *Dombey and Son* (1844-46) (Chapter 39), Charles Dickens writes: 'Clemency is the brightest jewel in the crown of a Briton's head.'

O rare Ben JONSON!
See **rare.**

Men wanted for hazardous JOURNEY
See **hazardous.**

JOURNEY'S End
The title of the play (1929) by R. C. Sherriff might seem to nod towards Shakespeare – 'Journeys end in lovers meeting' (*Twelfth Night*, II.iii.44), or 'Here is my journey's end' (*Othello*, V.ii.268), or Dryden, 'The world's an inn, and death the journey's end' (*Palamon and Arcite*). But it is impossible to be certain. In his autobiography *No Leading Lady* (1968), Sherriff writes of the titles he rejected, like 'Suspense' and 'Waiting', and then adds:

> One night I was reading a book in bed. I got to a chapter that closed with the words: 'It was late in the evening when we came at last to our Journey's End'. The last two words sprang out as the ones I was looking for. Next night I typed them on a front page for the play, and the thing was done.

He does not say what the book was.

A KESTREL for a Knave

The novel with this title by Barry Hines (1968) – filmed simply as *Kes* (1969) – tells of a boy misfit who learns about life through training a kestrel. The title comes from *The Boke of St Albans*, 1486, and a Harleian manuscript: 'An Eagle for an Emperor, a Gyrfalcon for a King; a Peregrine for a Prince, a Saker for a Knight, a Merlin for a Lady; a Goshawk for a Yeoman, a Sparrowhawk for a Priest, a Musket for a Holy water Clerk, a Kestrel for a Knave.'

I would KICK him up the arse, Alfred

A report in *The Times* Diary (29 March 1983) recalled a speech at the Royal Academy in 1949 when the president was Sir Alfred Munnings. One of his guests was Winston Churchill, who had just been admitted to the academy, and Munnings supposedly ruffled the politician's feathers by saying in his speech: 'Seated on my left is the greatest Englishman of all time. I said to him just now: "What would you do if you saw Picasso walking ahead of you down Piccadilly?" – and he replied: "I would kick him up the arse, Alfred".'

Alas, the BBC recording of the event fails to confirm that he ever said this. Not a born speaker, to put it mildly, what he said was, 'Once he said to me, "Alfred, if you met Picasso coming down the street, would you join with me in kicking his something-something?"

'I said, "Yes, sir, I would!" '

The Times report also suggested that, 'as the laughter died, Munnings yelled at the top of his voice: "Blunt, Blunt [i.e., Sir Anthony Blunt, the art connoisseur later unmasked as a traitor] –

you're the one who says he prefers Picasso to Sir Joshua Reynolds!' If he did yell it he was very quiet about it because the barb is not audible on the recording.

Thou shalt not KILL; but need'st not strive/ Officiously to keep alive

Arthur Hugh Clough's *The Latest Decalogue* (1862) was an *ironical* version of the Ten Commandments – so this line was not serious advice to doctors (in which sense it has been quoted, however).

The KING can do no wrong

Sir William Blackstone (1723-80), in his *Commentaries on the Laws of England,* wrote: 'That the king can do no wrong, is a necessary and fundamental principle of the English constitution.'

That is the only citation in the *ODQ.* Nevertheless, the concept was not original to Blackstone. Judge Orlando Bridgeman said it in the trial of the regicides after the restoration of the monarchy in 1660. But he went on to say that ministers *could* do wrong *in the king's name* and the fault should, therefore, be held against the ministers.

The saying also occurs in John Selden's *Table-Talk* (1689), 'The King can do no wrong, that is no Process can be granted against him', and there is a legal maxim to the same effect, expressed in Latin: '*Rex non potest peccare*'.

Then later, in 1822, giving judgment in the case of the goods of King George III, deceased, Mr Justice John Nicholl said: 'The King can do no wrong; he cannot constitutionally be supposed capable of injustice.' And, *mutatis mutandis,* Richard Nixon tried to assert the same principle on behalf of the American presidency in his TV interviews with David Frost in May 1977: 'When the President does it, that means it is not illegal.'

The KING is dead, long live the king!

This declaration was first used in 1461 upon the death of King Charles VII of France: '*Le roi est mort, vive le roi!*'

Julia Pardoe, in her *Life of Louis XIV,* describes how that king's death was announced by the captain of the bodyguard from a window of the state apartment: 'Raising his truncheon above his head, he broke it in the centre, and throwing the pieces among the crowd exclaimed in a loud voice, "*Le Roi est mort!*" Then seizing another staff, he flourished it in the air as he shouted, "*Vive le Roi.*" '

The custom ended with the death of Louis XVIII. The expression is now used allusively to denote a smooth transition of power of any sort. The *Independent* (25 January 1988): 'The cry went up: "The Liberal Party is dead. Long live the Liberal Party".'

The Once and Future KING
T. H. White's Arthurian romance *The Once and Future King* (1958) takes its title from *'Hic jacet Arthurus, rex quondam rexque futurus'*. This is what Sir Thomas Malory in the *Morte d'Arthur* (1469-70) said was written on the tombstone of King Arthur.

The KING'S life is moving peacefully towards its close
On Monday 20 January 1936, King George V lay dying at Sandringham. At 9.25 p.m., Lord Dawson of Penn, the king's doctor, issued a bulletin which he had drafted on a menu-card. It said: 'The King's life is moving peacefully towards its close.' This was taken up by the BBC. All radio programmes were cancelled and every quarter of an hour the announcer, Stuart Hibberd, repeated the medical bulletin until the king died at 11.55 p.m.

In December 1986, Dawson's biographer suggested, in *History Today*, that the doctor had in fact hastened the king's departure with lethal injections of morphine and cocaine at the request of the queen and the future Edward VIII. Dawson's notes revealed that the death was induced at 11 p.m. not only to ease his pain but to enable the news to make the morning papers, 'rather than the less appropriate evening journals'. *The Times* was advised that important news was coming and to hold back publication.

In an astonishing remark later, Margot Asquith said to Lord David Cecil: 'The King told me he would never have died had it not been for that fool Dawson of Penn.'

They buried him among the KINGS
See **buried.**

KISS me, Hardy
Well, what did Horatio Nelson say as he lay dying on HMS *Victory* at Trafalgar in 1805, having been severely injured by a shot fired from a French ship?

It has been said that, according to the Nelson family, he was in the habit of saying 'kismet' (fate) when anything went wrong. It is therefore not too unlikely that he said, 'Kismet, Hardy' to his flag captain, and that witnesses misheard.

In fact, the recording angel had to work overtime when Nelson lay dying. He said so much. The first reliable report of what went on was by Dr Beatty, the ship's surgeon, included in *Despatches and Letters of Lord Nelson* (ed. Nicholas, 1846):

> Captain Hardy now came to the cockpit to see his Lordship a second time. He then told Captain Hardy that he felt that in a few minutes he should be no more, adding in a low tone, 'Don't throw me overboard, Hardy.' The Captain answered, 'Oh, no, certainly not.' Then replied his Lordship, 'You know what to do. Take care of my dear Lady Hamilton. Kiss me, Hardy.' The Captain now knelt and kissed his cheek, when his Lordship said, 'Now I am satisfied. Thank God I have done my duty.'

This seems to be quite a reasonable description and, if Hardy did actually kiss him (a gesture that surely couldn't be mistaken), why should Nelson not have asked him to?

Robert Southey in his *Life of Nelson*, published earlier, in 1813, also supports the 'kiss me' version (his account is almost identical to Beatty's).

When the KISSING had to stop

The title of Constantine Fitzgibbon's 1960 novel about a Russian takeover of Britain was drawn from Browning's poem *A Toccata at Galuppi's*:

> What of soul was left, I wonder,
> When the kissing had to stop?

Particularly following an ITV dramatization in 1962, the phrase entered the list of journalistic format phrases, verging on the clichéd, with 'When the ———— had to stop' embracing any type of subject matter.

Every soldier has the baton of a field-marshal in his KNAPSACK

See **baton**.

I KNOW Where I'm Going

The film (UK 1945) takes its title from an Irish song which also provides its theme song. Co-writer and director, Michael Powell, explains in *A Life in Movies* (1986) that his wife suggested the title to him while travelling on 'the Number 9 bus to Piccadilly Circus . . . And standing there in the swaying bus, she sang it:

> 'I know where I'm going
> And I know who goes with me
> I know whom I love
> But the dear [devil/de'il/Lord, in some versions] knows
>   whom I'll marry.'

By which time, 'we were opposite Fortnum and Masons'.

To KNOW him is to love him

This is the title of a song, written by Phil Spector, which reached
No. 2 in the British charts in 1958. The words have a biblical ring
to them, but whether Phil Spector was ever aware of the words of
No. 3 in *C.S.S.M. Choruses* (3rd ed., 1928, by the Children's
Special Service Mission, London) we may never know. Written
by R. Hudson Pope, it goes:

> All glory be to Jesus
> The sinner's only Saviour,
> Whose precious blood for sin atones
> And blots it out for ever.
> To know Him is to love Him,
> To trust Him is to prove Him,
> And those He saves He ne'er forsakes –
> No, never, never, never!

Robert Burns came very close to the phrase on a couple of
occasions. In 'Bonnie Lesley', 'To see her is to love her/ And love
but her for ever', and in 'Ae Fond Kiss', 'But to see her was to
love her,/ Love but her, and love for ever.'

LADIES never move

A correspondent suggested, *en passant*, that it was Lord Curzon, the Tory politician, Indian viceroy, and so on, who originated the saying, 'She should *lie* back and enjoy it' (q.v., below). I puzzled over this for a number of years, unsure in what circumstances he might have said it and how it could ever be verified.

Then I came across what he *really* said (and perhaps my correspondent may be forgiven for his confusion). According to *The Oxford Book of Political Anecdotes*, Curzon when instructing his second wife on the subject of love-making, said, 'Ladies never move.'

The book of *New Statesmen* competition winners called *Salome Dear, Not With a Porcupine* (1982 – edited by Arthur Marshall) prefers, 'A lady does not move' (and proceeds to provide the circumstances in which it *might* first have been said).

When a LADY says no, she means perhaps

In October 1982, Lord Denning was quoted as having commented on the difference between a diplomat and a lady, at a meeting of the Magistrates Association, in these words: 'When a diplomat says yes, he means perhaps. When he says perhaps, he means no. When he says no, he is not a diplomat. When a lady says no, she means perhaps. When she says perhaps, she means yes. But when she says yes, she is no lady.'

Whether Denning claimed it as his own, I don't know, but in Hans Severus Ziegler's *Heitere Muse: Anekdoten aus Kultur und Geschichte* (1974), the passage appears in a (possibly apocryphal) anecdote concerning Bismarck at a ball in St Petersburg. His partner, whom he had been flattering, told him, 'One can't believe a word you diplomats say' and provided the first half of the description as above. Then Bismarck replied with the second half.

The LADY with the Lamp

Thus was dubbed Florence Nightingale (1820-1910), philanthropist and nursing pioneer, in commemoration of her services to soldiers at Scutari during the Crimean War (1853-56). She inspected hospital wards at night, carrying a lamp – a Turkish lantern consisting of a candle inside a collapsible shade. The phrase (with 'a' lamp) appears to have been coined by Longfellow in his poem *Santa Filomena* (1858 – i.e., very shortly after the events described):

> Lo! in that hour of misery
> A lady with a lamp I see
>   Pass through the glimmering gloom,
>   And flit from room to room.
> And slow, as in a dream of bliss
> The speechless sufferer turns to kiss
>   Her shadow, as it falls
>   Upon the darkening walls.

On her death, Moore Smith & Co. of Moorgate, London published a ballad with the title 'The Lady with *the* Lamp' which begins:

> The Lady with the Lamp –
> Let this her title be
> Remembered through the ages
> That will dawn and flee.
>
> Straight to an Empire's heart
> Her noble way she trod.
> She lives, she lives for ever
> Now she rests, she rests with God.

The film biography (1951), with Anna Neagle as Miss Nightingale, was called *The Lady with a Lamp* was based on a play by Reginald Berkeley.

The LADY'S not for turning
See **turning.**

Back to the LAND
See **back.**

Two countries separated by a common LANGUAGE
See **countries.**

LARS Porsena
In the 1920s, Robert Graves wrote a small book with the title *Lars Porsena, or the Future of Swearing and Improper Language.* As titles go, it is a subtly allusive one. In Lord Macaulay's poem 'Horatius' from his *Lays of Ancient Rome* (1842), you will remember that Lars Porsena did a lot of swearing:

> Lars Porsena of Clusium
>   By the nine gods he swore
> That the great house of Tarquin
>   Should suffer wrong no more.

My LAST appeal to reason
See **appeal.**

The LAST of the Summer Wine
This BBC TV comedy series (1974-) about a trio of old school friends in a Yorkshire village, finding themselves elderly and unemployed, has a title which sounds as though it should be a quotation (perhaps cf. *The Days of Wine and Roses* from Ernest Dowson's *'Vitae Summa Brevis').* However, according to *Radio Times* (February 1983), Roy Clarke, the programme's writer, says it is 'not a quotation, merely a provisional title which seemed to suit the age group and location. I expected it to be changed but no one ever thought of anything better.'

The LAW is an ass
Very pedantic it may be, but strictly speaking, if one is quoting Charles Dickens, what Mr Bumble says in *Oliver Twist* (Chapter 51) is: 'If the law supposes that . . . the law is a ass – a idiot.' He is dismayed that the law holds him responsible for his wife's actions.

LEAD on Macduff
Strictly speaking, it should be:

> *Lay on,* Macduff;
> And damn'd be he that first cries, 'Hold enough!'

Shakespeare, *Macbeth* (V.iii.33)

It would be interesting to know at what stage people started saying 'Lead on, Macduff' to mean, 'You lead the way, let's get

WHY DO WE QUOTE . . . ?

L

started . . .'. Partridge/Catchphrases has an example from 1912, but I suspect it started long before then. There has been a change of meaning along the way. Macbeth uses the words 'lay on' as defined by *OED* as: 'to deal blows with vigour, to make vigorous attack, assail'. The shape of the phrase was clearly so appealing that it was adapted to a different purpose.

A living LEGEND – a legend in one's own lifetime

Both of these phrases are now clichés of tribute. In a speech marking the retirement of George Thomas, Speaker of the House of Commons, in May 1983, Mrs Margaret Thatcher said: 'A great many have occupied your chair but it is a measure of your Speakership that you have become a legend in your own lifetime.'

On 25 August 1984, the *Guardian* reported that Tony Blackburn, a disc jockey, was writing his autobiography: 'It's called The Living Legend – The Tony Blackburn Story,' he explains, more or less tongue-in-cheek. 'They call me the Living Legend at Radio One . . . I'm known as the Survivor around there.'

The Oxford Companion to English Literature (1985) has this: 'In 1888 [Robert Louis] Stevenson had set out with his family entourage for the South Seas, becoming a legend in his lifetime.'

Where did it all begin? A possibility exists that the first person to whom both versions of the epithet were applied (and within a couple of pages of each other), actually deserved them. Lytton Strachey in *Eminent Victorians* (1918) wrote of Florence Nightingale: 'She was a legend in her lifetime, and she knew it . . . Once or twice a year, perhaps, but nobody could be quite certain, in deadly secrecy, she went for a drive in the park. Unrecognised, the living legend flitted for a moment before the common gaze.'

(In about 1976, I noted that Christopher Wordsworth, a literary critic, reviewing a novel by Clifford Makins, a sporting journalist, described the author as having been, 'a legend in his own lunchtime'.)

Me no LEICA

A small joke, but a good one. There was a vogue for dismissive one-line criticisms of plays and films in the 1930s, 1940s, and 1950s, when suitable opportunities presented themselves. It was either when Christopher Isherwood's Berlin stories were turned, first into a play, *I am a Camera*, or subsequently into a film, that

one critic summed up his/her reaction with the words 'Me no
Leica'. This has been variously attributed to George Jean Nathan,
C. A. Lejeune, Walter Kerr and Kenneth Tynan. It is a comment
on the transitory nature of much criticism that one cannot say for
sure who did originate the joke.

One may be on firmer ground with a comment passed about a
show called *Yes or No* that came off after three nights at the
Ambassadors Theatre, London in the autumn of 1938. The critic
Hannen Swaffer is said simply to have written: 'No!'.

LET my people go!
The film *Exodus* (1960), based on the novel by Leon Uris about
the early years of the state of Israel, was directed by Otto
Preminger and lasted about 220 minutes. The story has it that
Mort Sahl, the American satirist, was invited by the director to a
preview. After three hours had ground by, he stood up and
implored: 'Otto – let my people go!'

I don't suppose he actually did, but that is now he tells the
story in a comedy routine contained on the LP, *The New Frontier*
(1961).

He was, of course, quoting Exodus 8:1-2: 'And the Lord spake
unto Moses, Go unto Pharaoh, and say unto him, Thus saith the
Lord, Let my people go, that they may serve me. And if thou
refuse to let them go, behold, I will smite all thy borders with
frogs . . .'.

A soft-porn stage revue in London in 1976 had the title, *Let My
People Come*.

An ambassador is . . . sent to LIE abroad
See **ambassador**.

When rape is inevitable, LIE back and enjoy it
This is best described – as it is in Paul Scott's novel *The Jewel in the
Crown* (1966) – as 'that old, disreputable saying'. Daphne
Manners, upon whose 'rape' the story hinges, adds: 'I can't say,
Auntie, that I lay back and enjoyed mine.'

It is no more than a saying – a 'mock-Confucianism' is how
Partridge/Slang describes it, giving a date *c.* 1950 – and one is
unlikely ever to learn when, or with whom, it first arose.

A word of caution to anyone thinking of using it. An American
broadcaster, Tex Antoine, said in 1975: 'With rape so predominant
in the news lately, it is well to remember the words of Confucius:

"If rape is inevitable, lie back and enjoy it".' ABC News suspended Antoine for this remark, then demoted him to working in the weather department and prohibited him from appearing on the air.

(Cf. '**ladies** never move' above.)

LIE down, I think I love you

This was considered a sufficiently well-established, smart jokey remark to be listed by the *Sun* (10 October 1984) as one of 'ten top chat-up lines'. I have a feeling it may also have been used in a song, or a cartoon, or just as graffiti a little before that. Indeed, there was a song entitled 'Lie Down (A Modern Love Song)' written and performed by the British group Whitesnake in 1978.

And then again, there was the Marx Brothers' line from *The Cocoanuts* (1929), 'Ah, Mrs Rittenhouse, won't you . . . lie down?'

As ever, there is nothing new under the sun. Horace Walpole, in a letter to H. S. Conway on 23 October 1778, wrote: 'This sublime age reduces everything to its quintessence; all periphrases and expletives are so much in disuse, that I suppose soon the only way to making love will be to say "Lie down".'

Cannot come, LIE follows

In Ralph Nevill's *The World of Fashion* (1923) (Chapter 5) we read that Lord Charles Beresford (1864-1919) was once summoned at the last moment to dine with the Prince of Wales (presumably the one who became Edward VII). He declined with a telegram, saying: 'Very sorry can't come. Lie follows by post.'

Great minds think alike. Marcel Proust in *Le Temps Retrouvé* (published 1927 after his death in 1922) writes of, 'One of those telegrams of which M. de Guermantes has wittily fixed the formula: "Can't come, lie follows".'

And was it not Oscar Wilde who turned down a dinner invitation because he had a subsequent engagement?

A LIE travels round the world while truth is putting on her boots

In November 1976, James Callaghan, then British Prime Minister, said in the House of Commons, 'A lie can be half way round the world before the truth has got its boots on.' From time to time since, this has been ascribed to him as an original saying. To Mark Twain has been attributed, 'A lie can travel half way round the world while the truth is putting on its shoes' – though this is probably no more than another example of the rule, 'When in doubt, say Mark Twain said it'.

The true originator was the Revd C. H. Spurgeon, the nineteenth-century Baptist preacher, who said: 'A lie travels round the world while truth is putting on her boots.'

In This Our LIFE

Halliwell describes this US film melodrama (1942), based on Ellen Glasgow's novel, as being about a neurotic girl who 'steals her sister's husband, leaves him in the lurch, dominates her hapless family and is killed while on the run from the police'. The title has a certain ring to it. Is it a phrase from a prayer perhaps? I would only note that twice within a scene in Shakespeare's *As You Like It* (II.i.) do we find the 'this our life' formula: 'And this our life, exempt from public haunt,/ Finds tongues in trees, books in the running brooks . . .', and 'Most invectively he pierceth through/ The body of country, city, court,/ Yea, and of this our life.'

I expect the film use is no more than conscious archaism, to produce a 'poetic' title.

LIFE is what happens to you while you're busy making other plans

In the lyrics of John Lennon's song 'Beautiful Boy' (included on the *Double Fantasy* album, 1980), this is one of two quotations. (The other is the slogan of Couéism: 'Every day in every way I'm getting better and better.')

In Barbara Rowe's *The Book of Quotes* (1979), she ascribes the saying to Betty Talmadge, divorced wife of Senator Herman Talmadge, 'Life is what happens to you when you're making other plans.' Dr Laurence Peter, in *Quotations for our Time* (1977), gives the line to Thomas La Mance, of whom I know no more than his name.

LIFE owes me nothing; one clear morn is boon enough . . .

In March 1982, Mrs Margaret Thatcher described in a BBC Radio interview the fears she had felt for the safety of her son, Mark, who had been lost in the desert while taking part in a Trans-Sahara car rally. She said she realized then that all the little things people worried about really weren't worth it. 'As the poet said,' she went on, '"One clear morn is boon enough for being born", and so it is.'

Curious about her reliance on the old formula, 'As the poet said . . . ', when not knowing the provenance of a quote, I wrote to Downing Street asking where on earth she had found these lines. At this point, the Falklands conflict broke out and Mrs Thatcher was no doubt otherwise occupied, so I thought I would hear no more. As soon as hostilities ceased, however, I received a photocopy of a poem, taken from a piece of paper that looked as though it had been carried around in the Prime Ministerial handbag for purposes of uplift, for many a year:

> Life owes me nothing;
>   one clear morn
> Is boon enough
>   for being born;
> And be it ninety years
>   or ten,
> No need for me
>   to question when.
> While life is mine,
>   I'll find it good.
> And greet each hour
>   with gratitude.
>
> ANONYMOUS

Subsequently, the Prime Minister revealed (in *Woman's Own*, 17 October 1984) that the poem was taken from 'Love's Tapestry Calendar 1966'.

(Lest my assertion be doubted that she *does* carry quotations around in her handbag, I would cite her former speechwriter Sir Ronald Millar, who told the *Sunday Times* [23 November 1980] that in his first effort he included a quote from Abraham Lincoln – 'Don't make the rich poorer, make the poor richer.' 'I gave her the draft,' he recounted, 'and she immediately delved into her handbag for a piece of yellowing paper on which was written the very same Lincoln quotation. "I take it everywhere with me," she said.')

LIFE wasn't meant to be easy
Malcolm Fraser (*b.* 1930), Prime Minister of Australia 1975-83, was noted, among other things, for having said, 'Life wasn't meant to be easy.' The phrase was used as the title of a book about him by John Edwards in 1977. Douglas Aiton asked Fraser in an interview for *The Times* (16 March 1981) if he had ever actually said it. Fraser replied,

I said something very like it. It's from *Back to Methusaleh* by Bernard Shaw . . . A friend I was visiting in hospital asked me why I didn't give up politics and return to the good life [on his sheep farm]. I said life wasn't meant to be like that. That would be too easy. So that's what it grew from. I wouldn't mind a cent for every time it's been quoted or misquoted. It's the best thing I ever said.

I suspect the derivation from Shaw was an afterthought. (Shaw's line in the play is, 'Life is not meant to be easy, my child; but take courage: it can be delightful.') In a Deakin lecture on 20 July 1971, which seems to have been his first public use of the phrase, Fraser made no mention of Shaw. Referring rather to Arnold Toynbee's analysis of history, Fraser said: 'It involves a conclusion about the past that life has not been easy for people or for nations, and an assumption for the future that that condition will not alter. There is within me some part of the metaphysic, and thus I would add that life is not meant to be easy.'

It is not, of course, a startlingly original view. In A. C. Benson's essays *The Leaves of the Tree* (1912), he quotes Brooke Foss Westcott, Bishop of Durham, as saying: 'The only people with whom I have no sympathy . . . are those who say that things are easy. Life is not easy, nor was it meant to be.'

I pray that the church is not struck by LIGHTNING

I was told in 1977 that this was the gist of a telegram sent by Evelyn Waugh to Tom Driberg MP on the occasion of the latter's marriage (to a woman). I did not find a reliable source until publication of *Brief Lives* by Alan Watkins (1982).

The wedding was remarkable – not only to Waugh – because Driberg was an active homosexual. According to Watkins, Waugh wrote – rather than telegraphed – to the effect: 'I will think of you intently on the day and pray that the church is not struck by lightning.' The letter is not included in Waugh's published correspondence. Watkins adds: 'This sentence . . . is, oddly enough, attributed to Aneurin Bevan and Winston Churchill also.'

I never met a man I didn't LIKE

Will Rogers (1879-1935), the folksy American 'cowboy comedian' of the 1930s, used to proclaim this. If nothing else, the line gave rise to an amusing car sticker, ascribed in the *Independent* (1987) to a disgruntled collaborator of the composer Marvin Hamlisch. It stated, 'Will Rogers never met Marvin Hamlisch.'

There is no LIMIT to what a man can do . . .
The propensity for American presidents to clutter their desks with plaques bearing uplifting messages dates back to the days of Harry S Truman at least. His 'the buck stops here' motto was apparently of his own devising. Jimmy Carter either retrieved the original or had a copy made and displayed it near his own desk when he was in the Oval Office.

Enter Ronald Reagan. According to the *Daily Mail* (18 April 1985),

> . . . besides a calendar, a pen set, a clock and a horseshoe, the First Desk is now home to no fewer than eight inspirational messages. They range from the consoling 'Babe Ruth struck out 1,330 times', through the boosting *'Illegitimi Non Carborundum'* . . . to the altruistic 'There is no limit to what a man can do and where he can go if he doesn't mind who gets the credit'.

The thin red LINE
See **red.**

The LION shall lie down with the lamb
Only indirectly. This simplified version derives from Isaiah 17:6: 'The wolf also shall dwell with the lamb, and the leopard shall lie down with the kid; and the calf and the young lion and the fatling together.'

LIONS led by donkeys
Such is an alleged German description of British soldiery in the First World War, but who said it is a little unclear. The saying is usually ascribed to Erich Ludendorff (1865-1937), the German general. Alan Clark, in his book called *The Donkeys* (1961), quotes the following exchange which suggests that Ludendorff had only a half-share in the coinage:

> LUDENDORFF: The English soldiers fight like lions.
> HOFFMAN: True. But don't we know that they are lions led by donkeys.

Clark gives the source as Falkenhayn's memoirs – presumably those of Field Marshal von Falkenhayn – but I have been unable to find the precise passage.

Does LITTLE Nell die?
See **Nell.**

Come on you sons of bitches! Do you want to LIVE for ever?

According to Flexner, American Marine Sergeant Daniel Daly is remembered for having shouted, during the Battle of Belleau Wood in June 1918, 'Come on, you sons of bitches! Do you want to live forever?'

He was not the first military man to use this formula for encouragement. Frederick the Great (1712-86) demanded of hesitating guards at Kolin (18 June 1757), *'Ihr Racker, wollt ihr ewig leben?'* ('Rascals, would you live for ever?') Mencken concludes that the cry is 'probably ancient' anyway.

LIVERPOOL is the pool of life

Returning to my home town in 1982, I was intrigued to find a sign in Mathew Street – sacred site of the erstwhile Cavern Club – saying:

> Liverpool is the pool of life.
>
> C. J. JUNG 1927

How clever to have found such a nice compliment in Jung, I thought to myself and left it at that. Then I began to wonder if there was any record of the Swiss psychologist ever having set foot in the fair city. I consulted his *Memories, Dreams, Reflections* (1963) and found none. It turned out that he was describing a dream he'd had. In the centre was a round pool, and in the middle of it a small island. While everything round about was obscured by rain, fog, smoke and dimly lit darkness, the little island blazed with sunlight. 'I had had a vision of unearthly beauty,' Jung says, 'and that was why I was able to live at all. Liverpool is the "pool of life". The "liver", according to an old view, is the seat of life – that which "makes to live".'

Unfortunately, even here, Jung is basing his supposition on fanciful etymology, presumably just having heard the name 'Liverpool', and never having been there. The derivation of the placename is 'pool with clotted water' – rather more to the point than 'pool of life'.

By 1987, I noticed, the sign had been taken down.

A LIVING legend . . . in one's own lifetime
See **legend**.

Dr LIVINGSTONE, I presume
See **presume.**

LONELY are the Brave
The film (USA 1962) was based on a novel by Edward Abbey called *Brave Cowboy*. The film title was not a quotation, so far as I can discover.

None But the LONELY Heart
See **none.**

The LONGEST Pleasure
The novel (1986) by Anne Mather includes the information that the title derives from Byron: 'Hatred is the longest pleasure.'

Consider what the LORD said to Moses
See **right.**

LOVE among the ruins
An evocative phrase, for some reason. The notion of love among classical ruins seems hauntingly appealing, rather as do the reminders of time and decay in Arcadia (cf. *'Et in Arcadia ego'*)

Evelyn Waugh entitled one of his shorter novels *Love Among the Ruins: A Romance of the Near Future* (1953). Angela Thirkell used the title for a novel in 1948 (turned into a TV movie in 1974 with Laurence Olivier and Katherine Hepburn) about an elderly actress who turns to a former lover for legal counsel in a breach of promise case.

Earlier than this, we have the painting by Sir Edward Burne-Jones (1833-98) where the lover and his lass embrace among fallen pillars and stones with mysterious inscriptions on them, hemmed in by the briar rose which rambles over all, and search for the way to Cythara where, in the end, they must separate. The subject comes from the *Hypnerotomachia*. The painting dates from 1870-73 and hangs in Wightwick Manor.

Earlier still is Robert Browning's poem with the title in *Men and Women* (1855).

To know him is to LOVE him
See **know.**

LOVE in a Cold Climate

Robert Southey, the poet, writing to his brother Thomas (28 April 1797) said: 'She has made me half in love with a cold climate.' Could this have helped to provide Nancy Mitford with the title of her 1949 novel?

Whatever the case, Evelyn Waugh was keen to assure her that she had chosen a good one. In a letter (10 October 1949), he told her: *'Love in a Cold Climate* has become a phrase. I mean when people want to be witty they say I've caught a cold in a cold climate and everyone understands.'

LOVE is a Many-Splendoured Thing

The novel by Han Suyin, *A Many-Splendoured Thing* (1952, filmed 1955 as *Love is a Many-Splendoured Thing)* alludes to Francis Thompson's posthumously published poem, *The Kingdom of God* (1913):

> The angels keep their ancient places;
> Turn but a stone and start a wing!
> 'Tis ye, 'tis your estranged faces,
> That miss the many-splendoured thing.

LOVE is two minutes . . . of squishing noises

Of recent *bons mots,* one of the most quoted – but variously so – is the opinion of 'Johnny Rotten' (John Lydon, *b.* 1957), who was at one time with the notorious punk group, the Sex Pistols.

Jonathon Green's *Dictionary of Contemporary Quotations* (1982) has the version: 'Love is two minutes fifty-two seconds of squishing noises. It shows your mind isn't clicking right.' This I take it is definitive, although in my *Graffiti 3* (1981) I had had a photograph taken the previous year in London of a wall bearing the legend: 'Love is three minutes of squelching noises. (Mr J. Rotten).'

Auberon Waugh in *Private Eye* (18 November 1983) settled for 'two and a half minutes of squelching' but provided the interesting information that, in an interview with Christena Appleyard in the *Mirror,* Rotten had wished to amend his aphorism. 'It is more like five minutes now, he says, because he has mastered a new technique.'

McConville and Shearlaw, in *The Slanguage of Sex* (1984), claim that as a result of Rotten's statement, 'squelching' became an expression for sexual intercourse. They suggest that he had referred to 'two minutes of squelching noises' in *New Musical Express* in 1978.

'Tis LOVE, 'tis love, that makes the world go round

'Love makes the world go round' is an English proverb, apparently borrowed from the French. In the form, 'Oh, 'tis love, 'tis love . . .', it is what the Duchess says to Alice in Lewis Carroll's *Alice's Adventures in Wonderland* (1865).

W. S. Gilbert, in *Iolanthe* (1882), has a song made up of proverbial sayings, including, 'In for a penny, in for a pound – /It's love that makes the world go round.' Ian Bradley, in his *Annotated Gilbert and Sullivan* (Vol. 1), notes how a previous commentator wondered if this had to do with the old saying 'It's drink that makes the world go round', and also finds it in *Our Mutual Friend* by Charles Dickens (published in the same year as *Alice*).

But earlier than these was a French song (published 1851, but written as early as 1700), *'C'est l'amour, l'amour/ Qui fait le monde/ À la ronde'*. There is now an English song, 'Love makes the world go round' by Noel Gay (written *c.* 1936).

These You Have LOVED

As the title of a BBC Radio record programme, this has a history going back to 1938 when Doris Arnold introduced favourite middle-of-the-road music. The title was still being used 40 years later. Originally it was chosen by way of allusion to the line 'These *I* have loved' in the poem 'The Great Lover' by Rupert Brooke. This is a 'list' poem in which Brooke mentions some of his favourite things (rather as the song with that title did in the much later musical *The Sound of Music*). Brooke's 'loves' included 'white plates and cups' and 'the rough male kiss of blankets'.

I LOVED you, so I drew these tides of men . . .

The epigraph of *The Seven Pillars of Wisdom* (1926, 1935) by T. E. Lawrence is the verse:

> I loved you, so I drew these tides of men into my hands
>   and wrote my will across the sky in stars.
> To earn you freedom, the seven pillared worthy house,
>   that your eyes might be shining for me
>   When we came.

The dedication is to 'S. A.'. In a fit of naivety, I once supposed that 'S. A.' stood for 'Saudi Arabia'. I might just as well have said 'South Africa'. Much more likely – though few things can be certain about that maddening self-promoter – the dedication was to Lawrence's Arab protegé, Selim Ahmed, whom he had brought on a visit to Oxford before the First World War and who had died in 1918.

Cheaper to LOWER the Atlantic

A joke in circulation after 1980 concerning the expensive cinema flop *Raise the Titanic!* was that Lord Grade, the film's producer, had said it 'would have been cheaper to lower the Atlantic'. Alas, on *Frost on Sunday* (TV-am, 23 November 1987) he denied he had said that. He had merely remarked, 'I didn't raise the *Titanic* high enough . . .'.

Sarcasm is the LOWEST form of wit
See **sarcasm.**

LUCKY Jim

Kingsley Amis's comic novel (1953) about a hapless university lecturer, Jim Dixon, takes its title from a not terribly relevant American song by Frederick Bowers (1874-1961) and his vaudeville partner Charles Horwitz (though it is usually ascribed to Anon.). It tells of a man who has to wait for his childhood friend to die before he can marry the girl they were once both after. Then, married to the woman and not enjoying it, he would rather he was dead like his friend: 'Oh, lucky Jim, how I envy him.'

Once aboard the LUGGER and the girl is mine!

'A male catchphrase either joyously or derisively jocular' notes Partridge/Catchphrases. It came originally from a late Victorian melodrama – either *My Jack and Dorothy* by Ben Landeck (*c.* 1890) or *The Gypsy Farmer* by John Benn Johnstone (*d.* 1891). In 1908, A. S. M. Hutchinson called a novel *Once Aboard the Lugger – the History of George and Mary.* I am also told that the phrase occurs in the music hall song 'On the Good Ship Yacki-Hicki-Doo-La', written and composed by Billy Merson in 1918 and recorded by him on Decca F2653.

Benham has a different version, as often. According to him, 'Once aboard the lugger and all is well' was said to have been an actor's gag in *Black Eyed Susan,* a pantomine *c.* 1830-40.

A house is a MACHINE for living in
See **house**.

MAGGIE May
Given the way the popular press has taken to referring to
'Maggie' Thatcher since she became Prime Minister in 1979 – I
suppose it makes headline writing easier – it was inevitable that
she would make use of the song title 'Maggie May' at some stage.
In April 1983, she was trying to appear coy about the timing of
the next general election and told the annual dinner of the
Confederation of British Industry that some people were talking
of the end of the Parliament, 'a little prematurely, I think'.

'It reminds me of the old song, "Maggie May". Some say
Maggie may, others say Maggie may not. I can only say that
when the time comes, I shall decide.'

I suspect this was not one of the quotations she carries about in
her handbag, but one into which she was lured by her speech
writers. As Eric Heffer, a Liverpool Labour MP swiftly pointed
out, 'Plainly the Prime Minister knew nothing of the historical
connections of this song about a notorious Liverpool prostitute
who swiped sailors' trousers,' he said – suggesting at the same
time that she should have 'sharp words' with her speech writers.

Maggie May's exploits were being sung about as long ago as
1830. A sailor laments:

> In the morning I awoke
> With my heart all sorn an broke,
> No jacket, trousers, waistcoat could I find.
> When I asked her where they were,
> She said to me, Kind sir,
> They're down in Stanley's pawnshop number nine.

> To the pawnshop I did go,
> No trousers, jacket, waistcoat could I find
> And a policeman came and took that girl away.
> For she robbed a Yankee whaler,
> She won't walk down Lime Street any more.

A number of groups (including the Beatles) revived the song at the time of Liverpool's resurgence in the early 1960s. Lionel Bart and Alun Owen wrote a musical based on her life and called *Maggie May* in 1964.

MAGIC circle

In British politics this usage was introduced by Iain Macleod in an article on the previous year's struggle for the leadership of the Conservative Party (*Spectator*, January 1964). He was describing the way in which the leader, although supposedly just 'emerging', was in fact the choice of a small group of influential Tory peers and manipulators. Presumably, he was influenced in his choice of phrase by the magicians' Magic Circle. The phrase has subsequently been applied to other semi-secret cabals to which those who might wish to belong are denied access. A year or two later, and as a result of this experience, the Tory leadership was decided instead by a ballot of Conservative MPs.

C'est MAGNIFIQUE, mais ce n'est pas la guerre

In the beginning was the remark, 'It is magnificent, but it is not war', which was made by Maréchal Bosquet (1810-61) about the Charge of the Light Brigade in 1854.

Then along came *Punch* during the First World War and said of margarine, '*C'est magnifique, mais ce n'est pas le beurre*' ('butter').

In about 1962, I first heard the Oxford joke about the façade of Worcester College which, having a splendid clock on it, gave rise to, '*C'est magnifique, mais ce n'est pas la gare*' ('station').

Accordingly, when I was launching *Quote . . . Unquote* in 1975, I devised a spot in which my guests would invent what might have been said in certain situations. For example, what would Napoleon have said if he had arrived at Euston instead of Waterloo? How about, *C'est magnifique, mais ce n'est pas la gare . . .*'? Alas, it didn't work out . . . and I soon dropped the idea.

MAIRZY doats and dozy doats

One of the most impenetrable graffiti jokes that ever came my way was, at least at first glance, the scribbled addition to a notice in Liverpool proclaiming: 'Mersey Docks and Harbour Board . . . and little lambs eat ivy.' This was recorded in 1944. The graffiti-writer had cleverly spotted that the rhythm of 'Mersey Docks and Harbour Board' exactly matched the first line of a song, and also that a Scouser would pronounce Mersey, 'mairzy'.

Purely generational. In 1943, a nonsense song was popular in Britain and American called Mairzy Doats and Dozy Doats (Mares Eat Oats and Does Eat Oats)' It went:

> I know a ditty nutty as a fruit cake
> Goofy as a goon and silly as a loon . . .
>
> Mairzy doats and dozy doats
> And liddle lamzy divey.
> A kiddley divey too,
> Wouldn't you?

The song was 'written' by Milton Drake, Al Hoffman and Jerry Livingston but, as the Opies point out in their *Oxford Dictionary of Nursery Rhymes*, there is a 'catch' which, when said quickly, appears to be in Latin:

> In fir tar is,
> In oak none is,
> In mud eels are,
> In clay none are.
> Goat eat ivy
> Mare eat oats.

Say the Opies, 'The joke may be traced back 500 years to a medical manuscript in Henry VI's time.'

If a MAN bites a dog, that's news
See **dog.**

What is that MAN for?
See **for.**

I MARRIED him for better or worse, but not for lunch
See **worse.**

Advice to persons about to MARRY – Don't
What is probably the most famous of all *Punch* jokes appeared on the January page of the 1845 Almanack. R. G. G. Price in his history of the magazine wonders whether it is perhaps 'the most

famous joke ever made' and remarks that 'it needs an effort to realise how neat, ingenious and profound it must have seemed at the time'.

It was based on an advertisement put out by a house furnisher of the day and was probably contributed by Henry Mayhew, better known for his serious surveys of *London Labour and the London Poor*, though others also claimed to have done so.

MEAN Streets

The phrase 'mean streets' – as used for the title of a 1973 film about an Italian ghetto in New York – probably alludes to a noted sentence by Raymond Chandler (1888-1959) in 'The Simple Art of Murder' (1950). 'Down these mean streets a man must go who is not himself mean; who is neither tarnished nor afraid' refers to the heroic qualities a detective should have.

However, the phrase had been used long before this. In 1894, Arthur Morrison wrote *Tales of Mean Streets* about impoverished life in the East End of London.

Only the MEDIOCRE are always at their best

I have seen this thought attributed to Max Beerbohm in the form, 'Only mediocrity can be trusted to be always at its best' (quoted in S. N. Behrman, *Conversations with Max*, 1960). Also to Jean Giraudoux and W. Somerset Maugham (the latter specifically with regard to writers).

Where do we find such MEN?

On the fortieth anniversary of the D-Day landings, President Reagan visited Europe and made a speech in which he eulogized those who had taken part in the event. 'Where do we find such men?' he asked.

On a previous occasion he had said:

> Many years ago in one of the four wars in my lifetime, an admiral stood on the bridge of a carrier watching the planes take off and out into the darkness bent on a night combat mission and then found himself asking, with no one there to answer – just himself to hear his own voice – 'Where do we find such men?'

But the very first time he had used the line he had made it clear where it came from and that it was fiction. The story comes from James Michener's novel *Bridges at Toko-Ri*, later filmed (1954) with William Holden who asks, 'Where do we get such men?' Over the years, fiction became fact for Reagan. Perhaps he could not, or was unwilling, to distinguish between the two.

On another occasion he told a meeting of the Congressional Medal of Honor Society about an aircraft gunner who couldn't leave his post as his plane was crashing. He is told by his commanding officer that he has won a 'Congressional Medal of Honor, posthumously awarded'. No such incident happened in real life, though it did in the film *Wing and a Prayer* (1944).

In 1985, Michael Rogin, a professor of political science at Berkeley, explored similar borrowings of film-lines in Reagan's speeches in a presentation entitled 'Ronald Reagan: The Movie'. Among the examples he found, both credited and uncredited, were these:

During the New Hampshire primary of 1980, Reagan won a dispute over who should speak in a debate by declaring, 'I am paying for this microphone, Mr Green! Never mind that the man's name was actually 'Breen', the line in the form, 'Don't you shut me off, I'm paying for this broadcast' was delivered by Spencer Tracy in the film *State of the Union* (1948).

In *Mr Deeds Goes to Town*, Gary Cooper extolled man's responsibility to help his fellow man thus:

> From what I can see, no matter what system of government we have, there will always be leaders and always be followers. It's like the road out in front of my house. It's on a steep hill. And every day I watch the cars climbing up. Some go lickety-split up that hill on high – some have to shift in to second – and some splutter and shake and slip back to the bottom again. Same cars – same gasoline – yet some make it and some don't. And I say the fellas who can make the hill on high should stop once in a while and help those who can't.

Reagan quoted the speech verbatim in selling his welfare voluntarism programme, though he *did* credit the source.

Reagan credited the film *Rambo* when he said, 'In the spirit of Rambo, let me tell you we're going to win this time.'

He used his own line from the film *King's Row* ('Where's the rest of me? – he'd just had his legs amputated) as the title of an early autobiography.

He used *Star Wars* the movie to promote 'Star Wars' the weapons system: 'It isn't about fear, it's about hope, and in that struggle, if you'll pardon my stealing a film line, "The force is with us".'

He repeatedly made use of the line 'Win this one for the

Gipper' from the film *Knute Rockne* (1940) until it became his own slogan.

See also 'Go ahead, make my *day*'.

Esau selleth his birthright for a MESS of potage

The expression 'to sell one's birthright for a mess of potage', meaning to sacrifice something for material comfort, has biblical origins but is not a quotation of a verse in the Bible. 'Esau selleth his birthright for a mess of potage' appears as a chapter heading for Genesis 25 in one or two early translations of the Bible, though not in the Authorized Version of 1611.

The word 'mess' is used in its sense of 'a portion of liquid or pulpy food'. 'Potage' is thick soup (cf. French *potage*).

The lady doth protest too much, METHINKS

Gertrude's line from Shakespeare's *Hamlet* (III.ii.225) is often evoked to mean, 'There's something suspicious about the way that person is protesting his/her innocence more than is natural.' However, what Hamlet's mother is actually doing is giving her opinion of *The Mousetrap*, the play-within-a-play. What Gertrude means to say is that the Player Queen is overdoing her protestations and she used the word 'protest' in the sense of 'state formally', not 'complain'.

MIDDLE of the road

Mrs Thatcher to James Prior (quoted in Kenneth Harris, *Thatcher*, 1988): 'Standing in the middle of the road is very dangerous, you get knocked down by traffic from both sides.'

'We know what happens to people who stay in the middle of the road. They get run over.' – Aneurin Bevan, quoted in the *Observer*, 9 December 1953.

I expect Confucius probably said it too.

The age of MIRACLES is not past

ODCIE explains this saying as meaning 'something good can happen, or has happened, that seems inexplicable, or is of a kind that might once have been considered to be the work of God'. And it adds that the use is 'usually as facetious comment on an unexpected but pleasurable event, a complete reversal of a situation to one's advantage etc.'.

An example of (almost) this phrase, dating from 1900, is contained in a letter written by Oscar Wilde in European exile:

'Frank Harris is very wonderful and really very good and *sympathique* . . . He keeps Bosie [Lord Alfred Douglas] in order: clearly the age of miracles is not over.'

Of course, the saying is a semi-ironic twist upon the much older proverbial saying 'The age of miracles is [. . .] past.' *CODP* finds two forms of this expression in Shakespeare – 'miracles are ceas'd' (*King Henry V*, I.i.67) and 'They say miracles are past (*All's Well that Ends Well*, II.iii.1).

One of Our Aircraft is MISSING

In *A Life in Movies*(1986), Michael Powell writes of a moment in the Second World War: 'After I returned from Canada and I had time to listen to the nine o'clock news on the BBC, I had become fascinated by a phrase which occurred only too often: "One of our aircraft failed to return".' So he decided to make a film about such a failed bombing mission. 'Our screenplay, which was half-finished, was entitled *One of Our Aircraft is Missing*. We were never too proud to take a tip from distributors, and we saw that the original title, *One of Our Aircraft Failed to Return*, although evocative and euphonious, was downbeat.' The film was released in 1941.

In 1975, Walt Disney came up with a film called *One of Our Dinosaurs is Missing*, which doubtless nods in the direction of the earlier film.

I don't like MONDAYS

The title of a hit song written and performed by Bob Geldof and the Boom Town Rats (1979) derives from the excuse given by Brenda Spencer, a San Diego schoolgirl, for opening fire and killing an elementary school principal and a custodian, and wounding nine others in January 1979. A journalist rang her up and asked her why she was doing it and she replied, 'Something to do. I don't like Mondays.'

MONEY is the root of all evil

Strictly speaking, it is, 'the *love* of money is the root of all evil' – 1 Timothy 6:10.

MONEY makes the world go around

With this phrase, we may have to thank the writers of the musical *Cabaret* for either creating an instant 'saying' or, perhaps in this instance, for introducing to the English language something that was long known in others. 'Money makes the world go around', echoing 'Tis, *love*, that makes the world go round' (q.v.), is not recorded in either the *ODP* or the *CODP*.

I see that it appears in the English-language key to the Flemish proverbs picture by David Teniers the Younger (1610-90), at Belvoir Castle. The painting shows an obviously wealthy man holding a globe. How odd that it should have taken a song in a 1960s musical to get this expression into English.

Si MONUMENTUM requiris . . .

The epitaph in St Paul's Cathedral to its architect, Sir Christopher Wren (1632-1723) is '*Si monumentum requiris, circumspice*' ('If you seek for a monument, look around you'). Traditionally, the composition of this inscription is attributed to his son.

Horace Smith (1779-1849) commented that it would be equally applicable to a physician buried in a churchyard.

When Dean Inge was at St Paul's, pointing out the need to keep a wary eye on the traffic if one wishes to cross the road safely, he gave the warning: '*Nisi monumentum requaeris, circumspice*' ('Unless you want a monument, look out . . .').

Favourites of the MOON
See **favourites.**

The MOON and Sixpence

The title of W. Somerset Maugham's novel (1919) was taken from a review of his earlier book *Of Human Bondage* in the *Times Literary Supplement* which had said that the main character, was 'like so many young men . . . so busy yearning for the moon that he never saw the sixpence at his feet'.

Nor the MOON by Night

Used as the title of a film (UK 1958) about a game warden in Africa, this is based on Psalm 121, the one that begins: 'I will lift up mine eyes unto the hills.' It goes on: 'The Lord is thy shade upon thy right hand. The sun shall not smite thee by day, nor the moon by night.' In the USA, the film was called *Elephant Gun*.

One clear MORN is boon enough
See **life.**

Never glad confident MORNING again
See **never.**

The firstest with the MOSTEST
See **firstest.**

Dead! . . . and never called me MOTHER!
See **dead.**

Why is a MOUSE when it spins?
I mentioned a nonsensical riddle on Channel 4's *Countdown* programme in 1987 and was amazed at the response I had from viewers. The riddle went:

> Q. Why is a mouse when it spins?
> A. The higher, the fewer.

Most people remembered it being told to them by teasing parents in the 1920s and 1930s. Mr John Mack of Surbiton suggested that it originated in repartee between Jasper Maskelyne and Oswald Williams in magic shows at St George's Hall in Langham Place, London in about 1930. If not originated, he says, it was certainly much used by them.

Mrs Jean E. French of Finchampstead suggested that it might not be nonsensical if you substituted the word 'when' for 'why' in posing the riddle. From this I wondered whether it had anything to do with 'Hickory, dickory, dock, the mouse ran up the clock, the clock struck one, the mouse fell down . . . '. A variation of the riddle (which doesn't help either) is:

> Q. Why is a mouse when it's spinning its web?
> A. Because the more the fewer the quicker.

Other viewers raked up these equally nonsensical riddles:

> Q. How is man when he's out?
> A. The sooner he does, the much.

> Q. What is the difference between a duck?
> A. One of its legs is both the same.

> Q. Which would you rather, or go fishing/
>   swimming/hunting?
> A. One rode a horse and the other rhododendron.

This last may not be a riddle at all. Partridge/Slang gives 'What shall we do, or go fishing' as a 'trick elaboration' of the straightforward 'What shall we do now?' (It is quoted in Dorothy L. Sayers, *The Nine Tailors*, 1934.) Compare: 'Which would you rather be – or a wasp?'

Finally, to restore sanity, here is an old riddle which *does* have an answer:

> Q.   Why is a sheet of foolscap like a lazy dog?
> A.   A sheet of foolscap is an ink lined plain. An inclined plain is a slope up. A slow pup is a lazy dog.

(See also 'Why is a *raven* like a writing desk?')

Ladies never MOVE
See **ladies.**

MURDER, She Wrote
In 1984 an American TV series began with Angela Lansbury as Jessica Fletcher, a widowed best-selling crime writer who became involved in solving actual murder cases. Modelled on Miss Marple perhaps, there was another nod in the direction of Agatha Christie in the title. *Murder She Said* had been the title given to a 1961 film version of the Miss Marple story *4.50 From Paddington*.

That echoed *Murder He Says*, a 1945 film, and 'Murder, He Says', the curious Frank Loesser lyric to music by Jimmy McHugh which was sung by Betty Hutton in the film *Happy Go Lucky* (1942).

MUSSOLINI made the trains run on time
See **trains.**

N. or M.

The answer to the first question in the catechism in the Prayer Book, 'What is your name?', refers only to the answerer's Christian name or names, and that is exactly what the letters mean: 'N' is the first letter of the Latin *nomen*, 'name'; 'M' is a contraction of NN standing for the plural *nomina*, 'names'.

Agatha Christie gave the title *N or M?* to a spy story in 1941.

NACHT und Nebel

'Night and Fog' was the title of a 1941 decree issued under Hitler's signature. It described a simple process: anyone suspected of a crime against occupying German forces was to disappear into 'night and fog'. Such people were thrown into the concentration camp system, in most cases never to be heard of again.

Alain Resnais, the French film director, made a cinema short about a concentration camp called *Nuit et Brouillard* (1955).

But where does the haunting phrase come from? In Wagner's opera *Das Rheingold*, '*Nacht und Nebel niemand gleich*' is the spell that Alberich puts on the magic Tarnhelm which renders him invisible and omnipresent. It means approximately, 'In night and fog no one is seen', or, 'Night and fog is the same as being no one, a non-person', or, 'Night and fog make you no one instantly'. Undoubtedly, this is where the Nazi use originated.

NASTY, brutish and short
See **brutish**.

The nation's airy NAVIES grappling in the central blue
See **airy**.

Does Little NELL die?

Six thousand book-loving Americans, according to one account, hurried to the docks in New York to ask this question of sailors arriving from England. Another version is that it was longshoremen demanding 'How is Little Nell?' or 'Is Little Nell dead?' As the Charles Dickens novel *The Old Curiosity Shop* (1841) was serialized, they were waiting for the arrival of the final instalment of the magazine to find out what happened to the heroine.

The answer is, of course, yes. Oscar Wilde commented, 'One must have a heart of stone to read the death of Little Nell without laughing.'

Hesitantly, one might draw a comparison with the question, 'Who shot JR?' in a late twentieth-century equivalent of the serialized novel, the TV series *Dallas*. The hero-villain, J. R. Ewing, of the soap opera about oil-folk, was shot in the cliff-hanging last episode of the US programme's 1979-80 season. The question of who had inflicted this far from mortal wound caused a sensation in the USA and the UK. Consequently, the first episode of the next series attracted 53.3 per cent of the American viewing audience, the highest-ever rating. (The guilty party was a jilted lover, played by Bing Crosby's daughter.)

NEVER glad confident morning again

This is very much on my list of over-used, mis-used quotations. It comes from Robert Browning's poem 'The Lost Leader' in which he regretfully portrayed Wordsworth as a man who had lost his revolutionary zeal.

A correct – and devastating – use of the phrase came on 17 June 1963 when the British Government under its Prime Minister Harold Macmillan was rocking over the Profumo scandal. In the House of Commons, Tory MP Nigel Birch said to Macmillan:

> I myself feel that the time will come very soon when my right hon. Friend ought to make way for a much younger colleague. I feel that that ought to happen. I certainly will not quote at him the savage words of Cromwell, but perhaps some of the words of Browning might be appropriate in his poem on 'The Lost Leader', in which he wrote: . . .

> Let him never come back to us!
> There would be doubt, hesitation and pain.
> Forced praise on our part – the glimmer of twilight,
> Never glad confident morning again!

'Never glad confident morning again!' – so I hope that the change will not be too long delayed.

Birch was right. A few months later Macmillan was out of office; another year, and so was the Government.

In November 1983, on the twentieth anniversary of President Kennedy's assassination, Lord Harlech, former British Ambassador to Washington, paid tribute thus in the *Observer* magazine: 'Since 1963 the world has seemed a bleaker place, and for me and I suspect millions of my contemporaries he remains the lost leader – "Never glad confident morning again".' Harlech may have wanted to evoke a leader who had been lost to the world, but surely it was a mistake to quote a *criticism* of one?

Also in November 1983, in the *Observer*, Paul Johnson wrote an attack (which he later appeared to regret) on Margaret Thatcher: 'Her courage and sound instincts made her formidable. But if her judgement can no longer be trusted, what is left? A very ordinary woman, occupying a position where ordinary virtues are not enough. For me, I fear it can never be "glad confident morning again".'

Still at it in 1988 was Shirely Williams. When part of the SDP united with the Liberals, she used the words about David Owen, the SDP's once and future leader.

I went to NEW ZEALAND but it was closed

This is a joke which gets rediscovered every so often. The Beatles found it in the 1960s; slightly before, Anna Russell, the musical comedienne, said it on one of her records. It has also been attributed to Clement Freud. But William Franklyn, son of the antipodean actor, Leo Franklyn, tells me that his father was saying it in the 1920s.

I expect W. C. Fields began saying 'I went to Philadelphia and found that it was closed' about the same time (if indeed he did).

If a man bites a dog, that's NEWS
See **dog**.

No more Mr NICE Guy

'Mr Nice Guy' is a nickname applied to 'straight' figures (especially politicians) who are possibly following someone who is palpably not 'nice' (Gerald Ford after Richard Nixon, for example). They then sometimes feel the need to throw off some of their virtuous image, as presidential challenger Senator Ed Muskie did in 1972 – and his aides declared, 'No more Mr Nice Guy'. In April 1973, Alice Cooper had a song entitled 'No More Mr Nice Guy' in the British charts.

Safire dates to the 'mid-1950s' the joke about Hitler agreeing to make a comeback with the words, 'But this time – no more Mr Nice Guy.'

There Shall be No NIGHT
The title of the play (1940) by Robert Sherwood apparently comes from Revelation 22:5.

So deep is the NIGHT
See **deep.**

NIGHT and Fog
See *Nacht.*

The NIGHT has a Thousand Eyes
First came a story by Cornell Woolrich (about a vaudeville entertainer who can predict the future), adapted as a film in 1948. Out of that came a song (to be followed by several others), all with this title, and all deriving from the poem by Francis William Bourdillon in *Among the Flowers* (1878):

> The night has a thousand eyes,
> And yet the day but one;
> Yet the light of the bright world dies
> With the dying sun.

When a lady says NO, she means perhaps
See **lady.**

Oh, my dear fellow, the NOISE . . . and the people!
Describing what it was like to be in battle, a certain Captain Strahan exclaimed the above. According to the *ODQ*, quoting the *Hudson Review*, Winter 1951, he said it after the Battle of Bastogne in 1944.

Various correspondents suggest it was earlier in the war than this, however. Roy T. Kendall writes to me,

I heard this phrase used, in a humorous manner, during the early part of 1942. It was related to me as having been said by a young Guards officer, newly returned from Dunkirk, who on being asked what it was like used the expression: the inference being a blasé attitude to the dangers and a disdain of the common soldiery he was forced to mix with.

Tony Bagnall Smith adds that the Guards officer was still properly dressed and equipped when he said it, and that his reply was, 'My dear, the noise and the people – how they smelt!'

NONE But the Lonely Heart

The novel (1943) by Richard Llewellyn and the film (USA 1944) appear to have an original and very distinctive title (just like the same author's *How Green Was My Valley*). Nevertheless, 'None But the Weary Heart' is the title often given to a song by Tchaikovsky (Op. 6, No. 6.) This originated as 'Mignon's Song' in the novel *Wilhelm Meister* by Goethe – *'Nur wer die Sehnsucht kennt'* ('Only those who know what longing is') – which was translated into Russian by Mey. The lyrics of Tchaikovsky's song have been translated into English as, 'None but the weary heart can understand how I have suffered and how I am tormented.'

NOSTALGIA isn't what it used to be

According to *Newsweek* (22 May 1978), Simone Signoret found the title of her autobiography chalked up on a wall in New York City. As such, it has become one of the most well-known examples of graffiti comment.

As 'Nostalgia ain't what it used to be' this has been attributed to the American novelist Peter de Vries.

The only thing necessary for the triumph of evil is for good men to do NOTHING

– so said Edmund Burke, or at least he is often quoted as having said so. Bartlett cited it in a letter from Burke to William Smith on 9 January 1795, but on checking it is not there.

In an exhaustive, almost exhausting, piece in *On Language* (1980) William Safire describes his unavailing attempts to find a proper source. In the House of Commons on 23 April 1770, Burke said 'When bad men combine, the good must associate; else they will fall one by one, an unpitied sacrifice in a contemptible struggle' – which seems to be heading somewhere in the right direction. But, for the moment, we have here another of those quotations which arrive apparently from nowhere, and get quoted and re-quoted without justification. On the other hand, Burke wouldn't have wished to disown it, would he?

NOTHING venture, nothing win
The first recorded use of the proverb in this precise form is in Sir Charles Sedley's comedy *The Mulberry Garden* (1668). However, the variants 'nothing venture, nothing gain' and 'nothing venture, nothing have' go back further, and may derive from a Latin original.

W. S. Gilbert used this form in the 'proverb' song in Act II of *Iolanthe* (1882). Sir Edmund Hillary, the mountaineer, used it as the title of his autobiography in 1975.

NUTS!
In December 1944, the Germans launched a counter-offensive in what came to be known as the Battle of the Bulge. General Anthony 'Old Crock' McAuliffe (1898-1975) was acting commander of the American 101st Airborne Division and was ordered to defend the strategic town of Bastogne in the Ardennes forest. This was important because Bastogne stood at a Belgian crossroads through which the advancing armies had to pass. When the Americans had been surrounded like 'the hole in a doughnut' for seven days, the Germans said they would accept a surrender. On 23 December, McAuliffe replied: 'Nuts!'

The Germans first of all interpreted this one word reply as meaning 'crazy' and took time to appreciate what they were being told. Encouraged by McAuliffe's spirit, his men managed to hold the line and thus defeat the last major enemy offensive of the war.

McAuliffe recounted the episode in a BBC broadcast on 3 January 1945:

> When we got it [the surrender demand] we thought it was the funniest thing we ever heard. I just laughed and said, 'Nuts', but the German major who brought it wanted a formal answer; so I decided – well, I'd just say 'Nuts' – so I had it written out: 'QUOTE, TO THE GERMAN COMMANDER: NUTS. SIGNED, THE AMERICAN COMMANDER UNQUOTE' . . .

When Agence France Presse sought a way of translating this they resorted to, '*Vous n'êtes que de vieilles noix.*' When McAuliffe's obituary came to be written, the *New York Times* observed: 'Unofficial versions strongly suggest that the actual language used by the feisty American general was considerably stronger and more profane than the comparatively mild "Nuts", but the official version will have to stand.'

OH! Calcutta!

Kenneth Tynan's sexually explicit stage revue, first presented on Broadway in 1969, took its title from a curious piece of word play. It is the equivalent of the French *'Oh, quel cul t'as'*, meaning – broadly speaking – 'Oh, what a lovely bum you've got.' French *cul* is derived from the Latin *culus*, 'buttocks' but, according to the context, may be applied to the female vagina or male anus.

Shakespeare in *The Second Part of King Henry VI* (IV.vii.26) calls the Dauphin of France, 'Monsieur Basimecu' because of his fawning manners – i.e., *'bus mine cue/ baise mon cul/ kiss my backside'*.

In her *Life of Kenneth Tynan* (1987), Kathleen Tynan states that she was writing an article on the surreaslist painter Clovis Trouille, one of whose works was a naked odalisque lying on her side to reveal a spherical backside. The title was 'Oh! Calcutta! Calcutta!' 'I suggested to Ken that he call his erotic revue *Oh! Calcutta! . . .* I did not know at the time that it had the further advantage of being a French pun.'

A professor of French who is an authority on puns suggests that this one may date from the *belle époque*.

All for ONE and one for all

See **all**.

Well, it's a-ONE for the money, a-two for the show

'. . . three to get ready, now go, cat, go!' The start to the Carl Perkins song 'Blue Suede Shoes' (immortalized by Elvis Presley in 1956) is the form of words that children traditionally use at the start of races. A version used in Britain and dating from 1888 is, 'One for the money, two for the show, three to make ready, and four to go.' Another version, from 1853, is 'One to make ready, and two to prepare; good luck to the rider, and away goes the mare.'

OPPORTUNITY knocks but once

A talent contest called *Opportunity Knocks* ran on British TV from 1956 to 1977. Introducing contestants, the host, Hughie Greene, would say: 'For —— of ——, opportunity knocks!' and so characteristic was the pronunciation that the phrase became his.

It derives, of course, from the rather more restrictive proverbial expression, 'Opportunity knocks *but once*.' As *CODP* notes, 'Fortune' occurs instead of 'opportunity' in earlier forms of the proverb and slightly different ideas are expressed – 'opportunity is said to knock once or more, but in other quotations, once only'.

From Sir Geoffrey Fenton's *Bandello* (1567) comes the example: 'Fortune once in the course of our life, doth put into our hands the offer of a good turn.'

Let's get OUT of here!

Hardly a mighty line but, according to the *Guinness Book of Film Facts and Feats* (1985), 'a recent survey of 150 American features of the period 1938-74 [revived on British television] showed that it was used at least once in 84 per cent of Hollywood productions and more than once in 17 per cent'. Hence, it is nominated as 'the most hackneyed line in movie scripts'. One would guess that 'Let's go!' is probably not far behind.

I am just going OUTSIDE, and I may be some time

When Captain Lawrence Oates (nicknamed 'Titus') (1880-1912) walked to his death on Captain R. F. Scott's 1912 polar expedition, in the vain hope of saving his companions, he defined courage for a generation of Englishmen. Oddly, his most famous remark is omitted by both *ODQ* and Bartlett.

Beaten to the South Pole by the Norwegian explorer, Amundsen, the small party fell victim to terrible weather conditions on the return journey to its ship. One man died and Oates, suffering from scurvy, from frostbitten and gangrenous feet, and from an old war wound, realized that he would be next. Without him slowing them down, the remaining three might stand a better chance of survival. With classic stiff-upper-lip understatement,

Oates was reported by Scott as having said, 'I'm just going outside, and I may be some time.'

As the only record of what Oates said was contained in Scott's diary, it has been suggested that the words were Scott's invention, but opinion suggests that it was an act perfectly in character and there would have been no need to invent them.

Nevertheless, Oates provided the basis of a joke expression or catchphrase to be used when a person is departing from company for whatever reason. When Trevor Griffiths came to write a TV drama series about Scott's expedition, called *The Last Place on Earth* (1985), he ruffled a few feathers by substituting the line, 'Call of nature, Birdie.'

All the world OWES me a living

I was first alerted to the provenance of this expression by its use as the epigraph to Graham Greene's novel *England Made Me* (1935):

> 'All the word owes me a living.'
>
> Walt Disney
> *(The Grasshopper and the Ants)*

Could Disney really claim credit for the phrase? Well, the cartoon in question – one of the first 'Silly Symphonies' – was released in 1934. It is based on the Aesop fable 'Of the ant and the grasshopper (as it is called in Caxton's first English translation, 1484) which tells of a grasshopper asking an ant for corn to eat in winter. The ant asks, 'What have you done all the summer past?' and the grasshopper can only answer, 'I have sung.' The moral is that you should provide yourself in the summer with that you need in winter.

Disney turns the grasshopper into a fiddler and gives him a song to sing (written by Larry Morey to music by Leigh Harline):

> Oh! the world owes me a living
> Deedle, diedle, doedle, diedledum.
> Oh! the world owes me a living
> Deedle, diedle, doedle, diedleum, etc.

I haven't seen the film, but I know this develops in time to:

> Oh, the world owes us a living *(rpt.)*
> You should soil your Sunday pants
> Like those other foolish ants,
> So let's play and sing and dance . . .

And then, when the error of his ways has been pointed out to him, the grasshopper sings:

> I owe the world a living *(rpt.)*
> I've been a fool the whole year long.
> Now I'm singing a different song,
> You were right and I was wrong.

This song became quite well known and presumably helped John Llewellyn Rhys choose *The World Owes Me a Living* for his 1939 novel about a redundant RFC hero who tries to make a living with a flying circus (filmed 1944).

It is a little odd rendered in this form, because on the whole it is not something a person would say about himself. More usually, another would say, pejoratively, 'The trouble with you is, you think the world owes you a living.'

I have discovered the phrase used only once before Disney. In W. G. Sumner's *Earth Hunger* (1896), he writes: 'The men who start out with the notion that the world owes them a living generally find that the world pays its debt in the penitentiary or the poorhouse.' Sumner was an American author but I'm not certain that the phrase originated in the USA.

PARIS is for lovers

This phrase is spoken in Billy Wilder's film *Sabrina (Sabrina Fair* in the UK) (1954). It almost has the ring of an official slogan, though this was long before the days of 'I Love New York' (1977) and 'Virginia is for Lovers' (1981).

Nor have I found a song including the phrase or using it as a title, though Cole Porter's musical *Silk Stockings* (Broadway, 1955) has a song called 'Paris Loves Lovers'.

I look upon the whole world as my PARISH

ODCIE explains this idiomatic phrase thus: 'One's interests and activities are very wide; one travels widely, is knowledgeable about many peoples and places' – in other words, one is not a million miles from regarding it as one's oyster.

The original remark from which it derives was specifically religious. John Wesley (1703-91), the founder of Methodism, included in his diary entry for 11 June 1739 a letter to Revd James Hervey in which he defended himself against charges that he had invaded the parishes of other clergymen.

> You . . . ask, 'How is it that I assemble Christians, who are none of my charge, to sing psalms and pray and hear the Scriptures expounded? and think it hard to justify doing this in other men's parishes, upon catholic principles . . .
>
> Seeing I have now no parish of my own, nor probably ever shall . . . Suffer me now to tell you my principles in this matter. I look upon all the world as my parish . . .
>
> This far I mean, that, in whatever part of it I am, I judge it meet, right, and my bounden duty to declare unto all that are willing to hear the glad tidings of salvation.

George Whitefield, the Methodist preacher who separated from the Wesleys shortly afterwards, probably picked it up from

John and used it in a letter of 10 November 1739. As a position, however, it is thought to have long been familiar to the older members of the 'Holy Club' as also to the Epworth Wesleys (*Journals,* Vol. 2).

And this, too, shall PASS away

Chuck Berry 'spoke' a song (1979) called 'Pass away' which begins:

> Once in Persia reigned a king
> Who upon his royal ring
> Carved these words so true and wise
> Which when held before his eyes
> Gave him counsel at a glance
> Of his life of change and chance
> Solemn words, and these are they:
> 'Even this shall pass away.'

George Harrison named his first (mostly solo) record album *All Things Must Pass* in 1970. These musicians were by no means the first people to be drawn to this saying.

As Abraham Lincoln explained in an address to the Wisconsin State Agricultural Society (no less) on 30 September 1859:

> An Eastern monarch once charged his wise men to invent him a sentence to be ever in view, and which should be true and appropriate in all times and situations. They presented him with the words, 'And this, too, shall pass away.' How much it expresses! How chastening in the hour of pride! How consoling in the depths of affliction!

The next year, Nathaniel Hawthorne wrote in *The Marble Faun* of the 'greatest mortal consolation, which we derive from the transitoriness of all things – from the right of saying, in every conjuncture, "This, too, will pass away".'

But who was the oriental monarch? Benham says the phrase was an inscription on a ring, according to an oriental tale, and the phrase was given by Solomon to a sultan who 'desired that the words should be appropriate at all time'.

Tomorrow to fresh fields and PASTURES new
See **fresh.**

Eating *PÂTÉS de foie gras* to the sound of trumpets
See **trumpets.**

It PAYS to advertise
See **advertise.**

PEACE at any price
'Peace at any price; peace and union' was the slogan of the American (Know-Nothing) Party in the 1856 American presidential election. The party supported ex-President Fillmore and the slogan meant that it was willing to accept slavery for blacks in order to avoid a civil war. Fillmore lost to James Buchanan.

It has been suggested that the phrase had been coined in 1848 or 1820 by Alphonse de Lamartine, the French Foreign Affairs Minister in the form, '*La paix à tout prix*' in his *Méditations Poétiques.* However, the Earl of Clarendon quoted an 'unreasonable calumny' concerning Lord Falkland in his *History of the Rebellion* (written in 1647) 'that he was so enamoured on peace, that he would have been glad the king should have bought it at any price'. The phrase has been used in connection with English politicians who objected to war under all conditions.

When Neville Chamberlain signed his pact with Hitler in 1938, many praised him for trying to obtain peace at any price.

PEACE with honour
On his return from signing the Munich agreement with Hitler in September 1938, Neville Chamberlain spoke from a window at 10 Downing Street — 'Not of design but for the purpose of dispersing the huge multitude below' (according to his biographer Keith Feiling). He said: 'My good friends, this is the second time in our history that there has come back from Germany to Downing Street peace with honour. I believe it is peace for our time. Go home and get a nice quiet sleep.'

Two days before, when someone had suggested the Disraeli phrase 'peace with honour', Chamberlain had impatiently rejected it. Now, according to John Colville, *Footprints in Time* (1976), he used the phrase at the urging of his wife.

Chamberlain's own phrase 'peace for our time' is often misquoted as 'peace *in* our time' — as by Noel Coward in the title of his 1947 play set in an England after the Germans have conquered. Perhaps Coward, and others, were influenced by the phrase from the Book of Common Prayer, 'Give peace in our time, O Lord.'

She sits among the cabbages and PEAS

In the 1920s and 1930s, Leslie Sarony, the British entertainer (1897-1985), wrote a song 'Mucking About the Garden' using the *nom de plume* 'Q. Cumber' or 'Q. Kumber'. Unfortunately, I have been unable to find the sheet music (published by L. Wright) to see if it really does contain the immortal line, 'She sits among the cabbages and peas/ Watching her onions grow', as has been suggested.

The only recording I have heard of the song, by George Buck, does not have it. I suspect that the recording by Sarony himself and Tommy Handley with Jack Payne (on Columbia 5555), which I have not heard, doesn't either.

What I can't work out is whether this is the same song as that apparently made famous by Marie Lloyd (1870-1922). According to the story, when forbidden by a watch committee to sing 'He/she sits among the cabbages and peas,' she substituted, 'He/she sits among the cabbages and leaks.'

Sarony's song would appear to have been written after Marie Lloyd's death. So this is a puzzle.

PECCAVI

'*Peccavi*' is the Latin phrase for 'I have sinned'. The *OED* sees it as part of the expression 'to cry *peccavi*', an acknowledgement or confession of guilt. The earliest citation given by the *OED* is Bishop John Fisher's funeral sermon at St Paul's for Henry VII (1509): 'King David that wrote this psalm, with one word speaking his heart was changed saying *Peccavi*.' This refers to Psalm 41:4, 'I said, Lord, be merciful unto me: heal my soul, for I have sinned against thee.'

But the phrase occurs in a number of other places in the Bible, mostly in the Old Testament – e.g., 'And Saul said unto Samuel, I have sinned' (1 Samuel 15:24).

The Latin word is often thought to have furnished a famous pun. Here is Charles Berlitz's version in *Native Tongues*: 'Sir Charles Napier, a British officer in India, was given command of an expedition to annex the kingdom of Sind in (1843) . . . To announce the success of his mission, he dispatched to the headquarters of the British East India Company a one-word message, the Latin word *peccavi*, which means "I have *sinned*".'

Alas, Napier did no such thing. It was *Punch* on 18 May 1844 which suggested that Caesar's '*Veni, vidi, vici*' was beaten for brevity by 'Napier's dispatch to Lord Ellenborough', *Peccavi*. ODQ credits the joke to Catherine Winkworth. She was a young girl, so it was sent into *Punch* on her behalf.

It seems, however, that the joke was soon taken as genuine, even at *Punch* itself. On 22 March 1856, the magazine (confusing sender and receiver in the original) included the couplet:

> '*Peccavi* – I've Scinde,' wrote Lord Ellen, so proud.
> More briefly Dalhousie wrote – '*Vovi* – I've Oude.'

The PEN is mightier than the sword

According to a piece in the London *Standard* diary following the Gorbachev-Reagan summit in November 1987, Parker Pens broke new ground by placing an advertisement in the *Moscow News* to draw attention to the fact that the treaty had been signed with one of their fountain pens. The ad's Russian slogan, translated directly, was, 'What is written with the pen will not be chopped up with an axe', which the *Standard* thought was the equivalent of 'The pen is mightier than the sword'.

Unfortunately, the *Standard* announced that 'The pen is, etc.' was the most famous maxim attributed to Cardinal Richelieu. Bong! It was a line said by Richelieu in Edward Bulwer-Lytton's play *Richelieu* (II.ii.) (1839):

> Beneath the rule of men entirely great,
> The pen is mightier than the sword.

– which is not quite the same as Richelieu himself having originated it.

As for the idea, it was not, of course, original to Bulwer-Lytton either. *CDP* finds several earlier attempts at expressing it. I would add this 'corollary' from Shakespeare's *Hamlet* (II.ii.344): 'Many wearing rapiers are afraid of goose-quills'.

We have become the sort of PEOPLE our parents warned us about

I first registered a possible origin of this expression at the time Michael Holroyd's two-volume biography of Augustus John was published (1974-75), in which it does *not* appear. However, somewhere else, perhaps in a review – this is just my inefficiency, I forgot to write down the reference – John was recorded as having observed to Nina Hamnett, an artistic hanger-on of the 1930s, 'We have become, Nina, the sort of people our parents warned us about.'

I expect it was a common expression dating from the between-

the-wars years, if not before. In 1981, I received a letter from
Bernard S. Davis living in Turkish Cyprus who wrote, 'An
acquaintance of mine, York-Lodge, a close friend of Claud
Cockburn and Evelyn Waugh, was continually saying, "We are
the sort of people our parents warned us against," and claiming it
as his own. This was about 1924.'

The saying has been reported to me as graffiti from New York
City in the early 1970s ('We are the people our parents warned us
about'), and a placard carried at a demonstration by homosexuals
in New York in 1970 stated, 'We're the people our parents
warned us against.'

Let the PEOPLE Sing

This was the title of a novel by J. B. Priestley, written so that it
could be first broadcast by the BBC in (of all months) September
1939. The story, about people fighting to save a village hall from
being taken over by commercial interests, was later made into a
film and released in 1942. Characters in it write a song with this
title that goes:

> Let the people sing,
> And freedom bring
> An end to a sad old story.
>
> Where the people sing,
> Their voices ring
> In the dawn of the people's glory.

There must have been something about the phrase. In
December 1939, a song with the title (music by Noel Gay, lyrics
by Ian Grant and Frank Eyton) was being recorded. It was
featured in the 1940 revue *Lights Up* and later, I believe, ENSA,
the forces' entertainment organisation, used it as its signature
tune.

On 1 April 1940, the BBC started a long-running series of
programmes with this title – featuring 'songs of the moment,
songs of the past, songs of sentiment, songs with a smile, songs
with a story, songs of the people'.

The phrase almost took on the force of a slogan. Angus Calder
in *The People's War* (1969) wrote of Ernest Bevin, the Minister of
Labour from October 1940:

Bevinism in industry was symbolized by the growing understanding of
the value of music and entertainment in helping people to work faster
. . . There were the BBC's *Workers' Playtime* and *Music While You Work*

which 'progressive' management relayed over loudspeakers several times a day . . . 'Let the People Sing', it might be said, was the spiritual essence of Bevinism.

The phrase appears to have originated with Priestley, though one might note the similarity to the hymns, 'Let all on earth their voices raise' and 'Let all the world in every corner sing'.

Come alive with PEPSI

The worldwide spread of the soft drinks Coca-Cola and Pepsi Cola has given rise to some difficulties in translating their slogans. It is said that 'Come alive with Pepsi' became in German, 'Come alive out of the grave', and, in Chinese, 'Pepsi brings your ancestors back from the dead'.

When Coca-Cola started advertising in Peking, 'Put a Smile on Your Face' was translated as 'Let Your Teeth Rejoice'. Odder still, the famous slogan 'It's the Real Thing' came out as 'The Elephant Bites the Wax Duck'.

Hoist with his own PETARD
See **hoist.**

A PICTURE is worth a thousand words

This famous saying – which occurs for example in the David Gates song 'If' (*c.* 1975) – is sometimes said to be a Chinese proverb. Bartlett lists it as such in the form, 'One picture is worth more than ten thousand words' and compares what Turgenev says in *Fathers and Sons*, 'A picture shows me at a glance what it takes dozens of pages of a book to expound.'

But *CODP* points out that it originated in an American paper *Printers' Ink* (8 December 1921) in the form 'One look is worth a thousand words' and was there ascribed by its actual author, Frederick R. Barnard, to a Chinese source (to give it instant proverbial status, I suppose).

PILLARS of Society

Meaning people who are the main supporters of church, state, institutions or principles (cf. 'pillars of state', 'pillar of faith') this phrase almost certainly derives from its use as William Archer's translation of the title of Henrik Ibsen's play *Samfundet's Støtter* (1877). When this play was first produced in London in 1880 it was, however, called *Quicksands*. In the play, the 'pillars of society' are described as being, not people as such, but 'the spirit of truth and the spirit of freedom'.

Partridge/Slang notes the punning 'pillars of society' – 'persistent black-ballers at club elections' (Royal Yacht Club, since *c.* 1920').

Like the feather PILLOW, bears the marks of the last person who has sat on him
Oddly, for a well-known political expression, this is hardly recorded in the major quotation dictionaries. It was said by Sir Douglas Haig (1861-1928) of the uninspiring Lord Derby (who in 1916 had taken Lloyd George's place at the War Office). It could be that the phrase is less than adequately attributed because it appeared first not publicly but in a private letter from Haig to his wife (14 January 1918) and was only revealed when Robert Blake brought out out his edition of Haig's private papers in 1952.

PIPER at the Gates of Dawn
The first album recorded by Pink Floyd in 1967 took its title – in somewhat sixties style – from the title of Chapter 7 of Kenneth Grahame's *The Wind in the Willows* (1908). 'The Piper at the Gates of Dawn' describes a lyrical, not to say mystical experience, that Mole and Ratty have when they hear the god Pan piping at dawn.

The Vice-Presidency isn't worth a PITCHER of warm spit
John Nance Garner's characterization of the American Vice-Presidency (a job which he held during Franklin D. Roosevelt's first two terms) is a bowdlerized form of what he actually said. It was 'warm piss' originally, but the listening reporter cleaned it up. Garner also said the job was 'a spare tire on the automobile of government' (statement to the press, 19 June 1934) and 'didn't amount to a hill of beans' (interview, November 1963).

The Longest PLEASURE
See **longest.**

The PLEASURE momentary, the position ridiculous, and the expense damnable.
So said the fourth Earl of Chesterfield (1694-1773) of sex. Or did he? His description was one of the first quotes I scribbled down inside the back cover of a battered copy of the *Penguin Dictionary of Quotations* (purchased 1960) when I first began mildly to note

them for myself. I now have no idea where I came across it and I have never encountered it 'collected' anywhere else. I can only assume that it is to be found in Chesterfield's letters to his illegitimate son (published 1774) in which he commented on all aspects of a gentleman's behaviour.

Lately, I have even begun to wonder whether it may be one of those sayings imposed on a well-known person by a lesser one, or whether it might be a translation from the French (La Rochefoucauld, perhaps?) For the moment, I remain baffled.

POISED between a cliché and an indiscretion
See **cliché.**

A semi-house-trained POLECAT
'Is it always his desire to give his imitation of a semi-house-trained polecat?' Quite a good example of political abuse to show that the art is not quite dead. This was Michael Foot, when leader of Britain's Labour Party, talking about Norman Tebbit, the prickly Conservative Party Chairman. Foot said it at an eve-of-poll rally in Ebbw Vale in 1983. He noted that he had said it first in the House of Commons 'a few years ago'. Foot lost the general election overwhelmingly. Tebbit continued to bite people in the leg for a few years more.

A POLITICIAN is a person who approaches every subject with an open mouth
This is another of those quotations which floats continually in search of a definite source and could have been said by anyone and everybody. Was it Oscar Wilde? Or Adlai Stevenson? Or Arthur Goldberg? Wilde and Stevenson are given by different contributors to *Kindly Sit Down,* a compilation of after-dinner speeches by politicians collected by Jack Aspinwall (1983). Stevenson and Goldberg are given in the *Penguin Dictionary of Modern Quotations.* In the absence of any hard evidence, I feel inclined to award the palm to Stevenson.

A week is a long time in POLITICS
See **week.**

A POOR thing but mine own
In 1985, a painter called Howard Hodgkin won the £10,000 Turner prize for a work (of art) called 'A Small Thing But My

Own'. It was notable that he used the word 'small' rather than 'poor'. Nevertheless, he was presumably alluding to Touchstone's line in Shakespeare's *As You Like It* (V.iv.57), 'A poor virgin, sir, an ill-favoured thing, sir, but mine own.' Here Touchstone is not talking about a work of art but about Audrey, the country wench he woos. The line is nowadays likely to be used (in mock-modesty) about a thing rather than a person.

The fretful PORPENTINE

His face was flushed, his eyes were bulging, and . . . his hair was standing on end – like quills upon the fretful porpentine, as Jeeves once put it when describing to me the reactions of Barmy Fotheringay-Phipps on seeing a dead snip, on which he had invested largely, come in sixth in the procession at the Newmarket Spring Meeting.

So, Bertie Wooster in *The Code of the Woosters* by P. G. Wodehouse, using one of his favourite Shakespearean images (from *Hamlet*, I.v.20 – though I doubt whether Wooster is aware of this).

In the original, it is the ghost of Hamlet's father who is telling the prince he 'could a tale unfold' which would make 'each particular hair to stand on end/ Like quills upon the fretful porpentine.' ('Porpentine' = porcupine.)

In 1986, I was told that some of the more literate regulars of a pub called The Porcupine in Charing Cross Road, London would talk of repairing to 'the Fretters'.

The POSITION ridiculous
See **pleasure.**

A POSTILLION Struck by Lightning
This was the somewhat peculiar title selected by Dirk Bogarde for the first volume of his autobiography (1977). Describing a holiday in early childhood (1920s presumably), he mentions an old phrase book (seemingly dated 1898) which contains lines like 'This muslin is too thin, have you something thicker?' 'My leg, arm, foot, elbow, nose, finger is broken' and 'The postillion has been struck by lightning'.

I'm not sure which phrasebook this was (though it does not appear to have been *English As She Is Spoke* –q.v. under *'English'* – in which the 'postillion' line does not appear). A writer in *The Times* (30 July 1983) noted, ' "Look, the front postillion has been struck by lightning" . . . supposed to feature in a Scandinavian phrase book: but it may well be apocryphal.' Until a source turns up, I'm inclined to agree.

In the third volume of Bogarde's autobiography, *An Orderly Man* (1983), describing the writing of the first, he says: 'My sister-in-law, Cilla, on a wet camping holiday somewhere in northern France . . . once sent me a postcard on which she said . . . she had been forced to learn a little more French than the phrase "Help! My postillion has been struck by lightning!" I took the old phrase for the title of my book . . .'.

Keep you POWDER dry

'Put your trust in God, my boys, and keep your powder dry' – thus said Oliver Cromwell during his Irish campaign in 1649. There is some doubt as to whether he really said it at all, as it was only ascribed to him about a century after his death by one Valentine Blacker in an Orange ballad.

The part about keeping one's powder dry is no more than sensible advice from the days when gunpowder had to be kept dry if it was to be used at all. The idiomatic injunction means 'remain calm and prepared for immediate action', 'be prudent, practical, on the alert'.

All POWER corrupts

Lord Acton (1834-1902) famously said, 'Power *tends* to corrupt and absolute power corrupts absolutely' [my italics] in a letter to Bishop Mandell Creighton on 3 April 1887 (published 1904). In any case, he had been anticipated by William Pitt, Earl of Chatham who had already said in the House of Lords (9 January 1770), 'Unlimited power is apt to corrupt the minds of those who possess it.'

PRESIDENT Can't Swim

There's no joke like an old joke – and there's one that politicians just love:

Lyndon B. Johnson (US President, 1963-68) once said of the media that if one morning he walked on top of the water across the Potomac River, the headline that afternoon would read, PRESIDENT CAN'T SWIM (quoted in *Time*, 28 December 1987).

Neil Kinnock, Leader of the British Labour Party: 'Worried about my media coverage, I consulted a fortune teller. She told me to perform miracles, so I walked across the Thames. Next day the *Sun* headline ran: Neil Kinnock fails to swim river' (quoted in *Sunday Today*, 17 May 1987).

The Rt Revd Desmond Tutu, Archbishop of Cape Town tells a joke about himself: 'Tutu and State President P. W. Botha are in a boat in Table Bay when a storm blows up. Tutu says: "It's all right, I'll get help" and walks across the water. The next day in the Afrikaans paper, the headline is: *"Tutu Kan Nei Swem Nie"* – Tutu can't swim' (quoted in the *Observer* Magazine, 20 March 1988).

Dr Livingstone, I PRESUME

The most famous greeting was put by Sir Henry Morton Stanley, the British explorer and journalist, to the explorer and missionary Dr David Livingstone at Ujiji, Lake Tanganyika on 10 November 1871. Stanley had been sent by the *New York Herald* to look for Livingstone who was missing on a journey in central Africa.

In *How I Found Livingstone* (1872), Stanley described the moment:

> I would have run to him, only I was a coward in the presence of such a mob – would have embraced him, only, he being an Englishman, I did not know how he would receive me; so I did what cowardice and false pride suggested was the best thing – walked deliberately to him, took off my hat and said: 'Dr Livingstone, I presume?'
> 'Yes,' said he, with a kind of smile, lifting his cap slightly.

One barmy suggestion is that Stanley was making a tongue-in-cheek reference to a moment in Sheridan's *School for Scandal* (Act 5, Scene 1) in which, after much mutual confusion, two of the main characters finally get to meet with the line, 'Mr Stanley, I presume?'

Perhaps it was not such a remarkable salutation after all. General R. E. Lee, when he entered Maryland at Williamsport on 25 June 1863, had been greeted by the spokesman of a women's committee of welcome with the words, 'This is General Lee, I presume?'

PRICK up your ears

In his diary for 18 February 1967, the playwright Joe Orton wrote: 'Started typing up my final version [of the first draft] of *Up Against It*. Kenneth suggested that I call it *Prick Up Your Ears*. But this is much too good a title to waste on a film.'

The 'Kenneth' was Kenneth Halliwell, Orton's flatmate who

murdered him later that year. It was indeed too good a title to waste on the abortive *Up Against It*, Orton's planned film for the Beatles. However, it was not used as the title of a film until 1987 when, fittingly, it was applied by Alan Bennett to his account of the Orton/Halliwell relationship and murder.

In 1978, John Lahr had used the phrase as the title of his biography of Orton. In his edition of the *The Orton Diaries* (1986), Lahr noted: 'The title is a triple-pun, "ears" being an anagram of "arse". Orton intended using it as the title for a farce about the backstage goings-on prior to a coronation.' When the film *Prick Up Your Ears* came out, there were reports of enthusiastic punsters of London climbing up to rearrange the lettering over cinema doors.

In 1978 I received a note from Fritz Spiegl in which he said: 'This crossword clue appeared in the *Financial Times* at the end of January about four years ago: "Listen carefully, or a sexual perversion (5, 2, 4, 4)".'

PRIDE and Prejudice

The title of Jane Austen's novel (written 1797 as 'First Impressions', published 1813) has been said to derive from the second chapter of Edward Gibbon's *The Decline and Fall of the Roman Empire*, published in 1776. Writing of the enfranchisement of the slaves, Gibbon says: 'Without destroying the distinction of ranks a distant prospect of freedom and honours was presented, even to those whom pride and prejudice almost disdained to number among the human species.'

What this had to do with Austen's subject-matter one can only guess at. Much more to the point, the phrase occurs no less than three times, in bold print, towards the end of Fanny Burney's *Cecilia* (1787):

> 'The whole of this unfortunate business', said Dr Lyster, 'has been the result of **Pride and Prejudice** . . . Yet this, however, remember; if to **Pride and Prejudice** you owe your miseries, so wonderfully is good and evil balanced, that to **Pride and Prejudice** you will also owe their termination.'

This seems the most likely cue to Jane Austen. On the other hand, *OED Supp.* does provide six citations of the phrase 'pride and prejudice' before Burney, one of which has capital Ps.

PRIDE goeth before a fall

This might seem to be a telescoped version of 'Pride goeth before destruction and an haughty spirit before a fall' (Proverbs 16:18) but the proverb seems to have developed independently. *CODP* cites Alexander Barclay's *The Ship of Fools* (1509), 'First or last foul pride will have a fall', and Samuel Johnson wrote in a letter (2 August 1784), 'Pride must have a fall.' I expect that at some stage the biblical wording was grafted on to the original proverb.

One of Swift's clichés in *Polite Conversation* (1738) is, 'You were afraid that Pride should have a Fall.'

The PRIVATE life of . . .

The original of all the 'Private Life of . . .' books and films was surely Korda's film *The Private Life of Henry VIII* (1933)[1]. The next year, Julian Huxley, with R. M. Lockley, produced a natural history film called *The Private Life of Gannets* (which won an Oscar).

Since then, in the cinema, we have had private lives of Don Juan (1934), Elizabeth and Essex (1939), Sherlock Holmes (1970), and so on. And on TV there have been numerous natural history films since the mid-1960s, e.g., the BBC's *The Private Life of the Kingfisher*.

There is, of course, a nudging note to the use of the phrase – as though we are not just being promised a glimpse of domestic happenings, but probably sex life, too.

PROMINENT because of the flatness of the surrounding countryside

It would be wrong of me to question why other people become obsessive about tracing quotations which mean nothing to me. Obsession is to the phrase detective what daffodils were to Wordsworth, to adapt something Philip Larkin once said.

So, I merely mention that Dr J. F. C. of Isleworth has had this quotation running around his head for 30 years. It relates to the estimate of a person's innate qualities and is usually stated as being, 'Prominent, mainly because of the flatness of the surrounding countryside.'

'I had always believed', he states, 'that it was first said by Karl Marx of John Stuart Mill when he was told the latter was "a

---

[1]*The Private Life of Helen of Troy* had, however, been directed by Korda in 1927.

prominent economist". I have consulted every dictionary of quotations I can lay may hands on – with no success.'

A *Quote . . . Unquote* listener, Peter Effer of Walthamstow, found this in Vol. 1, Chapter 16 of *Das Kapital* by Karl Marx: 'On a level plain, simple mounds look like hills; and the insipid flatness of our present bourgeoisie is to be measured by the altitude of its "great intellects".' Marx comments thus after having demolished one of Mill's arguments. Clearly this was the genesis of the quotation as it was referred to me.

The lady doth PROTEST too much
See **methinks.**

Now Barabbas was a PUBLISHER
See **Barabbas.**

QUEEN Anne is dead

This is a phrase used to put down someone who has just told you some very old news or what you know already. Mencken glosses it slightly differently: 'Reply to an inquiry for news, signifying that there is none not stale.' He also supplies the alternative 'Queen Elizabeth is dead' (which I have never heard used) and says that both forms appear to date from *c.* 1720. In George Colman the Younger's play, *The Heir-at-Law* (1797) there occurs the line, 'Tell 'em Queen Anne's dead.'

She actually died in 1714. Partridge/Slang dates 'Queen Anne is dead' to 1722, in a ballad cited by Apperson, 'He's as dead as Queen Anne the day after she dy'd' (which doesn't seem to convey the modern meaning of the expression); 'Queen Elizabeth is dead' to 1738 in Swift's *Polite Conversation* – 'What news, Mr Neverout? *Neverout:* Why, Madam, Queen Elizabeth's dead'; and puts 'My Lord Baldwin is dead' to *c.* 1670-1710.

An American equivalent is, 'Bryan has carried Texas.'

QUEEN Elizabeth slept here

This is a line that has been used to promote visits to English stately homes – and some inns – probably since such visiting began in the eighteenth century. Elizabeth I was an inveterate traveller and guest. By 1888, Jerome K. Jerome was writing in *Three Men in a Boat:* 'She was nuts on public houses, was England's Virgin Queen. There's scarcely a pub of any attractions within ten miles of London that she does not seem to have looked in at, stopped at, or slept at, some time or other.'

In the USA, the equivalent slogan is 'George Washington slept here' (as in the title of Kauffman and Hart's play, 1940, filmed 1942, which, when adapted by Talbot Rothwell for the Strand

Theatre, London, later in the 1940s, was called ... *Queen Elizabeth Slept Here*).

QUIET calm deliberation disentangles every knot

When Harold Macmillan was Prime Minister (1957-63) he wrote out in longhand a motto for his private office and the Cabinet room at 10 Downing Street. It came from W. S. Gilbert's lyrics for *The Gondoliers* (1889):

> In a contemplative fashion,
>   And a tranquil frame of mind,
> Free from every kind of passion,
>   Some solution let us find.
> Let us grasp the situation,
>   Solve the complicated plot –
> Quiet, calm deliberation
>   Disentangles every knot.

QUO Vadis?

Knowing how squeamish Hollywood producers are about incomprehensible or even slightly difficult titles (changing English film titles at the slightest hint of difficulty) it is interesting that they let this one by in 1951 (the previous two versions were Italian). Did American audiences really know the words or what they meant?

The words *'Quo vadis?'* – meaning 'Whither goest thou?' – come from the Latin translation (the Vulgate) of John 13:36 in which, 'Simon Peter said unto him, Lord, whither goest thou? Jesus answered him, Whither I go, thou canst not follow me now'; and from John 16:5 in which Christ comforts his disciples before the Crucifixion. They also occur in Genesis 32:17, though not relevantly.

The words also occur in the Acts of St Peter among the New Testament Apocrypha in which, after the Crucifixion, Peter, fleeing Rome, encounters Christ on the Appian Way. He asks Him, *'Domine, quo vadis?'* ('Lord, whither goest thou?') and Christ replies, *'Venio Roman, iterum crucifigi'* ('I am coming to Rome to be crucified again.') This encourages Peter to return to his own martyrdom there.

Spike Milligan maintains that, because films of the 1950s always had to have a love song, there was one called 'Quo Vadis, I Love You', but I suspect he may be having us on. (However, there was definitely a 'Love Theme from *Quo Vadis?*') Earlier than all this, in 1909, there was an opera with the title by Jean Nouguès, based on the novel by a Pole, Henryk Sienkiewicz.

(Probably the most difficult title Hollywood has ever tried to inflict on non-American audiences is *99 and 44/100 Per Cent Dead* [1974]. Even if you could find a way of pronouncing it, it only meant anything to you if you were aware that from *c.* 1882 there had been an advertisement, familiar to Americans, for Ivory Soap – '99 44/100 Per Cent Pure'. Even *Variety* found the film 'as clumsy as its title' and it was tardily renamed *Call Harry Crown.)*

I hate QUOTATIONS

Ironically, the *ODQ* has Ralph Waldo Emerson writing in his journal for May 1849, 'I hate quotations' and, ho ho, very ironic. Even toilers in the quotation vineyard feel like echoing this thought from time to time when they hear yet another person about to launch into some over-familiar line with, 'As the poet has it . . .', or 'As George Bernard Shaw once said . . .'.

Oddly enough, and ironically, what the *ODQ* has is a *misquotation*. What Emerson actually wrote was: '*Immortality*. I notice that as soon as writers broach this question they begin to quote. I hate quotation. Tell me what you know.' *(Journals and Miscellaneous Notebooks,* Vol. 11.)

So it's 'quotation' not 'quotations'. There is a difference after all.

Verify your QUOTATIONS
See **verify.**

The RACE to the sea

This phrase comes from the autumn of 1914 during the early months of the First World War. In his *English History 1914-45*, A. J. P. Taylor writes:

> Both combatant lines hung in the air. Some 200 miles of open country separated the German and French armies from the sea. Each side tried to repeat the original German strategy of turning the enemy line. This was not so much a 'race to the sea', its usual name, as a race to outflank the other side before the sea was reached. Both sides failed.

Martin Gilbert uses the phrase evocatively of a phase of the Second World War in Chapter 21 of Vol. 6 of his biography of Winston Churchill: 'As dawn broke on May 26 [1940], the news from France dominated Churchill's thoughts, and those of his advisers and staff. The road to Dunkirk was open. The race to the sea was about to begin.' (In his own *The Second World War*, Vol. 2, Churchill entitled the chapter dealing with Dunkirk, 'The March to the Sea.')

RANDOM Harvest

The novel (1941) by James Hilton and the film (USA 1942) take their title – as Hilton notes – from an error in German wartime propaganda when they claimed to have attacked the town of 'Random'. This was on the basis of a British communiqué which had said that 'bombs were dropped at random'.

When RAPE is inevitable, lie back and enjoy it

See **lie.**

O RARE Ben Jonson!

Ben Jonson's epitaph in Westminster Abbey was composed in 1637, the year he died, by John Young. According to abbey tradition (recounted in its official guide book, 1971 revision), Jonson died in poverty and had himself directed that he be buried upright to save space. So he was, in the north aisle, with a small square stone over him.

As for the epitaph, 'Another tradition says, "it was done at the charge of Jack Young, afterwards knighted, who, walking here when the grave was covering, gave the fellow eighteen pence to cut it".'

The inscription has also been ascribed to the playwright, D'Avenant (*d.* 1668) who succeeded Jonson as unofficial Poet Laureate. His own gravestone in the abbey reads, 'O RARE S WILLIAM DAVENANT.'

Whoever composed it, and it is a small point in a century when the spelling of names was notably free-form (cf. Shakespeare's 57 varieties), the stonemason put 'Johnson' instead of 'Jonson' on the gravestone. On his later monument, the name is correctly spelled.

You dirty RAT!
See **dirty.**

RATS deserting a sinking ship
The basic idiom here is 'like rats leaving/deserting a sinking ship/ – i.e., hurriedly, desperately. This comes from the English proverb to the effect that 'rats desert/forsake/leave a falling house/sinking ship'. *ODP* finds an example of the 'house' version in 1579 and of the 'ship' (in Shakespeare) in 1611. Brewer adds: 'It was an old superstition that rats deserted a ship before she set out on a voyage that was to end in her loss.'

The word 'rat' to mean 'a politician who deserts his party' was used by the first Earl of Malmesbury in 1792 (*OED*). In the USA it made its first appearance in the saying 'like a rat deserting a sinking ship' around 1800 (Safire).

A number of good jokes have grown from this usage. In Malcolm Muggeridge's diary for 14 February 1948 (published 1981), he notes: 'Remark of Churchill's was quoted to me about the Liberal candidature of Air Vice-Marshal Bennett in Croydon. "It was the first time", Churchill said, "that he had heard of a rat actually swimming out to join a sinking ship".'

In his diary for 26 January 1941, John Colville noted that Churchill had reflected on the difficulty of 'crossing the floor' (changing parties) in the House of Commons: 'He had done it and he knew. Indeed he had re-done it, which everybody said was impossible. They had said you could rat but you couldn't re-rat.'

(When TV-am, the breakfast television company had a disastrous start in 1983 and was pulled round, in part, by the introduction of a puppet called Roland Rat, an unnamed spokesman from the rival BBC said, 'This must be the first time a rat has come to the aid of a sinking ship.')

Why is a RAVEN like a writing desk?

In *Alice's Adventures in Wonderland* (1865) by Lewis Carroll, the Hatter poses this riddle at the mad tea-party, but Carroll stated positively that there was no answer. Nevertheless, various people have tried to supply one:

'A quill' – what a raven and a writing desk would have had in common in the last century (Christopher Brown of Portswood, Southampton).

'They both begin with the letter R' (Leo Harris).

'Because it can produce a few notes, tho they are very flat; and it is never put with the wrong end in front' – these were Lewis Carroll's own possible solutions (1896 edition).

'Because the notes for which they are noted are not noted for being musical notes' (Sam Loyd).

'Edgar Allan Poe' – he wrote on both a raven and a writing desk (Sam Loyd).

'Because bills and tales (tails) are among their characteristics; because they stand on their legs; conceal their steels (steals); and ought to be made to shut up' (Sam Loyd).

'Because it slopes with a flap' (A. Cyril Pearson).

'Because there is a "B" in "both"' (Dr E. V. Rieu).

(Some of these solutions are included in *The Annotated Alice,* ed. Martin Gardner, 1960.)

In *The Yeoman of the Guard* (1888), W. S. Gilbert also posed a riddle without an answer. Jack Point, the Strolling Jester, asks: 'Why [is] a cook's brain-pan . . . like an overwound clock?' but he is interrupted before the solution can be given. 'Just my luck,' he exclaims, 'my best conundrum wasted!'

Ian Bradley in his *Annotated Gilbert and Sullivan* (Vol. 2) notes that Sir Henry Lytton once asked Gilbert what the answer to his conundrum was 'and was told by the librettist that he would leave it in his will. Needless to say, when he died, it wasn't there. The truth is that Gilbert had never bothered about answering his own riddle.'

The RAZOR'S Edge

The novel (1944) by W. Somerset Maugham takes its title from the Katha-Upanishad: 'The sharp edge of a razor is difficult to pass over; thus the wise say the path to Salvation is hard.'

REAP the Wild Wind

This is the title of a US film made in 1942. Apparently, the title is original, though presumably it alludes to, 'They have sown the wind, and they shall reap the whirlwind' (Hosea 8:7).

The REASON the sun never sets on the British Empire . . .

With reference to the British, the basic expression, 'His Majesty's Dominions, on which the sun never sets' was coined in *Noctes Ambrosianae* in April 1829. The author was 'Christopher North' (Professor John Wilson). By 1844, Charles Dickens was writing in *Dombey and Son*: 'No tax-gatherer in the British Dominions – that wide-spread territory on which the sun never sets, and where the tax-gatherer never goes to bed.'

However, the expression had been used earlier about the Spanish Empire. 'Why should the brave Spanish soldier brag the sun never sets in the Spanish dominions? (Captain John Smith, 1631); 'It may be said of them [the Hollanders] as of the Spaniards, that the sun never sets on their dominions' (Thomas Gage, 1648). Sir Walter Scott said in his *Life of Napoleon*, 1827: 'The sun never sets on the immense empire of Charles V.'

But who said, 'I know why the sun never sets on the British Empire: God wouldn't trust an Englishman in the dark'? Nancy McPhee in her *Book of Insults* (1978) attributes this to one Duncan Spaeth: but who he?

All I know is that in June 1981, an Irish Republican placard, held up during a visit by Prince Charles to New York City, read: 'The sun never sets on the British Empire because God doesn't trust the Brits in the dark.'

The thin RED line

A report by William Howard Russell in *The Times* (25 October 1854) described the first stage of the Battle of Balaclava in the Crimean War (the Charge of the Light Brigade followed a few hours later). Russell (1820-1907) wrote of the Russian charge repulsed by the British 93rd Highlanders: 'The ground lies beneath their horses' feet; gathering speed at every stride, they dash on towards that thin red streak topped with a line of steel.'

By the time he was writing his book, *The British Expedition to the Crimea* (1877), Russell was writing, 'The Russians dashed on towards *that thin red line tipped with steel*' [his italics]. Thus was created the jingoistic Victorian phrase 'the thin red line', standing for the supposed invincibility of British infantry tactics. It was celebrated in a painting by Lady Butler (1846-1933) called, I believe, 'The Thin Red Line' and in Kipling's poem 'Tommy' from *Departmental Ditties* (1890) which goes: 'But it's "Thin red line of 'eroes" when the drums begin to roll.'

La REINE le veult

In Britain, the royal assent to parliamentary bills is still given in Norman French (written, never spoken). So, it is either *'Le Roy'* or *'La Reine le veult'* – 'the King/Queen allows it'. The negative form would be *'Le roi/la reine s'avisera'* ('will consider it'), though this veto has not been used since Queen Anne opposed a Scottish Militia Bill in 1707 (Brewer).

I shall RETURN

In my *Sayings*, I considered General Douglas MacArthur's famous boast at some length. Forced to pull out of the Philippines by the Japanese, he left Corregidor on 11 March 1942. He made his commitment to return not while in the Philippines but during a stop at the railway station in Adelaide, South Australia, on his way to Melbourne.

The phrase was suggested to MacArthur by Carlos P. Romulo, a Filipino diplomat who later twice became his country's Foreign Minister. He had been a journalist before the Second World War and served as a brigadier general on MacArthur's staff. He died, aged 86, in 1984.

Of the various uses to which the catchphrase or slogan has been put, it is interesting that it was used as the *British* title of the US film *An American Guerilla in the Philippines* (1950).

The RICH man in his castle,
The poor man at his gate

The enormously popular hymn, 'All things bright and beautiful' (1848) by Mrs Cecil Frances Alexander is in danger of being known as the hymn from which a verse had to be dropped. Causing all the trouble is the third verse with its apparent acceptance of, to modern ears, an unacceptable status quo.

In Barbara Pym's novel *No Fond Return of Love* (1961), 'Dulcie sang in a loud indignant voice, waiting for the lines

> 'The rich man in his castle, the poor man at his gate,
> God made them, high or lowly, and ordered their estate.

'but they never came. Then she saw that the verse had been left out. She sat down, feeling cheated of her indignation.'

Mrs Alexander (1818-95), born in County Wicklow, was the wife of a bishop of Derry and archbishop of Armagh. Most modern hymnbook compilers omit the verse from the hymn. *Songs of Praise Discussed* (1933) calls it an 'appalling verse . . . She must have forgotten Dives, and how Lazarus lay "at his gate"; but then she had been brought up in the atmosphere of a land-agent on an Irish estate. The *English Hymnal* led the way in obliterating this verse from the Anglican mind.'

The verse remains in *Hymns Ancient and Modern* (Standard Edition, reprinted 1986), but it has disappeared from the *Irish Hymnal*. The authors of *The Houses of Ireland* (1975) note that by the present century, 'the ecclesiastical authorities had decided that God's intentions are not to preclude movement within the social system. However, few of her contemporaries doubted that Mrs Alexander's interpretation was correct.'

Will no man RID me of this turbulent priest?
See **turbulent.**

The RIDDLE of the Sphinx
The riddle is: 'What animal walks on four feet in the morning, two feet at noon, and on three feet in the evening – but has only one voice? Its feet vary, and when it has most it is weakest.' The answer is: man – because he crawls on all fours as an infant, walks on two feet when full grown, but in old age moves upon his feet and a staff.

As mentioned in *Oedipus Rex* by Sophocles, Oedipus answered the riddle correctly when he encountered the Sphinx on the road to Thebes. The Sphinx killed herself in despair, and the Thebans made Oedipus their king out of gratitude. If he had not answered correctly, the Sphinx would have killed him.

Consider what the Lord said to Moses
– and I think he was RIGHT
For a long time I was under the impression this was something

that Field Marshal Montgomery – that blushing violet – had actually said. Then I came across the line in a sketch called 'Salvation Army' performed by Lance Percival as an army officer with a Montgomery accent on BBC TV's *That Was The Week That Was* (1962/63).

And then I discovered in the Lyttelton-Hart-Davis letters (Vol. 4 – relating to 1959) the same joke in the form, 'Did you hear of the parson who began his sermon, "As God said – and rightly . . ."'.

So that was it, except that on 7 June 1977, in a sermon for the Queen's Silver Jubilee service at St Paul's, Archbishop Donald Coggan came along and said: 'We listened to these words of Jesus [St Matthew 7:24] a few moments ago.' Then he exclaimed: 'How right he was!'

One is reminded irresistibly of Lorenz Hart's stripper's song 'Zip' from *Pal Joey* (1940):

> I was reading Schopenhauer last night,
> And I think that Schopenhauer was right . . .

The RIGHT Stuff

Tom Wolfe helped repopularize the phrase 'the right stuff' in the sense of the qualities needed by test pilots and would-be astronauts in the early years of the US space programme when he chose it as the title of his book about them (1979, filmed 1983).

But the 'right sort of stuff' had been applied much earlier to qualities of manly virtue, good officer material and even good cannon fodder. Partridge/Slang has an example from the 1880s. In this sense, the phrase was used by Ian Hay as the title of a novel – 'some episodes in the career of a North Briton' – in 1908.

It is now a handy journalistic device: an *Independent* headline over a story about the ballet *Ondine* (13 May 1988) was, 'The Sprite Stuff'; in the same month, *The Magazine* had 'The Right Stuff' as the title of an article on furnishing fabrics.

The 'right stuff' has also been used as an expression meaning 'alcohol', and Martini has been promoted since 1970 as 'the Right One'.

One More RIVER

This was the American title of the 1934 (USA) film based on John Galsworthy's 1933 novel *Over the River* (which was how the film was known in the UK). The altering of the title for the American market would suggest an allusion to the traditional song 'One More River to Cross' (a.k.a. 'Noah's Ark' and referring to the Jordan):

> Old Noah once he built the Ark
> There's one more river to cross.
> And patched it up with hick'ry bark
> There's one more river to cross.
>
> One more river, and that's the river of Jordan,
> One more river
> There's one more river to cross.

Across the RIVER and Into the Trees
See **across.**

RIVERS of blood
On 20 April 1968, Enoch Powell (*b*. 1912), the Conservative Opposition Spokesman for Defence made a speech in Birmingham on the subject of immigration. He concluded with the words: 'As I look ahead, I am filled with foreboding. Like the Roman, I seem to see "the River Tiber foaming with much blood".'

The next day, Powell was dismissed from the Shadow Cabinet for a speech 'racialist in tone and liable to exacerbate racial tensions'. What became known as his 'Rivers of Blood' speech certainly produced an astonishing reaction in the public, unleashing anti-immigrant feeling that had largely been pent up until this point. He received 100,000 letters of support within a few days.

Much later, Powell said that, in retrospect, he would have changed the reference to the Tiber. He would have quoted the remark in Latin to emphasize that he was only evoking a classical prophecy of doom and not actually predicting a bloodbath. In Virgil's *Aeneid* (Book 6, line 87), the Sibyl of Cumae has the line: '*Et Thybrim multo spumantem sanguine cerno*'.

'Rivers of blood' was thus quite a common turn of phrase before Powell made it notorious. Speaking on European unity (14 February 1948), Churchill said: 'We are asking the nations of Europe between whom rivers of blood have flowed to forget the feuds of a thousand years.'

The ROAR of the greasepaint
See **greasepaint.**

Childe ROLAND to the Dark Tower came
See **Childe.**

Love among the RUINS
See **love.**

RULE, Britannia
See **Britons.**

From RUSSIA with Love
The title of Ian Fleming's James Bond novel (1957) and,
especially, its use when filmed (1963), provided a format phrase
for journalists which rapidly became clichéd. Everything was
'from (somewhere) with love'. Fritz Spiegl, in *Keep Taking the
Tabloids* (1983), notes but two sample headlines: 'From Maggie
without love!' and 'From the Rush Hour with Love'.

SABRINA Fair

Billy Wilder's 1954 film *Sabrina*, based on a play by Samuel Taylor, was about the daughter (Audrey Hepburn) of a chauffeur who gets wooed by both of the two brothers who employ her father. Known simply as *Sabrina* in the USA, the film was released as *Sabrina Fair* in Britain. Now this could have been because the distributors thought that English cinema-goers would relish an allusion to the poetic name for the River Severn, as applied to the nymph in Milton's masque *Comus* (1634):

> Sabrina fair,
>   Listen where thou art sitting
> Under the glassy, cool, translucent wave,
>   In twisted braids of lilies knitting
> The loose train of thy amber-dropping hair.

On the other hand, the distributors might have been sending them a message that the film had nothing at all to do with Sabrina, a busty (41-18-36) model, who was at that time featured on TV shows with Arthur Askey, the comedian.

Alas, this second theory does not fit, as Norma Sykes (her real name) did not appear until 1956 and, in fact, she took her stage-name from the title of the film. So, it must have been the allusion to Milton after all.

SARCASM is the lowest form of wit

A *Quote . . . Unquote* listener asked me who said this. I was completely stumped and remain so. It sounds familiar – but, I think, deceptively so. It is probably a blend of two sayings. Thomas Carlyle remarked that 'Sarcasm is the language of the devil' (*Sartor Resartus*, 1833/34), and 'punning is the lowest form of wit' derives from Dryden's dismissal of Ben Jonson's 'clenches' as 'the lowest and most grovelling kind of wit.'

Eric Partridge begins his section on 'Puns' in *Usage and Abusage* (1973 edition) with, 'The pun is the lowest form of wit'.

Bears the marks of the last person who SAT on him
See **pillow.**

SAVAGE indignation
'Swift sleeps under the greatest epitaph in history' said W. B. Yeats. Dr Jonathan Swift is buried in St Patrick's Cathedral, Dublin (where he served as dean 1713-45) and the inscription on a tablet near his grave includes the words: *'Ubi saeva indignatio ulterius cor lacerare nequit'* – which is translated, in full, as 'Here lies the body of Jonathan Swift for thirty years dean of this cathedral, where savage indignation can no longer gnaw his heart. Go, traveller, and imitate, if you can, one who played a man's part in defence of Liberty.' The part quoted in Latin above was composed by Swift himself.

I disapprove of what you SAY, but will defend to the death your right to say it
This is attributed to Voltaire, notably by S. G. Tallentyre, in *The Friends of Voltaire* (1907). But Tallentyre gave the words as a free paraphrase of what Voltaire wrote in his *Essay on Tolerance*: 'Think for yourself and let others enjoy the privilege to do so, too.'

Then along comes Norbert Guterman to claim that what Voltaire *did* write in a letter of February 1770 to a M. le Riche was: 'Monsieur l'abbé, I detest what you write, but I would give my life to make it possible for you to continue to write.'

So, whether or not he used the precise words, at least Voltaire believed in the principle behind them.

The SCUM of the earth
As with almost everything attributed to the first Duke of Wellington, this description of his men in a despatch to Lord Bathurst, the War Minister, in 1813, requires a hefty footnote. Harold Whelan supplied it in a letter to the *Sunday Times* on 23 June 1985:

> The words 'We have in the service the scum of the earth as common soldiers' were said in July 1813, after the battle of Vittoria, when

Wellington's troops ('our vagabond soldiers') were 'totally knocked up' after a night of looting . . .

The words 'I don't know what effect these men will have on the enemy, but by God they frighten me' referred to some of his generals, and not to his regimental officers or to the rank and file . . . They come from a despatch to Sir Colonel Torrens, military secretary at the Horse Guards, and were written in August 1810.

On more than one occasion Wellington spoke in complimentary terms about the common soldiers under his command.

The Scum of the Earth is the title of a novel by Arthur Koestler (1941). The expression predates Wellington. Dr John Arbuthnot in *John Bull* (1712) (III.vi.25) has 'Scoundrels! Dogs! the Scum of the Earth!'

He lived by the SEA, died on it, and was buried in it

Referring to Sir Francis Drake, this was quoted by President Reagan on 28 January 1986 in his tribute to those who had died in the *Challenger* space shuttle disaster. He seemed to be drawing some sort of parallel.

I have been unable to find the source of his quotation. It almost sounds like an allusion to G. M. Trevelyan's comment about Nelson in his *History of England*, that he was 'always in his element and always on his element'.

I can, however, point to more satirical use of 'sea' phraseology. Malcolm Muggeridge cites Horace Walpole's gloomy description of a low point in Britain's fortunes: 'Everything is at sea – except the fleet.' When Ramsey Macdonald died on a cruise ship in 1937, it was said of him that, 'He died – as he lived – at sea.'

The SEA, The Sea

The title of Iris Murdoch's novel (1978) is, one assumes, by way of an allusion to Xenophon's story of the Greeks who shouted *'Thalatta, thalatta!'* (*Anabasis*, IV.vii.24).

I believe that the Chevalier Sigmund Neukomm (1778-1858) also wrote a song with this title. It was certainly parodied in H. J. Byron's version of *Aladdin* with reference to tea-clippers in 1861:

> The Tea! The Tea!
>   Refreshing Tea.
> The green, the fresh, the ever free
>   From all impurity.

A Man for All SEASONS
Robert Bolt's title for his 1960 play about Sir Thomas More (filmed 1967) has provided a popular phrase for an accomplished, adaptable, appealing person – also a format, verging on the cliché, whereby almost anything can be described as 'a ——— for all seasons'.

The playwright found his title in a description of More (1478-1535) by a contemporary, Robert Whittington: 'More is a man of angel's wit and singular learning; I know not his fellow. For where is the man of that gentleness, lowliness and affability? And as time requireth, a man of marvellous mirth and pastimes; and sometimes of as sad a gravity: as who say a man for all seasons.'

Whittington (*c.* 1480-*c.* 1530) wrote the passage for schoolboys to put into Latin in his book *Vulgaria* (*c.* 1521). It translates a comment on More by Erasmus who wrote in his preface to *In Praise of Folly* (1509) that More was *'omnium horarum hominem'*.

Believe only half of what you SEE
See **believe**.

A SELF-MADE man who worships his creator
Mencken attributes this to one Henry Clapp, *c.* 1858, about Horace Greeley (1811-72), the American journalist. He also gives it as said by John Bright about Benjamin Disraeli in *c.* 1868. If his dates are right, Clapp is the clear winner.

To SERVE Them All My Days
The title of the novel (1972) by R. F. Delderfield sounds as if it ought to be a quotation, but contains no more than echoes of several religious lines: 'And to serve him truly all the days of my life' from the catechism in *The Book of Common Prayer*: 'To serve thee all my happy days', from the hymn 'Gentle Jesus, meek and mild' in the Methodist Hymnal; the Devon carol, 'We'll bring him hearts that love him/ To serve him all our days'; and the Sunday school hymn: 'I must like a Christian/ Shun all evil ways,/ Keep the faith of Jesus,/ And serve him all my days.'

Had I but SERVED God as diligently as I have done the King . . .
Cardinal Wolsey's remark about Henry VIII was made to Sir William Kingston, Constable of the Tower of London, when Wolsey was under arrest for high treason in November 1530: 'I

see the matter against me how it is framed. But if I had served God as diligently as I have done the King, he would not have given me over in my grey hairs.'

These were not his actual 'last words', as is sometimes suggested, though they were spoken on his deathbed. His last words appear to have been: 'Master Kingston, farewell. My time draweth on fast. Forget not what I have sent and charged you withal. For when I am dead you shall, peradventure, understand my words better.'

Wolsey was not executed but died in Leicester on his way to the Tower. Shakespeare in *King Henry VIII* (III.ii.455) takes the report of Wolsey's death in Raphael Holinshed's *Chronicle* (1587) – which is more or less as in the first paragraph above – and comes up with slightly different wording for Wolsey's exit from the play. To Cromwell, his servant, he says:

> Had I but serv'd my God with half the zeal
> I serv'd my king, he would not in mine age
> Have left me naked to mine enemies . . .
>   Farewell
> The hopes of court, my hopes in heaven do dwell.

The situation in Germany is SERIOUS but not hopeless
See **situation**.

Give us a child until it is SEVEN, and it is ours for life
See **give**.

SEX and the Single Girl
See **single**.

SHE didn't say yes, she didn't say no
The song 'She Didn't Say Yes' by Jerome Kern and Otto Harbach from the musical *The Cat and the Fiddle* (1931) was memorably quoted by Harold Macmillan when Prime Minister in October 1962. Speaking to the Conservative Party conference at Llandudno he referred to the Labour Party's attitude to the Government's attempts (from July 1961) to open negotiations for Britain's entry to the European Common Market.

'What did the socialists do? . . . They solemnly asked Parliament not to approve or disapprove, but to "take note" of our decision. Perhaps some of the older ones among you [oh, wonderful Macmillanism!] will remember that popular song –

> 'She didn't say yes, she didn't say no,
> She didn't say stay, she didn't say go.
> She wanted to climb, but dreaded to fall,
> She bided her time and clung to the wall.''

Private Eye magazine – perhaps inspired by a recent American record which had taken President Kennedy's inaugural speech and added a music track – put out a record of Macmillan 'singing' the song to a tinny 1960s backing. Very droll it was, too, and now sadly evocative of a bygone era.

SHE Who Must Be Obeyed

The original 'she' in the novel *She* (1887) by H. Rider Haggard was the all-powerful Ayesha, 'who from century to century sat alone, clothed with unchanging loveliness, waiting till her lost love is born again'. But also, 'she was obeyed throughout the length and breadth of the land, and to question her command was certain death'.

From the second of these two quotations we get the use of the phrase by barrister Horace Rumpole with regard to his formidable wife in the 'Rumpole of the Bailey' stories by John Mortimer (in TV plays from 1978, and novelizations therefrom). Hence, too, one of the many nicknames applied to Margaret Thatcher – 'She-Who-Must-Be-Obeyed'.

Like being savaged by a dead SHEEP

When he was Chancellor of the Exchequer, the British Labour politician Denis Healey (*b.* 1917) said of an attack by his Conservative opposite number, Sir Geoffrey Howe, that it was 'like being savaged by a dead sheep'. This memorable shaft occurred in a House of Commons debate on 14 June 1978 about some of Mr Healey's many budget proposals.

It was subsequently claimed that Sir Roy Welensky, one-time Prime Minister of Rhodesia, had said of an attack by Iain Macleod, a former Colonial Secretary, that it was like being 'bitten by a dead sheep'.

Healey kept mum about any prior inspiration for his remark until the 1987 general election when, according to Alan Watkins in the *Observer* (8 June), he started claiming he had taken it from a Winston Churchill remark about Clement Attlee. There is a certain inevitability about this, but it sounds plausible, though Churchill strenuously denied most of the cruel remarks attributed to him about Attlee.

A SHINING city on a hill
See **city.**

My SHINING Hour
I am told that Johnny Mercer (1909-76) found the title-lyric of
his song 'My Shining Hour' (first sung in the film *The Sky's the
Limit,* 1943) in the Isaac Watts poem 'Against Idleness and
Mischief' (1715):

> How doth the little busy bee
>   Improve each shining hour,
> And gather honey all the day
>   From every opening flower!

If Mercer did, he had, of course, been beaten to it by Lewis
Carroll who parodied the Watts poem in *Alice's Adventures in
Wonderland* (1865) as 'How doth the little crocodile/ Improve his
shining tail'.

One Brief SHINING Moment
In 1983, on the twentieth anniversary of President Kennedy's
assassination, William Manchester wrote a memorial volume
under the title *One Brief Shining Moment.* The title came from a
favourite lyric of the late president in the Lerner and Loewe
musical *Camelot*:

> Camelot . . .
> Where once it never rained till after sundown
> By eight a.m. the morning fog had flown
> Don't let it be forgot
> That once there was a spot
> For one brief shining moment
> That was known as Camelot.

The musical was first produced on Broadway in December
1960 just before Kennedy took office and the name 'Camelot'
came to be applied to the romantic concept of his presidency. As
Alan Jay Lerner wrote in *The Street Where I Live* (1978), when
Jackie Kennedy quoted the lines in an interview with *Life*
magazine after the assassination in 1963, '*Camelot* had suddenly
become the symbol of those thousand days when people the
world over saw a bright new light of hope shining from the White
House . . . For myself, I have never been able to see a
performance of *Camelot* again.'

SIC transit gloria mundi

The phrase meaning 'So passes away the glory of the world' – perhaps now mostly used ironically when something has failed – is a quotation from *Of the Imitation of Christ* (*c.* 1420) by Thomas à Kempis (1380-1471) (*'O quam cito transit gloria mundi'* – 'O, how quickly the world's glory passes away'). It is used at the coronation ceremony of popes when a reed surmounted with flax is burned and a chaplain intones, *'Pater sancte, sic transit gloria mundi'* to remind the new Holy Father of the transitory nature of human vanity (Brewer).

ODQ, however, says it was used at the crowning of Alexander V at Pisa in July 1409, and is of earlier origin, which, if so, would mean that it was à Kempis who was doing the quoting.

The SIGN of a misspent youth
See **billiards.**

SILENCE is golden

This recommendation to people to remain silent is from a Swiss inscription written in German and best known in the English translation by Thomas Carlyle: *'Sprechen ist silbern, Schweigen ist golden'* – 'Speech is silvern, silence is golden'. The original is sometimes given in the form *'Reden ist Silber, Schweigen ist Gold'* – (*'Reden'* = 'speech').

SILLY Billy

The most notable person to be given this nickname was William Frederick, second Duke of Gloucester (1776-1834), uncle of William IV, although it was also applied to the king himself. In the wrangles between Whigs and Tories, when the king supported the former, Gloucester is reported to have asked, 'Who's Silly Billy now?'

Partridge/Slang has Henry Mayhew in 1851 finding 'Silly Billy . . . very popular with the audience at the fairs' (as a name used by a clown for a foolish person).

In the 1970s, Mike Yarwood, the TV impressionist, put it in the mouth of the British Labour politician, Denis Healey, because it went rather well with Healey's *persona* and distinctive vocal delivery. Healey then imitated art by saying it himself.

According to Alan Watkins in the *Observer* (13 January 1985), Randolph Churchill, the Conservative politician (and son of Winston), was also noted for using the expression.

Mrs SIMPSON'S pinched our king
See **hark.**

SINEWS of peace
Winston Churchill's speech at Fulton, Missouri, on 5 March 1946, introduced the old phrase 'Iron Curtain' to a wider audience. The title of his speech was 'The Sinews of Peace'. This was an allusion to the phrase *'nervi belli pecunia'* from Cicero's *Philippics* where the 'sinews of war' are 'money'. The 'sinews of peace' recommended by Churchill in dealing with the Soviet Union amounted to recourse to the newly formed United Nations Organization.

I SING the body electric
Lest any reader has seen the film *Fame* (1980) and wondered how it is that a pupil of the New York High School for the Performing Arts calls a rather grand composition 'I Sing the Body Electric', well, the title came from Walt Whitman. Whitman certainly can't be blamed for the lyrics beyond that: 'I sing the body electric . . . I celebrate the "me" yet to come and toast to my own reunion when I become one with the sun . . .'.

The SINGER Not the Song
This film (UK 1960) was based on a novel (1959) by Audrey Erskine Lindop. She took her title from a West Indian calypso.

Sex and the SINGLE Girl
Helen Gurley Brown's sex advice book (1962) was followed by a film (1964) which used the title but nothing else. Thus was born the journalistic format phrase 'Sex and the ———' or 'Sex and the Single ———'. Fritz Spiegl in *Keep Taking the Tabloids* (1983) finds the newspaper headlines, 'Sex and the Parish Priest', 'Sex and the Single Siberian' and 'Sex and the Kindly Atheist'.

The SITUATION in Germany is serious but not hopeless
'. . . the situation in Austria is hopeless but not serious'. In *Quotations for Speakers and Writers* (1970), this is described as an 'Austrian proverb collected by Franklin Pierce Adams'.

In 1965 a little-shown film was made about two American airmen captured by a mild-mannered German (Alec Guinness) who hasn't the heart to tell them the war is over. Taken from the novel *No Hiding Place* by Robert Shaw, the film was called *Situation Hopeless But Not Serious*.

Oh! I have SLIPPED the surly bonds of earth

In his TV broadcast (28 January 1986) after the space shuttle *Challenger* disaster, President Reagan said: 'We will never forget them nor the last time we saw them this morning as they prepared for their journey and waved goodbye and slipped the surly bonds of earth to touch the face of God.'

This immediately sent people the world over on fruitless journeys to their quotation books. He was quoting 'High Flight', a sonnet written by John Gillespie Magee who was an American-born pilot with the Royal Canadian Air Force in the Second World War. He died at the age of nineteen in 1941 during a mission from Britain. He is buried in Scopwick burial ground (not cemetery) near Lincoln.

The poem 'High Flight' – sometimes referred to as 'the pilot's creed' – was published in 1943 in a volume called *More Poems from the Forces* (which was 'dedicated to the USSR'):

> Oh! I have slipped the surly bonds of earth,
>   And danced the skies on laughter-silvered wings;
> Sunward I've climbed, and joined the tumbling mirth
>   Of sun-split clouds – and done a hundred things
> You have not dreamed of – wheeled and soared and swung
>   High in the sunlit silence. Hov'ring there
> I've chased the shouting wind along and flung
>   My eager craft through footless halls of air.
>
> Up, up the long, delirious, burning blue
>   I've topped the wind-swept heights with easy grace
> Where never lark, nor even eagle flew –
>   And, while with silent lifting mind I've trod
> The high, untrespassed sanctity of space,
>   Put out my hand and touched the face of God.

SMALL is beautiful

The title of the book published in 1973 by Professor E. F. Schumacher (1911-77) provided a catchphrase and a slogan for those who were opposed to a trend in business and organizations that was very apparent in the 1960s and 1970s and who wanted 'economics on a human scale'. However, it appears that he very nearly didn't come up with the phrase. According to his daughter and a correspondent (*Observer*, 29 April/ 6 June 1984), the book was going to be called 'The Homecomers'. His publisher, Anthony Blond, suggested 'Small*ness* is Beautiful', and then Desmond Briggs, the co-publisher, came up with the eventual wording.

There are no SNAKES to be met with throughout the whole island

This is the entire contents of Chapter 72 of *The Natural History of Iceland* by a Dane called Horrebow (1758). Dr Samuel Johnson used to boast of being able to repeat the whole chapter (Boswell's *Life*, 13 April 1778).

Sometimes Ireland rather than Iceland is mentioned in telling the 'joke', presumably on the grounds that St Patrick drove out all the snakes from that country by ringing a bell.

SNOBBERY with violence

In its obituary for Colin Watson, the detective story writer (21 January 1983), *The Times* mentioned his *Snobbery with Violence* – a survey of the modern crime story, 1971 – 'from which the phrase comes.'

As usual, there is an earlier example: in Alan Bennett's play *Forty Years On* (1969) a character talks of, 'Sapper, Buchan, Dornford Yates, practitioners in that school of Snobbery with Violence that runs like a thread of good-class tweed through twentieth-century literature.'

We are all SOCIALISTS nowadays

King Edward VII is said to have said this, when Prince of Wales, in a speech at the Mansion House, London, on 5 November 1895 – though I can find no mention of him making any such speech on that day. His biographer, Sir Philip Magnus, makes no mention of him doing so and the *ODQ* dropped the entry after pointing out in the corrigenda to the 1941 edition that the saying should more correctly be ascribed to Sir William Harcourt (1827-1904). He is quoted as saying it in *Fabian Essays* (1889, edited by Bernard Shaw) (i.e., six years before the supposed 1895 speech). Harcourt was Lord Rosebery's (Liberal) Chancellor of the Exchequer and an impassioned enemy of the House of Lords. He introduced estate duty tax in his budget of 1894.

Whoever said it first, the foundation was laid for a much later remark by Jeremy Thorpe, the Liberal politician, in a speech in the House of Commons on 6 March 1974. After a general election which resulted in no party having a clear majority – a Liberal coalition with the Conservatives had been mooted but rejected – he observed, 'Looking around the House, one realizes that we are all minorities now.'

Under this SOD, another lies

I had always thought this to be a joke gravestone inscription until being told of an 'epitaph' on the fourteenth Earl of Strathmore and Kinghorne (*d.* 1944), maternal grandfather of the present Queen. A Scottish poet calle Clarke (who also wrote 'The Skull') is supposed to have written:

> Neath this sod another lies,
> An aristocrat of Scots assize,
> Long dead but not forgotten.
> When writhe and maggots eat his eyes,
> They'll cause his lordship no surprise,
> For while he lived, the man was rotten.

This was quoted in 1947. Somewhat later Paul Dehn won a *New Statesman* competition with this epitaph on John Gordon, columnist on the *Sunday Express*:

> Believing that his hate for queers
>   Proclaimed his love of God,
> He now (of all queer things, my dears)
>   Lies under his first sod.

The SOFT underbelly of Europe
See **underbelly.**

Every SOLDIER has the baton of a field-marshal in his knapsack
See **baton.**

SOMEBODY'S Husband, Somebody's Son

The title of Gordon Burn's (1984) book about the 'Yorkshire Ripper' derives from the prolonged police hunt for the killer. George Oldfield, leading the hunt, appeared on the Jimmy Young radio show on 9 February 1978 and 'urged the predominantly female audience to search their collective conscience and report any man of their acquaintance who they suspected of behaving oddly. Husband, father, brother, son – it shouldn't matter.' After another killing, a Yorkshire clergyman, the Revd Michael Walker told his congregation on Palm Sunday 1979, 'He [the Ripper] needs help, he is somebody's child, husband or father.'

Peter Sutcliffe (*b.* 1946), who murdered some thirteen women in the period 1975-80, was given his nickname by a Yorkshire local newspaper after he had murdered his third victim in February 1977. *The Times* did not use the 'Ripper' tag in 1977 but was doing so by February 1978.

Dark night of the SOUL
See **dark.**

The SOUND OF Two Hands Clapping
See **clapping.**

SPARKS fly upward
Stewart Granger, the film actor, and Frank Chapple, the former trade union leader, both chose the same biblical quotation for their memoirs: Granger's was *Sparks Fly Upward* (1981) and Chapple's was *Sparks Fly* (1984).

Chapple had been leader of the Electricians' Union and 'sparks' has been the nickname given to members of that trade since the First World War at least.

Both authors drew on the Book of Job 5:7: 'Man is born unto trouble, as the sparks fly upward.'

SPECIAL relationship
This term is used most often about relationships between countries – the earliest *OED Supp.* citation is for one between Britain and Galicia in 1929 – but it particularly refers to that supposed to exist between Britain and the United States especially on the basis of historical ties and a common language. The notion was principally promoted by Winston Churchill in his attempts to draw the USA into the 1939-45 war, though whether he used the phrase prior to 1941, I do not know. In the House of Commons on 7 November 1945, Churchill said: 'We should not abandon our special relationship with the United States and Canada about the atomic bomb.' In his 1946 'Iron Curtain' speech at Fulton, Missouri, he asked, 'Would a special relationship between the United States and the British Commonwealth be inconsistent with our over-riding loyalties to the World Organization?' (i.e., the UN).

Love is two minutes ... of SQUELCHING/SQUISHING noises
See **love.**

The STARS Look Down

The title of the novel (1935, filmed 1939) by A. J. Cronin alludes, I think, to a situation rather than quoting anything specific: i.e., the controllers of earthly destiny looking down on human behaviour. The idea also pops up in a song of the 1940s called 'Tonight' (also known as 'Perfidia'), written by Milton Leeds to music by Alberto Dominguez: 'While the Gods of love look down and laugh at what romantic fools we mortals be.' There is here a more obvious allusion to the situation in Shakespeare's *A Midsummer Night's Dream* (III.ii.115) when the sprite Puck says to Oberon, King of the Fairies: 'Lord, what fools these mortals be!' In *Coriolanus* (V.iii.184), we find: 'The gods look down, and this unnatural scene/ They laugh at.'

When people are STARVING in India . . .

I am indebted to *The Complete Directory to Prime Time Network TV Shows* (1981) for the information that when a proposed US series called *B.A.D. Cats* crashed in 1980, Everett Chambers, its executive producer, said, 'We bought $40,000 worth of cars to smash up, and we never got a chance to smash them up. I think that's kind of immoral, $40,000 worth of cars to smash up when people are starving in India.'

I had always taken this to be a (British) nanny's expression, but the nearest I can find, recorded in *Nanny Says* by Sir Hugh Casson and Joyce Grenfell (1972) is, 'Think of all the poor starving children who'd be grateful for that nice plain bread and butter.' Wasn't it also advised that it was polite to leave a little food on the side of the plate 'for the starving in India' if not for 'Mr Manners'?

The STATELY homes of England

Although this phrase is best known in Noel Coward's delightful 1938 song with the same title (from the show *Operette*), it began life in a ballad 'The Homes of England' (1827) by Mrs Hemans (1793-1835):

> The stately homes of England
> How beautiful they stand!
> Amidst their tall, ancestral trees,
> O'er all the pleasant land.

That's one small STEP for a man, one giant leap for mankind

I have described at length in my *Sayings* how Neil Armstrong claimed that this was what he actually said when stepping on to the moon's surface for the first time on 20 July 1969. The indefinite article before 'man' was, however, completely inaudible, thus ruining the sense.

Reference books have been thrown into confusion ever since. Several follow the version – 'One small step for [. . .] man, one big step [*sic*] for mankind' (my brackets) – which appeared in the magazine *Nature* in 1974.

The *Observer* 'Sayings of the Week' column in the week following the landing had, 'That's one small step for [. . .] man, one giant leap for all [*sic*] mankind' (my brackets). Either way, Armstrong launched an imperishable format. Here is but one example of it in use: 'SMALL STEP FOR NON-WHITE MANKIND' (*The Times*, 29 October 1983).

The correct version has even been set to music. I have heard the Great Mormon Tabernacle Choir sing:

> One small step for a man, one giant leap for mankind –
> It shows what a man can do, if he has the will.

The heart and STOMACH of a king

What Elizabeth I is supposed to have said in a speech to her army of twenty thousand gathered at Tilbury prior to the Spanish Armada in 1588 is:

My loving people, we have been persuaded by some that are careful for our safety to take heed how we commit ourselves to armed multitudes, for fear of treachery. But I assure you I do not desire to live to distrust my faithful and loving people. Let tyrants fear. I have always so behaved myself that, under God, I have placed my chiefest strength and safeguard in the loyal hearts and goodwill of my subjects; and therefore I am come amongst you, as you see, resolved, in the midst and heat of the battle, to live or die amongst you all, to lay down for my God, and for my kingdom, and for my people, my honour and my blood, even in the dust.

I know I have the body of a weak and feeble woman, but I have the heart and stomach of a king, and of a king of England too; and think foul scorn that Parma or Spain, or any prince of Europe, should dare to invade the borders of my realm; to which, rather than any dishonour shall grow by me, I myself will take up arms, I myself will be your general, judge, and rewarder of every one of your virtues in the field. I know already for your forwardness you have deserved rewards and crowns; and we do assure you, in the word of a prince, they shall be duly paid you.

In *History Today* (May 1988), Felix Barker contended that the queen might never have used these words because of the absence of any contemporary accounts of her doing so. The sole source is an undated letter (not published until 1691) to the Duke of Buckingham from Leonel Sharp, a chaplain who was at Tilbury but who had a reputation for being 'obsequious and ingratiating' (according to the *DNB*).

The only contemporary account of the speech is by a poet called James Aske but it contains none of the above phrases. Why did no one else quote the good bits at the time, Felix Barker wondered, if they had in fact been said?

For reasons of delicacy, presumably, when Flora Robson came to give the speech in the film *Fire Over England* (1937), she found herself saying, 'But I have the heart and valour of a king' rather than the traditional 'heart and stomach'.

Collapse of STOUT party
See **collapse.**

Not As a STRANGER
The novel with this title (1954) by Morton Thompson and the film (USA 1955) appear not to be quoting. The song which came out of the film goes, 'Not as a stranger, dear, but my own true love . . .'

The STUFF that dreams are made on
If one is quoting Prospero's words from Shakespeare's *The Tempest* (IV.i.156) – 'We are such stuff/ As dreams are made on' – it is definitely 'on' not 'of' (though Shakespeare did use the 'of' form elsewhere).

So, well done, the writer of the *Guardian* headline, 9 May 1988: 'Stuff that dreams are made on' and, rather less well done, Humphrey Bogart as Sam Spade in *The Maltese Falcon* (1941). 'What is it?' he is asked before speaking the last line of the picture, and replies: 'The stuff that dreams are made of.' Absolutely no marks to the cast of the 1964 Cambridge Footlights revue, *Stuff What Dreams Are Made Of*.

From the SUBLIME to the ridiculous

. . . there is but one step.' This is usually quoted now without the final qualifying phrase. The proverb most probably came to us from the French. Napoleon is said to have uttered on one occasion (after the retreat from Moscow in 1812): '*Du sublime au ridicule il n'y a qu'un pas.*'

However, Thomas Paine had already written in *The Age of Reason* (1795): 'The sublime and the ridiculous are often so nearly related, that it is difficult to class them separately. One step above the sublime, makes the ridiculous; and one step above the ridiculous, makes the sublime again.'

The SUN Also Rises

This tantalizingly odd title to a novel (1926) by Ernest Hemingway appears to be original. However, it lead to the Hollywood joke, 'The son-in-law also rises' when Louis B. Mayer promoted his daughter's husband (David O. Selznick) in *c.* 1933. The novel was originally known as *Fiesta* in the UK.

Thank heavens, the SUN has gone in, and I don't have to go out and enjoy it

These are sometimes quoted as though they were Logan Pearsall Smith's last (i.e., dying) words – in *A Dictionary of Famous Quotations* (1962), for example. They are not, though the misunderstanding is understandable. They appear in a work called *Last Words* (1933). Smith did not die until 1946 when, according to James Lees-Milne, *Caves of Ice* (1983), his actual last words were, 'I must telephone to the Pope-Hennessys.'

The reason the SUN never sets on the British Empire

See **reason**.

Oh! I have slipped the SURLY bonds of earth

See **slipped**.

The SURVIVAL of the fittest

Herbert Spencer wrote in *Principles of Biology* (1864-67): 'This survival of the fittest which I have here sought to express in mechanical terms is that which Mr Darwin has called "natural selection, or the preservation of favoured races in the struggle for life".'

In other words, Spencer, in talking of evolution, was pointing to the survival of the most suitable, not of the most physically fit.

(When the Abbé Emmanuel Joseph Siéyès – who had played a somewhat Vicar of Brayish role in the French Revolution – was asked *c.* 1795 what he did during the Reign of Terror, he replied simply: 'I survived' – '*J'ai vécu*').

SUSSEX by the Sea

This comes from the song with this title with words and music by W. Ward-Higgs (*d.* 1936):

> We plough and sow and reap and mow,
> And useful men are we . . .
> You may tell them all that we stand or fall
> For Sussex by the sea.

That song was published in 1908 but the phrase 'Sussex by the sea' also occurs in a poem called 'Sussex' (1902) by Rudyard Kipling.

So who got there first? Looks like Kipling. Incidentally, the English county has since been cut in two. Both bits are still by the sea, however.

President can't SWIM
See **president.**

The Nine TAILORS

In the Dorothy L. Sayers novel (1934), 'Tailor Paul' is the name of one of the church bells of 'Fenchurch St Paul' which play a significant part in the plot. The saying 'Nine tailors make a man' is quoted on the last page of the novel.

So what we have in the title is a blend. In bell-ringing it was possible to indicate the gender of the dead person for whom the bells were being tolled. 'Nine tailors' or 'nine tellers' (strokes) meant a man.

The bell-ringing use of the phrase nevertheless echoes an actual proverb, 'It takes nine tailors to make a man' which apparently came to us from the French *c.* 1600. The meaning seems to be that a man should buy his clothes from various outlets. One source suggests that it is said in contempt of tailors. Apperson shows that, until the end of the seventeenth century, there was some uncertainty about the number of tailors mentioned. In *Westward Hoe* by John Webster and Thomas Dekker (1605) it appeared as three.

And thereby hangs a TALE

As a story-telling device, this is still very much in use – we might use it to indicate that some tasty titbit is about to be revealed. It occurs a number of times in Shakespeare. In *As You Like It* (II.vii.28) Jaques, reporting the words of a 'motley fool' (Touchstone) moralizing about time, says:

> And so from hour to hour, we ripe and ripe,
> And then, from hour to hour, we rot and rot:
> And thereby hangs a tale.

Other examples occur in *The Merry Wives of Windsor* (I.iv.143) and *The Taming of the Shrew* (IV.i.50). In *Othello* (III.i.8), the Clown says, 'O, thereby hangs a tail', emphasizing the innuendo that may or may not be present in the other examples.

TELL-TALE Tits

The title of the spicy memoirs of the actress Fiona Richmond (published 1987) probably seemed to promise more lubricity than the phrase was originally meant to deliver. As Iona and Peter Opie record in *The Lore and Language of Schoolchildren*:

> Tell tale tit
> Your tongue shall be slit,
> And all the dogs in the town
> Shall have a little bit

– has been 'stinging in the ears of blabbers for more than two hundred years' (since 1780, at least).

TENDER is the Night

The novel (1934) by F. Scott Fitzgerald and the film (1961) take their title from the 'Ode to a Nightingale' by Keats: 'Already with thee! tender is the night.'

TENDER Loving Care

Understandably, this a phrase that appears irresistible to song-writers. The catalogue of the BBC Gramophone Library reveals a considerable list:

As 'T.L.C.', there is a song by Lehman: Lebowsky: C. Parker dating from 1960 (and translated as 'Tender Loving *and* Care'). Also with this title, there is a Motown song by Jones: Sawer: Jerome (1971), an instrumental by R. L. Martin: Norman Harris (1975); and a song by the Average White Band and Alan Gorrie.

As 'Tender Lovin' Care' there is a song written by Brooks: Stillman (1966) and one written and performed by Ronnie Dyson (1983).

As 'Tender Loving Care', there is a song written by Mercer: Bright: Wilson, and recorded in 1966 by Nancy Wilson. It was also used as the title of an album by her.

It has also been suggested to me that 't.l.c.' has been used in advertisements by BUPA, the medical insurance scheme, or by Nuffield Hospitals. Have I imagined it being used in washing powder ads, too – for Dreft perhaps? The *OED Supp.* recognizes the phrase as a colloquialism denoting, 'especially solicitous care such as is given by nurses' and cites the *Listener* (12 May 1977): 'It is in a nurse's nature and in her tradition to give the sick what is well called "TLC", "tender loving care", some constant little service to the sick.'

Well, there's no phrase like an old phrase. In Shakespeare, *The Second Part of King Henry VI* (III.ii.277/9) we read:

> *Commons. (Within):* [i.e., a rabble offstage] An answer
>   from the King, or we will all break in!
> *King:* Go, Salisbury, and tell them all from me,
>   I thank them for their tender loving care.

Fold their TENTS like the Arabs
See **fold.**

Because it's THERE
See **because.**

THESE You Have Loved
See **loved.**

THINGS ain't what they used to be
The title of the Frank Norman/Lionel Bart musical *Fings Ain't Wot They Used T'be* (1959) — which popularized an already existing catchphrase in a particular form — gave rise to one of the nicest juxtaposition jokes I have spotted. In an edition of the *Liverpool Echo* of *c.* 1960, an advertisement for the Royal Court Theatre announced:

THIS WEEK & NEXT
THEATRE CLOSED FOR ALTERATIONS
Box Office Now Open for
Lionel Bart's Smash Hit Musical
'FINGS AIN'T WOT THEY USED T'BE'

It should be remembered that a song by Mercer Ellington and Ted Persons, published in 1939, was called 'Things Ain't What They Used To Be'.

THINGS fall apart; the centre cannot hold
See **centre.**

I THINK I go home
At one time, 'I tink I go home', spoken in a would-be Swedish accent, was as much part of the impressionist's view of Greta

Garbo as 'I want to be alone'. One version of how the line came to be spoken is told by Norman Zierold in *Moguls* (1969):

> After such films as *The Torrent* and *Flesh and the Devil*, Garbo decided to exploit her box-office power and asked Louis B. Mayer for a raise – from three hundred and fifty to five thousand dollars a week. Mayer offered her twenty-five hundred. 'I tink I go home,' said Garbo. She went back to her hotel and stayed there for a full seven months until Mayer finally gave way.

Alexander Walker, in *Garbo* (1980), recalls, rather, what Sven-Hugo Borg, the actress's interpreter, said of the time in 1926 when Mauritz Stiller, who had come with her from Sweden, was fired from directing *The Temptress:* 'She was tired, terrified and lost . . . as she returned to my side after a trying scene, she sank down beside me and said so low it was almost a whisper, "Borg, I think I shall go home now. It isn't worth it, is it?"'

Walker comments: 'That catch-phrase, shortened into "I think I go home", soon passed into the repertoire of a legion of Garbo-imitators and helped publicize her strong-willed temperament.'

A caricatured Garbo was shown hugging Mickey Mouse in a cartoon film in the 1930s. 'Ah tahnk ah kees you now' and 'ah tink ah go home,' she said. This cartoon was, incidentally, the last item to be shown on British television before the transmitters were closed down on the brink of war on 1 September 1939.

THIRTY is a Dangerous Age, Cynthia
The title of an early (and very mild) Dudley Moore film comedy (1967) would seem to allude, however distantly and unknowingly, to *Den farlige alder* ('The dangerous age'), a book in Danish by Karin Michaelis (1910). In that case, the dangerous age is forty.

In the Moore film, as far as I can recall, it was very important for him to write a musical, or perhaps get married, before he was thirty. I think, however, that the 'dangerous age' can occur almost any time. It might be said of teenagers first encountering the opposite sex, 'Well, that's the dangerous age, of course' as much as it might be said of married folk experiencing the 'seven-year itch'.

The TIMES **is a tribal noticeboard**
See **tribal**.

THUS far shalt though go and no further
Hearing the Revd Ian Paisley, the Ulster loyalist, booming this out
in 1974 (in the form, 'So far and no further'), I was not entirely
surprised to find that the 'first use' seems also to lie in an Anglo-
Irish context. Charles Stewart Parnell, the champion of Irish
Home Rule, said in Cork in 1885: 'No man has a right to fix the
boundary of the march of a nation; no man has a right to say to
his country, Thus far shalt thou go and no further.'

On the other hand, the Book of Job 38:11 has: 'Hitherto shalt
thou come, but no further: and here shall thy proud waves be
stayed.'

There is always room at the TOP
CODP lists this as a proverb 'commonly used to encourage
competition', but doesn't record the occasion when Daniel
Webster (1782-1852), the American politician, said it. Responding
to a suggestion that he shouldn't become a lawyer because the
profession was overcrowded, he said, 'There is always room at
the top.'

John Braine's novel *Room at the Top* was published in 1957.
At one point, its hero is told: 'You're the sort of young man we
want. There's always room at the top.'

The Church of England is the TORY party at prayer
See **church**.

***TOUT** passe, tout casse, tout lasse*
('Everything passes, everything perishes, everything palls'.) This
anonymous French expression amounts, I suppose, to much the
same as, 'And this, too, shall *pass* away' (q.v.) but deserves to be
better known.

Please send photograph of TRACTOR
See **words**.

At least Mussolini made the TRAINS run on time
– i.e., efficiency may be the saving grave of a fascist dictatorship.
But did Mussolini ever boast that he would do so, possibly in the
words, 'I will make the trains run on time and create order out of
chaos'? Or did he ever claim afterwards that this is what he had
done? It would be good to have chapter and verse on this. One of
his biographers says he did eventually boast of the efficiency of

Italian railways, though quite how efficient they were is open to some doubt. Perhaps they just ran *relatively* more on time than they had done before. But they had managed all right for the famous 'March on Rome' (October 1922) which – despite its name – was largely accomplished by rail.

Across the River and Into the TREES
See **across.**

The TREES do not grow up to the sky
Is this one of those actual Russian folk proverbs, or a made up one? And what does it mean, for heaven's sake? John Colville quotes Churchill as saying it on 6 January 1953 in a situation where he is recommending a 'wait and see' policy. The full version seems to be, 'The trees are tall but they do not reach to the sky.' In other words, 'trees may be tall, but they're not that tall'. Later in the same year, on 9 November, in his speech at the Lord Mayor's banquet, Churchill said:

> Another old saying comes back to my mind which I have often found helpful or at least comforting. I think it was Goethe who said, 'The trees do not grow up to the sky'. I do not know whether he would have said that if he had lived through this frightful twentieth century where so much we feared was going to happen did actually happen. All the same it is a thought which should find its place in young as well as old brains.

Goethe? So perhaps it isn't Russian after all. Nevertheless, the great utterer of obscure proverbial sayings was Nikita Khrushchev. 'If you start throwing hedgehogs under me, I shall throw two porcupines under you.' 'If you cannot catch a bird of paradise, better take a wet hen.' 'Those who wait for the Soviet Union to abandon communism must wait until a shrimp learns to whistle.'

But people have also made them up. Anon. devised one for Khruschev himself: 'Great oafs from little ikons grow.' Dr Walter Heydecker sent this one into a *New Statesman* competition: 'Even a short leg reaches the ground.'

The Times is a TRIBAL noticeboard
A candidate for the editorship of the paper's woman's page in the 1960s described *The Times* as a 'tribal noticeboard'. This so tickled the editor, Sir William Haley, that he gave her the job. The candidate was, I now learn, Suzanne Puddefoot.

TRUE, O King!
When I have made an obvious statement, perhaps even a pompous one, my wife has a way of saying to me, 'True, O King!' I wondered where she had picked up this habit until one day I happened to see an old film of Charles Laughton indulging in a public reading from the Bible, as he was latterly wont to do. He was telling the story of Nebuchadnezzar and the gentlemen who were cast into the burning fiery furnace. 'Did not we cast three men bound into the midst of fire?' Nebuchadnezzar asks (Daniel 3.24). 'They answered and said unto the king, True, o king.'

The nearest Shakespeare gets is the ironical '"True"? O God!' in *Much Ado About Nothing* (IV.i.68), though he has any number of near misses like 'true, my liege', 'too true, my lord' and 'true, noble prince'.

Just to show that my wife is not alone, Mrs H. Joan Langdale of Tunbridge Wells wrote to me in June 1988 to say, 'My father, a classical scholar and an Anglican priest, used to use your wife's quotation "True, O King!" and always added, "Live for ever".'

Eating *pâtés de foie gras* to the sound of TRUMPETS
The Revd Sydney Smith is usually credited with this definition of heaven, but *ODQ* misleadingly manages to suggest he was quoting someone else. The best source (which *ODQ* confuses) is Hesketh Pearson's *Smith of Smiths* (1934) which has, 'My idea of heaven, is eating *pâtés de foie gras* to the sound of trumpets.'

Economical with the TRUTH
See **economical**.

A lie travels . . . while TRUTH is putting on her boots
See **lie**.

Why must the Devil have all the best TUNES?
See **devil**.

Will no man rid me of this TURBULENT priest?
King Henry II's rhetorical question regarding Thomas à Beckett – which was unfortunately acted upon by the archbishop's murderers in 1170 – is ascribed to 'oral tradition' by *ODQ* in the form: 'Will no one revenge me of the injuries I have sustained from one turbulent priest?'

The young king, who was in Normandy, had received reports

that the archbishop was ready 'to tear the crown from' his head. 'What a pack of fools and cowards I have nourished in my house', he cried, according to another version, 'that not one of them will avenge me of this turbulent priest!' Yet another version has, 'of this upstart clerk'.

An example of the phrase used allusively in conversation was played on tape at the conspiracy-to-murder trial involving Jeremy Thorpe MP in 1979. In one tape, Andrew Newton, speaking of the alleged plot, said: 'They feel a Thomas à Beckett was done, you know, with Thorpe sort of raving that would nobody rid me of this man.'

The lady's not for TURNING

In a speech to the Conservative Party conference at Brighton in 1980, Mrs Margaret Thatcher came up with, what is, in a sense, her most-remembered formally spoken 'line': 'To those waiting with bated breath for that favourite media catchphrase, the U-turn, I have only one thing to say. You turn if you want to. The lady is not for turning.'

One presumes she realized she was alluding to the title of Christopher Fry's play *The Lady's Not For Burning* (1948). According the *Sunday Times* (23 November 1980),

> . . . the man who had coined the phrase was sitting in the hall, nervous and discomfited. Sir Ronald Millar, 61-year-old playwright of musicals and farces, would have preferred his friend the Prime Minister to have said 'the lady's not for turning' with an elided 's' exactly as in the original title of Christopher Fry's play.

'TWAS ever thus . . .'

An exclamation meaning almost the same as the more modern, 'So what's new?' It does not occur in Shakespeare or the Bible. In fact, the only examples I have turned up so far are:

. . . as the first line of 'Disaster' by C. S. Calverley (*d.* 1884): ''Twas ever thus from childhood's hour!' This is a parody of lines from Thomas Moore's 'The Fire Worshippers' in *Lalla Rookh* (1817): 'Oh! ever thus from childhood's hour!'

. . . as the title, ''Twas Ever Thus' given to the parody of the same poem by Henry S. Leigh (1887-83). His version begins, 'I never rear'd a young gazelle'.

Give me TWENTY-SIX soldiers of lead . . .

The typographer F. W. Goudy (1865-1947) wrote in *The Type*

Speaks, 'I am the leaden army that conquers the world – I am TYPE' – but I rather suspect he was merely reworking an old riddle.

The *ODQ* finds in 1867 the saying, 'With twenty-six lead soldiers [the characters of the alphabet set up for printing] I can conquer the world', and points to the (probably independently arrived at) French riddle: '*Je suis le capitaine de vingt-quatre soldats, et sans moi Paris serait pris*,' to which the answer is '*A.*' ('I am the captain of twenty-four [*sic*] soldiers and without me Paris would be taken' – remove the '*a*' from '*Paris*' and it becomes '*pris*' or '*taken*'.) I find the phrase used as the title of a spiritual quest book, *Twenty-Six Lead Soldiers*, by Dan Wooding (1987): 'A top Fleet Street journalist and his search for the truth . . .'. He attributes the saying to 'Karl Marx or Benjamin Franklin . . .'

TWILIGHT of empire
I suppose this refers to Britain at any time after the death of Queen Victoria in 1901 or when the colonies started moving towards independence. Malcolm Muggeridge puts in a bid for coining the expression. In his diary entry for 21 December 1947 he calls it a 'phrase which occurred to me long ago'.

UNACCUSTOMED as I am to public speaking
On 26 July 1897, Winston Churchill made his first political speech at a Primrose League gathering near Bath.

> If it were pardonable in any speaker to begin with the well worn and time honoured apology, 'Unaccustomed as I am to public speaking', it would be pardonable in my case, for the honour I am enjoying at this moment of addressing an audience of my fellow-countrymen and women is the first honour of the kind I have ever received.

It is somehow reassuring that even an orator of future greatness should have fallen back on a dreadful cliché to begin his first effort. I wonder how long it has really been used as a speechmaker's introductory gambit?

Opening a Red Cross bazaar at Oxford, Noel Coward once began: 'Desperately *accustomed* as I am to public speaking . . . .'.

The soft UNDERBELLY of Europe
The phrase 'soft underbelly', meaning a vulnerable part, appears to have originated with Winston Churchill in the Second World War. Speaking to the House of Commons on 11 November 1942, he said: 'We make this wide encircling movement in the Mediterranean . . . having for its object the exposure of the under-belly of the Axis, especially Italy, to heavy attack.'

In *The Second World War* (Vol. 4), Churchill describes a meeting with Stalin before this date, in August 1942, at which he had outlined the same plan: 'To illustrate my point I had meanwhile drawn a picture of a crocodile, and explained to Stalin with the help of this picture how it was our intention to attack the soft belly of the crocodile as we attacked his hard snout.'

Somewhere, subsequently, the 'soft' and the 'underbelly' must have joined together to produce the phrase in the form in which it is now used.

UNDERNEATH the spreading chestnut tree

Some sort of prize should surely be awarded to Longfellow for providing in 'The Village Blacksmith' (1842) one of the most parodied and plundered verses. He started with:

> Underneath the spreading chestnut tree
> The village smithy stands;
> The smith a mighty man is he
> With large and sinewy hands
> And the muscles of his brawny arms
> Are strong as iron bands.

In the nineteenth century there were musical settings of this verse by several composers, but that by W. H. Weiss (1820-67) was the most popular (1854).

There was then a lull until a song was written called 'The Chestnut Tree' in 1938. This was a joint effort by Jimmy Kennedy, Tommie Connor and Hamilton Kennedy:

> Underneath the Spreading Chestnut Tree
> I loved her and she loved me.
> There she used to sit upon my knee
> 'Neath the Spreading Chestnut Tree.
>
> There beneath the boughs we used to meet,
> All her kisses were so sweet.
> All the little birds went tweet tweet tweet
> 'Neath the Spreading Chestnut Tree.

The actual blacksmith only manages to make an appearance in this song by exclaiming 'Chest . . . nuts!' – which gave rise to interesting gestures by performers. Instructions were given for these on the sheet music of this 'novelty singing dance sensation'.

During the build-up to the Second World War, between the Munich Agreement and the end of 1939, there then arose a playground rhyme in Britain which went:

> Under the spreading chestnut tree,
> Neville Chamberlain said to me:
> 'If you want to get your gas mask free,
> Join the blinking A.R.P.'

In fact – as Norman Longmate points out in *How We Lived Then* (1973) – this was not true. You were given a free gas mask anyway, but the A.R.P. (Air Raid Precautions) people were given more sophisticated ones.

In George Orwell's novel *1984* (1948), there is another variation:

> Under the spreading chestnut tree
> I sold you and you sold me:
> There lie they, and here lie we
> Under the spreading chestnut tree.

Arnold Silcock's *Verse and Worse* (1952) includes this anonymous parody:

> Under a spreading gooseberry bush the village burglar lies,
> The burglar is a hairy man with whiskers round his eyes
> And the muscles of his brawny arms keep off the little flies.
>
> He goes on Sunday to the church to hear the Parson shout
> He puts a penny in the plate and takes a pound note out
> And drops a conscience-stricken tear in case he is found out.

The latest word I have on the subject is from American graffiti, collected before 1980:

> Beneath the spreading chestnut tree
> The village idiot sat –
> Amusing himself
> By abusing himself
> And catching it all in his hat.

Make four people UNHAPPY instead of two

In my very first quotation book I made a mistake by attributing to Tennyson a view on the marriage of Thomas and Jane Carlyle. When it was suggested that the marriage had been a mistake – because with anyone but each other they might have been perfectly happy – I said that Tennyson had opined: 'I totally disagree with you. By any other arrangement *four* people would have been unhappy instead of *two.*'

This remark should have been credited to Samuel Butler (1835-1902). In a letter to a Miss Savage, 21 November 1884, he wrote: 'It was very good of God to let Carlyle and Mrs Carlyle marry one another and so make only two people miserable instead of four, besides being very amusing.'

I see that my inaccurate version has now entered *The Faber Book of Anecdotes* (1985).

The UNPLUMB'D, salt, estranging sea

The last sentence of *The French Lieutenant's Woman* (1969) by John Fowles is: 'And out again, upon the unplumb'd, salt, estranging sea.' Keen students of Matthew Arnold's 'To Marguerite – Continued' will immediately note an allusion to:

> A God, a God their severance ruled!
> And bade betwixt their shores to be
> The unplumb'd, salt, estranging sea.

He has VAN Gogh's ear for music

Appearing on *Quote . . . Unquote* in 1977, Kenneth Williams came up with a rather good showbiz story. He said that Orson Welles had said of the singing of Donny Osmond (then a popular young star): 'He has Van Gogh's ear for music.'

In fact, Orson Welles didn't say it, nor was it about Donny Osmond, but the reasons why the joke had been reascribed and redirected are instructive. It was, in fact, Billy Wilder, the film director, who made the original remark. He has a notably waspish wit but is, shall we say, not such a household name as Orson Welles. He lacks, too, Welles's Falstaffian stature and his, largely unearned, reputation in the public mind for saying witty things.

And Wilder said it about *Cliff* Osmond, an American comedy actor who appeared in Wilder's *Kiss Me Stupid, The Fortune Cookie* and *The Front Page*. As far as I know, he is unrelated to Donny Osmond but, apparently, he had to be replaced in the anecdote because he lacked star status.

VENGEANCE is mine, saith the Lord

No, he doesn't, nor does Paul the Apostle in his epistle to the Romans (12:19):

> 'Dearly beloved, avenge not yourselves, but rather give place unto wrath: for it is written, Vengeance is mine; I will repay, saith the Lord.
>   Therefore if thine enemy hunger, feed him; if he thirst, give him drink: for in so doing thou shalt heap coals of fire on his head.

Paul is quoting 'To me belongeth vengeance, and recompence' which occurs in Deuteronomy 32:35 and is also alluded to in Psalms 94:1 and Hebrews 10:30.

VENI, vidi, vici

According to Suetonius, 'I came, I saw, I conquered' was an inscription displayed in Latin to Julius Caesar's Pontic triumph of 47 BC. According to Plutarch, it was written in a letter by Caesar, announcing the victory of Zela (in Asia Minor) which concluded the Pontic (Black Sea) campaign. In North's 1570 translation of Plutarch, he states:

> Julius Caesar fought a great battle with King Pharnaces and because he would advertise one of his friends of the suddenness of this victory, he only wrote three words unto Anicius at Rome: *Veni, Vidi, Vici*: to wit, I came, saw, and overcame. These three words ending all with like sound and letters in the Latin, have a certain short grace, more pleasant to the ear, than can well be expressed in any other tongue.

Shakespeare alludes to Caesar's 'thrasonical brag' in four plays, including *Love's Labour's Lost* (IV.i.68) and *As You Like It* (V.ii.30).

VERIFY your quotations

Apologizing for an inaccurate account to the House of Commons of when he had first heard the words 'unconditional surrender', Winston Churchill writes in *The Second World War*, Vol. 4: 'It was only when I got home and searched my archives that I found the facts as they have been set out here. I am reminded of the professor who in his declining hours was asked by his devoted pupils for his final counsel. He replied, "Verify your quotations".'

Well, not exactly a 'professor', and not exactly his dying words, and not 'quotations' either. Dr Martin Joseph Routh (1755-1854 – i.e., he lasted a very long time) was President of Magdalen College, Oxford, for 63 years. Of the many stories told about Routh, Churchill was groping towards the one where he was asked what precept could serve as a rule of life to an aspiring young man. Said Routh, 'You will find it a very good practice always to verify your references, sir!'

This story was first recorded in this form in 1878, as Churchill and his amanuenses might themselves have verified. Perhaps he was recalling instead the Earl of Rosebery's version, given in a speech on 23 November 1897: 'Another confirmation of the advice given by one aged sage to somebody who sought his guidance in life, namely, "Always wind up your watch and verify your quotations"' (Benham).

Arrest several of these VICARS

Tom Stoppard once claimed that the funniest line anywhere in English farce was to be found in Philip King's *See How They Run* (first performed in 1944). It was: 'Sergeant, arrest several of these vicars.'

Alas, the actual line is not quite that good. For reasons it would be exhausting to go into, the stage gets filled with various people who are, or are dressed up as, vicars, and the order is given: 'Sergeant, arrest most of these people.'

The VICE-PRESIDENCY isn't worth a pitcher of warm spit

See **pitcher.**

V for VICTORY

The 'V for Victory' slogan of the Second World War started as a piece of officially encouraged graffiti inscribed on walls in occupied Belgium by members of the anti-German 'freedom movement'. The Flemish word for freedom begins with a V – *vrijheid* – and the French word for victory is, of course, *victoire.* The idea came from Victor de Laveleye, the BBC's Belgian programme organizer, who, in a broadcast on 14 January 1941, suggested that listeners should adopt the letter 'V' as 'a symbol of their belief in the ultimate victory of the allies'. They were to go out and chalk it up wherever they could.

From Belgium, the idea spread into the Netherlands and France and 'multitudes' of little Vs started appearing on walls in those countries. In a BBC English-language broadcast to resistance workers in Europe on 31 July 1941, 'Colonel Britton' (Douglas Ritchie) said:

> It's about the V – the sign of victory – that I want to talk to you now. All over Europe the V sign is seen by the Germans and to the Germans and the Quislings it is indeed the writing on the wall. It is the sign which tells them that one of the unknown soldiers has passed that way. And it's beginning to play on their nerves.
>
> They see it chalked on pavements, pencilled on posters, scratched on the mudguards of German cars. Flowers come up in the shape of a V; men salute each other with the V sign separating their fingers. The number five is a V and men working in the fields turn to the village clocks as the chimes sound the hour of five.

The 'Colonel' also encouraged the use of the V sound – three short taps and a heavy one:

When you knock on a door, there's your knock. if you call a waiter in a restaurant, call him like this: 'Eh, *garçon* [taps rhythm on wine glass] . . . Tell all your friends about it and teach them the V sound. If you and your friends are in a café and a German comes in, tap out the V sign all together.

From these broadcasts emerged the evocative slogan, 'The night is your friend, the "V" is your sign.' Winston Churchill spoke of the V-sign as a symbol of the 'the unconquerable will of the people of the occupied territories'.

The symbol was expressed in other ways, too. The opening three notes of Beethoven's Fifth Symphony corresponded to the (... —) of the V in Morse Code and, accordingly, the music was used in BBC broadcasts to occupied Europe.

People gave the 'V for Victory' salute with parted middle index fingers – though Winston Churchill confused matters by presenting his fingers the wrong way round in a manner akin to the traditionally obscene gesture. His private secretary, John Colville, noted in his diary on 26 September 1941: 'The P.M. *will* give the V sign with two fingers in spite of the representations repeatedly made to him that this gesture has quite another significance.'

As to how *that* came about . . . in his book *Year of the King* (1985), the actor Anthony Sher quotes an interesting historical 'fact' dug up in *Henry V* rehearsals: 'The two-fingered sod-off sign comes from Agincourt. The French, certain of victory, had threatened to cut off the bow-fingers of all the English archers. When the English were victorious, the archers held up their fingers in defiance.'

Perhaps Churchill wasn't so far out after all.

A VIEW to a Kill

The title of the umpteenth James Bond film (1985) must have puzzled many cinemagoers who then quietly said to themselves 'it must have something to do with killing' and forgot about it.

The original title of the Bond short story by Ian Fleming (published in 1960 with *For Your Eyes Only* and, one gathers, having no other connection with the film) is rather more meaningful. It is '*From* a View To a Kill'.

As such it is very close to the title of Anthony Powell's 1933 novel *From a View to a Death* which is a direct quotation from the song 'D'ye ken John Peel', written in 1832 by the appropriately named John Woodcock Graves:

> Yes, I ken John Peel, and Ruby too,
> Ranter and Ringwood, Bellman and True,
> From a find to a check, from a check to a view,
> From a view to a death in the morning.

In foxhunting terminology, a 'check' is a loss of scent, a 'view (halloo)' is the huntsman's shout when a fox breaks cover, and a 'kill' or a 'death' is what it says.

Inside with the five wise VIRGINS, or outside . . .

A favourite story, sometimes taken with a pinch of salt, comes in the category of 'sermons we would like to have heard'. Dr Henry Montagu Butler (1833-1918), Headmaster of Harrow, then, from 1886, Master of Trinity College, Cambridge, was preaching a sermon in the college chapel when he asked: 'Would you, my dear young friends, like to be inside with the five wise virgins or outside, alone, and in the dark, with the five foolish ones?'

The source for this is Edward Marsh in *Ambrosia and Small Beer* (1964).

VOX populi

In British broadcasting of the 1950s and 1960s, there was a vogue for what was known in the business as 'vox pops' – namely, street interviews with passers-by presenting views on issues of the day which, with luck, were amusingly expressed and – for reasons of balance – effectively cancelled each other out. *'Vox populi'* – (Latin for 'voice of the people') is, naturally, of venerable origin.

Alcuin (735-804) wrote in a letter to the Emperor Charlemagne in AD 800: *'Nec audiendi sunt qui solent dicere, "Vox populi, vox Dei"; cum tumultuositas vulgi semper insaniae proxima sit'* – 'Nor should we listen to those who say, "The voice of the people is the voice of God", for the turbulence of the mob is always close to insanity.' So, clearly, even though he didn't like it, the phrase was not of his making.

'Fox populi' was a nickname applied to Abraham Lincoln (presumably on account of his looks or his populism) by *Vanity Fair* magazine, London, in 1863.

The same year, the American General W. T. Sherman, in a letter to his wife on 2 June, wrote 'Vox populi, vox humbug' – by which he meant, 'The voice of the people is humbug.'

Now VOYAGER

The novel (1941) by Olive Higgins Prouty and the film (USA 1942) both quote Walt Whitman: 'Now voyager, sail thou forth to seek and find'.

Because his skin smelt of WALNUTS

When Dame Rebecca West, the writer, died in March 1983, mention was made of her affair, 70 years previously, with H. G. Wells. The *Guardian* (16 March) said she had been attracted to him 'because he smelt of walnuts' (he, more predictably, had been attracted by her 'hard mind').

No source was given for West's assertion, but it chimes with another mention of H. G. Wells given in Ted Morgan's biography of W. Somerset Maugham. When Maugham asked Moura Budberg (another lover of H. G. Wells) what she saw in the paunchy, played-out writer, she replied, 'He smells of *honey*'.

Whatever Wells smelt of, it seems to have been effective and surely ought to have been bottled and put on the market.

There ain't gonna be no WAR

See **gonna.**

The people our parents WARNED us about

See **people.**

To meet one's WATERLOO

– i.e., to meet one's ultimate challenge and fail, as Napoleon did at the battle in 1815. Possibly the earliest use of this expression was by the American lawyer, Wendell Phillips, in the form, 'Every man meets his Waterloo at last' (at Brooklyn, 1 November 1859). He was referring to the failure of an attack by his fellow abolitionist, John Brown, on an arsenal in Virginia two weeks before.

On the other hand, earlier examples in the *OED* show that, almost from the word go, a 'Waterloo' entered the language in this sense. Byron, in 1816, called Armenian 'a Waterloo of an alphabet'. And John Aiton, in his *Manual of Domestic Economy for Clergymen* (1842), wrote: 'If there must be a Waterloo, let it be a conflict for all the minister's rights, so that he may never require to go to law in his lifetime again.'

The battle of WATERLOO was won on the playing fields of Eton

This opinion was first ascribed to the first Duke of Wellington in Count Charles de Montalembert's *De L'Avenir Politique de l'Angleterre* in 1856. The Frenchman stated that the Duke returned to Eton in his old age and, recalling the delights of his youth, exclaimed: 'It is here that the battle of Waterloo was won' (i.e., he made no mention of playing fields).

Burnam 2 notes that Sir Edward Creasy built on this in *Memoirs of Eminent Etonians* (though as this was published in 1850, I'm not sure how). Anyhow, he had the Iron Duke passing the playing fields in old age and saying, 'There grows the stuff that won Waterloo.'

Then in 1889, a third writer, Sir William Fraser, in *Words on Wellington*, put together Montalembert's remark with Creasy's playing fields to produce the popularly known version.

The seventh Duke tried to pour more cold water on the matter in letters to *The Times* sometime prior to his death in 1972:

> During his old age Wellington is recorded to have visited Eton on two occasions only and it is unlikely that he came more often. He attended the funeral of his elder brother in College Chapel in October 1842 and he accompanied the Queen when she came to Eton with Louis Philippe in October 1844. On the first occasion, he attended the ceremony only and went away when it was over: and, on the second, he is hardly likely to have talked about the battle of Waterloo. Wellington's career at Eton was short and inglorious and, unlike his elder brother, he had no particular affection for the place . . . Quite apart from the fact that the authority for attributing the words to Wellington is of the flimsiest description, to anyone who knows his turn of phrase they ring entirely false. It is, therefore, much to be hoped that speakers will discontinue using them either, as is generally the case, in order to point out their snobbishness, which is so alien to ideas generally now held, or else to show that Wellington was in favour of organized games, an assumption which is entirely unwarranted.

Perhaps the nearest the first duke came to any sort of compliment to the effect his old school had on him was, 'I really believe I owe my spirit of enterprise to the tricks I used to play in the garden' [of his Eton boarding-house] – quoted in Vol. 1 of Elizabeth Longford's biography (1969).

But the saying, however apocryphal, still exerts its power. One H. Allen Smith (*b.* 1906) said: 'The battle of Yorktown was lost on the playing fields of Eton' (Yorktown, in Virginia, was the scene of the surrender of British forces at the end of the War of Independence, 1781). George Orwell (an Old Etonian himself) averred: 'Probably the Battle of Waterloo *was* won on the playing fields of Eton, but the opening battles of all subsequent wars have been lost there' (*The Lion and the Unicorn*, 1941).

WATER, water, everywhere and not a drop to drink
That is how everyone remembers it, but what Samuel Taylor Coleridge wrote in his poem 'The Ancient Mariner' (1798) was:

> Water, water everywhere,
> And all the boards did shrink;
> Water, water, everywhere
> *Nor any* drop to drink.

What are the Wild WAVES Saying?
I treasure an advertisement for Igranic wireless coils, dating from the early 1920s, which plays upon the idea of radio waves and asks, 'What are the wild waves saying?'

This is the title line of a Victorian song with words by J. E. Carpenter (1813-85) and music by Stephen Glover (1813-70):

> What are the wild waves saying,
> Sister, the whole day long:
> That ever amid our playing,
> I hear but their low, lone song?
> Not by the seaside only,
> There it sounds wild and free;
> But at night when 'tis dark and lonely,
> In dreams it is still with me.

The song is a duet between Paul and Florence Dombey and based on an incident in *Dombey and Son* (1848) by Charles Dickens. Nowhere in the novel does Dickens use the words, 'What are the *wild* waves saying?' although the book is fairly awash with the idea of a 'dark and unknown sea that rolls round all the world' (Chapter 1, end). At the end of Chapter 8, in Brighton, young Paul Dombey says to his sister, Florence, 'I want to know what it says . . . The sea, Floy, what is it that it keeps on saying?' Then, a line or two later: 'Very often afterwards, in the midst of their talk, he would break off, to try to understand what it was that the waves were always saying; and would rise up in his couch to look towards that invisible region, far away.' The title of Chapter 16 is 'What the Waves were always Saying'.

The WAY to the Stars
The title of the film (UK 1945), set near an RAF airfield during the Second World War, and based on Terence Rattigan's stage play *Flare Path*, presumably alludes to the RAF motto '*Per ardua ad astra*' ('through striving, to the stars').

However, I notice in Bartlett that '*Sic itur ad astra*', from Virgil's *Aeneid* (Book 9, line 641), is translated as, 'That's the way to the stars.'

In the USA, perhaps to avoid any such questions, the film was called *Johnny in the Clouds* (after the line 'Johnny head-in-air' from the poem 'For Johnny' by John Pudney, which is recited in the film).

A WEEK is a long time in politics
When I asked him, Harold Wilson (*b*. 1916), later Lord Wilson, uncharacteristically was unable to remember when he first uttered the much-quoted dictum, 'A week is a long time in politics.' For someone who, as Labour Prime Minister 1964-70, 1974-76, used to be able to cite the columns of *Hansard* in which his speeches appeared, this was a curious lapse. When I approached him on the matter in 1977, he also challenged the accepted interpretation of the words – which most people would think was along the lines of 'What a difference a day makes', 'Wait and see', and 'Don't panic, it'll all blow over.'

'It does not mean I'm living from day to day,' he said, but was intended as 'a prescription for long-term strategic thinking and planning, ignoring the day-to-day issues and pressures which may hit the headlines but which must not be allowed to get out of focus while longer-term policies are taking effect.'

Inquiries among political journalists led to the conclusion that, in its present form, the phrase was probably first used at a meeting between Wilson and the parliamentary lobby correspondents in the wake of the sterling crisis shortly after he first took office as Prime Minister in 1964. However, Robert Carvel of the London *Evening Standard* recalled Wilson at a Labour Party conference in 1960 having said, 'Forty-eight hours is a long time in politics.'

In the late 1980s, Channel 4 carried a weekly review with the title *A Week in Politics*, clearly alluding to Wilson's phrase.

WENT the Day Well?

At the start of the 1942 British film *Went the Day Well?* there appears on screen the anonymous epigraph:

> Went the day well?
>> We died and never knew.
> But, well or ill,
>> Freedom, we died for you.

At the time the film was released, a classics teacher suggested that this was a version of a Greek epitaph, but I have no note of which one he was referring to. In the USA, the film was retitled *48 Hours*. It was based on a short story by Graham Greene, entitled *The Lieutenant Died Last*, and tells of a typical English village repelling Nazi invaders in its midst. The epigraph presumably refers to the villagers who die defending 'Bramley End'.

The question, 'Went the day well?' sounds as if it ought to come from Shakespeare's *Henry V*, although it does not. However, in the battle in *King John*, the king has the understandable query, 'How goes the day with us?' (V.iii.1).

Go WEST, young man!

This advice is an early example of a misattribution that refuses to be corrected. Its originator was John Babsone Lane Soule who first wrote it in the Terre Haute (Indiana) *Express* in 1851 when, indeed, the thing to do in the United States was to head westwards, where gold and much else lay promised. However, Horace Greeley repeated it in *his* New York newspaper, the *Tribune*, and, being rather more famous – a candidate for the presidency and all – it stuck with him. Greeley reprinted Soule's article to show where he had taken it from, but to no avail.

The original sentence was, 'Go west, young man, and grow up with the country.'

Go West Young Man was a film vehicle for *Mae* West (rather than anything to do with *the* West) in 1936. *Go West Young Lady* followed in 1940. There have been two films called *Go West*, the more notable of which was the 1940 one, often called *The Marx Brothers Go West*.

To 'go west', meaning 'to die' is a completely separate coinage, I believe. It dates back to the sixteenth century and alludes to the setting of the sun.

The WHEEL is come full circle

Now a cliché, this expression probably owes its fame to the fact that Edmund the Bastard says it in Shakespeare's *King Lear* (V.iii.173). He is referring to the wheel of Fortune, he being at that moment back down at the bottom where he was before it began to revolve.

WHERE there is hatred . . .

On first becoming Prime Minister, Mrs Margaret Thatcher stood in Downing Street on 4 May 1979 and said:

> I would just like to remember some words of St Francis of Assisi which I think are really just particularly apt at the moment − 'Where there is discord, may we bring harmony; where there is error may we bring truth; where there is doubt, may we bring faith; and where there is despair, may we bring hope.

According to Sir Ronald Millar, one of her speechwriters at the time, it was he who, at four o'clock on Mrs Thatcher's first morning as PM, gave her the words to read out, 'ignoring the advice of harder-nosed associates who thought the sentiments too trite even for that emotional occasion' (*Sunday Times*, 23 November 1980).

It was inevitable that the quotation would, in time, be held against her. Two years later, almost to the day, Labour's Peter Shore, then Shadow Chancellor, told a May Day rally: 'She has brought not love, not pardon, not union, not hope, not joy. Instead, we have had injury, discord, despair, darkness, sadness and indeed hate.'

Bartlett has a fuller version and a different translation, saying no more than that the words are 'attributed' to St Francis (*c.* 1181-1226). In 1988, this was the version entitled 'Prayer for Peace' that was available (unattributed) in Britain on prayer cards. There was even a version on a tea-towel on sale at York Minster. At the Basilica of St Francis at Assisi, it was, of course, available in any number of languages:

> Lord, make me an instrument of your peace.
> Where there is hatred, let me sow love.
> Where there is injury, pardon.

Where there is doubt, faith.
Where there is despair, hope.
Where there is darkness, light.
Where there is sadness, joy.
O Divine Master, grant that I may not so much seek
To be consoled as to console,
To be understood as to understand,
To be loved as to love.

For it is in giving that we receive,
It is in pardoning that we are pardoned,
It is in dying that we are born to eternal life.

Actually there is some doubt as to whether St Francis had anything to do with the prayer at all. A former Bishop of Ripon, writing to the *Church Times*, suggested the prayer had probably been written in France in 1912.

The Great WHITE Way
This name for Broadway, popular in the first half of the twentieth century, derives from the title of a novel (1901) by Albert Bigelow Paine. For a while, the theatre district was also known as 'the Gay White Way' – which, today, might only lead to misunderstanding.

Caesar's WIFE must be above suspicion
It was Julius Caesar himself who said this of his wife, Pompeia, when he divorced her in 62 BC. In North's translation of Plutarch's *Lives* – which is how the saying came into English in 1570 – Caesar is quoted thus: 'I will not, sayd he, that my wife be so much as suspected.'

Pompeia was Caesar's second wife. According to Suetonius, in 61 BC she took part in the women-only rites of the Feast of the Great Goddess. But it was rumoured that a profligate called Publius Clodius attended the ceremony wearing women's clothes and that he had committed adultery with Pompeia. Caesar divorced Pompeia and, at the subsequent inquiry into the desecration, was asked why he had done so. 'Caesar's wife must be above suspicion,' he replied. He later married Calphurnia.

An example of the phrase in use occurs in Lord Chesterfield's letters: 'Your moral character must be not only pure, but, like Caesar's wife, unsuspected.' This should not be confused with what a newly elected mayor (quoted by G. W. E. Russell in

Collections and Recollections, 1898) once said. During his year of office he felt he should lay aside all his political prepossessions and be, like Caesar's wife, 'all things to all men'.

If it's only WIND I'll call it . . .

F. E. Smith, first Earl of Birkenhead, taunted Lord Chief Justice Hewart about the size of his stomach. 'What's it to be – a boy or a girl?'

Replied Hewart: 'If it's a boy I'll call him John. If it's a girl I'll call her Mary. But if, as I suspect, it's only wind, I'll call it F. E. Smith.'

I printed that anecdote in my book *Quote . . . Unquote* (1978). The story had come to me from a woman who said it had been told to her brother 'by a stranger in a bus queue in Harrogate in 1923'. Smith died in 1930, Hewart in 1943.

According to Humphrey McQueen in *Social Sketches of Australia* (1978), the Antipodean version has Sir George Houstoun Reid (1845-1918) replying, in answer to the question, apropos his stomach, 'What are you going to call it, George?': 'If it's a boy, I'll call it after myself. If it's a girl, I'll call it Victoria after our Queen. But if, as I strongly suspect, it's nothing but piss and wind, I'll call it after you.'

According to the *Faber Book of Anecdotes* (1985), the US version has President Taft (*d.* 1930) making this retort to Senator Chauncey Depew (*d.* 1929).

God tempers the WIND to the shorn lamb

In Laurence Sterne's *Sentimental Journey* (1768), we find: 'How she had borne it . . . she could not tell – but God tempers the wind, said Maria, to the shorn lamb.' That is to say, God arranges matters so as not to make them unduly harsh for the unfortunate.

As such, this is possibly one of the most preposterously untrue of all proverbial sayings. For a proverb it is, not an original remark of Sterne's, as is sometimes supposed, although Sterne's wording is how it is now used. *CODP* finds a French version in 1594.

The Last of the Summer WINE
See **last.**

Comin' in on a WING and a Prayer
See **comin'.**

The WINTER of discontent

Shakespeare's *Richard III* begins, famously, with Gloucester's punning and original metaphor:

> Now is the winter of our discontent
> Made glorious summer by this son of York;
> And all the clouds that lour'd upon our House
> In the deep bosom of the ocean buried

– even if the editor of the Arden edition does describe the entire image as 'almost proverbial'. Probably made all the more memorable by Laurence Olivier's delivery of these lines in the 1955 film, the phrase 'winter of discontent' suffered the unpleasant fate of becoming a politician's and journalist's cliché following the winter of 1978-79 when British life was disrupted by all kinds of industrial protests against the Labour Government's attempts to keep down pay rises. Most notably, rubbish remained uncollected and began to pile up in the streets, and a gravediggers' strike in one area reputedly left bodies unburied.

This 'winter of discontent' (as it is still referred to in 1988) may perhaps have contributed to the Conservative victory at the May 1979 general election. The question I have been asked is, who first referred to it as such?

Mrs Margaret Thatcher, opening her election campaign on TV (2 April 1979) said, 'We have just had a devastating winter of industrial strife – perhaps the worst in living memory, certainly the worst in mine', which is almost it, but not quite.

The first example I have found in a far-from-exhaustive search through the files is in the *Sun* (30 April): 'WINTER OF DISCONTENT. Lest we forget . . . the *Sun* recalls the long, cold months of industrial chaos that brought Britain to its knees.' Then, after the election, the phrase is revived in the *Observer* (9 September). The sub-title to an article is, 'Do we face a winter of discontent? Adrian Hamilton and Robert Taylor report on the union and employer mood'.

At the end of that month, on the 26th, the *Daily Express* began a report of a speech by Mrs Thatcher at Milton Keynes, thus: 'STRIKE AT YOUR PERIL! Maggie spells out price of conflict this winter. Mrs Thatcher yesterday put a price on another winter of discontent. It would be lost jobs, she said.'

As far as I can make out, she didn't actually use the phrase itself. I rather think that it was a journalistic imposition and, as with the *Observer's* use, it is interesting to note that the 'winter'

225

referred to is the forthcoming one of 1979-80 rather than the previous one.

The *Observer* was still ringing changes on the original on 7 February 1982: 'WHY FOOTBALL MUST SURVIVE ITS WINTER OF PENURY AND DISCONTENT'.

He who is not WITH us is against us
See **against.**

A WOMAN is only a woman, but a good Cigar is a Smoke
This view, which would now be seen as an outrageous example of male chauvinism, is expressed in Rudyard Kipling's poem 'The Betrothed' (1886). Lest Kipling, as usual, should take more blame than he should for what one of his characters says, it is worth pointing out that the man in question (the poem is in the first person) is choosing between his cigars and his betrothed, a woman called Maggie.

The situation arose in an actual breach of promise case, *c.* 1885, in which the woman had said to the man, 'You must choose between me and your cigar.'

The poem ends:

> Light me another Cuba — I hold to my first-sworn vows.
> If Maggie will have no rival, I'll have no Maggie for Spouse!

WOMEN'S faults are many
See **faults.**

The 10 Commandments contain 297 WORDS . . .
I recently saw in a book of 'amazing facts' a report to the effect that although the Ten Commandments contain 297 words and Lincoln's Gettysburg Address a mere 266, an EEC directive on butter had no less than 26,911 words . . .

At once, I knew this to be untrue – not that I checked whether there was any such EEC directive. It is simply that this 'fact' is merely a colourful jibe at bureaucracy in general and has been around for a very long time.

Max Hall in 'The Great Cabbage Hoax: A Case Study' (*Journal of Personality and Social Psychology*, 1965, Vol. 2, No. 4) made a thorough survey of its origins. These seemed to lie with the US Office of Price Administration during the Second World War, although the joke really only began to spread widely in 1951, during the US involvement in the Korean War. Numerous examples were found in press and broadcasting of the rumour that the then Office of Price Stabilization had a 26,911-word cabbage order. This was compared with the brevity of the Gettysburg Address, the Ten Commandments and the Declaration of Independence. In another version, the cabbage order became a 12,962-word regulation on manually operated foghorns.

As with rumours of a more inflammatory kind, is it not amazing that such a story can keep on turning up – even when the true facts have been established (there was no cabbage order of any kind from the OPA or the OPS)?

I am in the process of tracing how another kind of jokey 'fact' gained currency. The *Mail on Sunday*, on 4 January 1987, printed what it claimed to be an advertisement from the *Mountain Echo* of Himeville in 'Drakesburg Mountain', South Africa (I think they meant the Drakensberg mountains, but never mind). It went: 'Man of 38 wishes to meet woman of 30 owning a tractor. Please enclose pic of tractor.'

Compare this with a citation from a book called *Glad to be Grey* by Peter Freedman, published two years earlier, in 1985: 'Young farmer with 100 acres would be pleased to hear from young lady with tractor. Please send photograph of tractor.' This was said to come from the personal column of the *Evesham Admag* in 1977.

Earlier, in 1983, in one of their programmes featured in the video *The Best of the Two Ronnies*, comedians Ronnie Barker and Ronnie Corbett evidently used the same gag – in this version one of them visits a psychiatrist and talks about cup-final tickets.

But we can go back much further. Roger S. Windsor writes (from Peru, as it happens):

> In January 1963 I was in my final year of veterinary studies at the Royal Veterinary College in Edinburgh and we organized the Annual Conference of the Association of Veterinary Students of Great Britain and Ireland. At one of our formal lunches . . . Arthur Smith (Captain of Scotland's rugby team) was the after-lunch speaker. He had recently returned from South Africa where he had captained the Lions. He told the story of an advertisement in the *Rand Daily Mail* before the Cape Town Test where a man advertised for a wife who had to be in possession of two tickets for the test. The advert ran: 'Please send a photograph . . . of the tickets.'

So that takes us to 1962, at least. But could the incident ever really have taken place anywhere, whether about tickets or tractors or whatever?

All the WORLD and his wife
– i.e., 'everybody'. The *ODQ* cites Christopher Anstey's use of this phrase in *The New Bath Guide* (1766):

> You may go to Carlisle's, and to Almack's too;
> And I'll give you my head if you find such a host,
> For coffee, tea, chocolate, butter, and toast:
> How he welcomes at once all the world and his wife,
> And how civil to folk he ne'er saw in his life.

But the phrase was quite clearly an established one by 1738 when Swift included it in *Polite Conversation*: 'Who were the Company? – Why; there was all the World and his Wife.'

There is an equivalent French expression, 'All the world and his father'.

This WORLD is a comedy to those that think, a tragedy to those that feel . . .
So wrote Horace Walpole to the Countess of Upper Ossory on 16 August 1776, and it is to him that the observation is usually credited. However, I am informed that Blaise Pascal (1623-62) had earlier said: *'La vie, c'est une tragédie pour celui qui sent, mais une comédie pour celui qui pense.'* Alas, I have no source for this.

All the WORLD owes me a living
See **owes**.

The WORLD, the Flesh and the Devil
This expression, with the words in the order given – as used, for example, in a 1959 film title – comes from the Litany in the *Book of Common Prayer*: 'From fornication, and all other deadly sin; and from all the deceits of the world, the flesh and the devil, Good Lord, deliver us.' Again, in the Collect for the eighteenth Sunday after Trinity, we find: 'Lord, we beseech thee, grant thy people grace to withstand the temptations of the world, the flesh, and the devil . . .'.

The same combination also occurs in the Catechism where the confirmee is asked what his godfathers and godmothers had promised for him at his baptism: 'First, that I should renounce the *devil* and all his works, the pomps and vanity of this wicked *world*, and all the sinful lusts of the *flesh*.'

In the sixteenth and seventeenth centuries, the words were

also grouped together in a different order to denote 'our ghostly enemies' – as, for example, 'the devil, the world, and the flesh' (1530).

When the WORLD was young

I take this to be a wistful expression not only of 'long ago' but also of a time more innocent than the present. It may derive ultimately from this verse in the Bible: 'For the world has lost his youth, and the times begin to wax old' (2 Esdras 14:10).

Precisely as 'When the World Was Young', I have found it used as the title of a painting (1891) by Sir E. J. Poynter PRA, which shows three young girls in a classical setting, relaxing by a pool.

WORRAworraworraworraworra

This is the noise ('not a growl, and it isn't a purr') made by Tigger, the bouncy tiger, in *The House at Pooh Corner* (1928) by A. A. Milne.

However, 'wurra-wurra-wurra' also occurs in Thackeray's *The Rose and the Ring* (1856), Chapter 15. Here it seems to denote eating noises – but from the same corner of the animal kingdom. Count Hogginarmo jumps into a circus ring, and then: 'Wurra wurra wurra wur-aw-aw-aw!!! in about two minutes, the Count Hogginarmo was GOBBLED UP by those lions: bones, boots and all, and there was an end of him.'

Earlier still, on 26 January 1788, when Captain Arthur Phillip's fleet landed at what would later be called Sydney Harbour in Australia, they were greeted by Aborigines crying, '*Warra, warra!*' (meaning, 'Go away!')

I married him for better or WORSE, but not for lunch

I thought I had first encountered this rather pleasing play on the words from the Anglican marriage service in an article by Ludovic Kennedy about the Duchess of Windsor (*Observer*, 2 December 1979, based on *The Windsor Story* by J. Bryan III and Charles J. V. Murphy): '[The Duke of Windsor] usually lunched alone on a salad while the duchess went out ("I married the Duke for better or worse but not for lunch").'

Then I noticed that in Partridge/Catchphrases (1977) it is listed as an 'Australian catchphrase used by a woman whose husband has retired, works at home or comes home for his midday meal', dating it from the 1940s and 'familiar to Britons since at least the latish 1960s'.

It's WORSE than a crime, it's a blunder!

There is no doubting that this was said about the execution of the Duc d'Enghien in 1804. Suspecting the Duc of being involved in royalist conspiracies against him, Napoleon had him found and executed – an act which hardened opinion against the French emperor. But who said it? The Comte Boulay de la Meurthe, Talleyrand, Fouche, and any number of others, including Napoleon himself, are said to have said it. In French, the remark is usually rendered as: *'C'est pire qu'un crime; c'est une faute!'*

Whoever said it first, the saying still comes in useful.

Cheer up! The WORST is yet to come

Partridge/Catchphrases manages no more than 'a US c.p. of ironic encouragement since *c.* 1918'. The most usual attribution, though, is to the American writer Philander Johnson (1866-1939) in his *Shooting Stars* (*c.* 1920). I have found it earlier, however, in *The Love Letters of Mark Twain* in a letter from Twain to his wife in 1893-94.

The similar expression, 'Cheer up . . . you'll soon be dead!' appears in several British entertainments in the period 1909-18.

The non-ironic line, 'The worst is yet to come', occurs in Tennyson's *Sea Dreams* (1864).

The worst pun on the phrase concerns the man who was eating a German meal but was encouraged to continue with the words, 'Cheer up, the *würst* is yet to come!'

She Done Him WRONG
See **done.**

YES, Minister

The title of the BBC TV comedy series about the relationship between Government ministers and the Civil Service in Britain (1980-85), although perhaps an obvious one to choose, nevertheless has a precise source. It comes from a description by Richard Crossman, a minister in Labour governments of the 1960s and 1970s, of his first day in office as a cabinet minister, in October 1964:

> Already I realize the tremendous effort it requires not to be taken over by the Civil Service. My Minister's room is like a padded cell, and in certain ways I am like a person who is suddenly certified a lunatic and put safely into this great vast room, cut off from real life . . . Of course, they don't behave *quite* like nurses because the Civil Service is profoundly deferential – 'Yes, Minister! No, Minister! If you wish it, Minister!'
>
> *(The Diaries of a Cabinet Minister*, Vol.1, 1975)

She didn't say YES, she didn't say no

See **she.**

Alas, poor YORICK . . . I knew him well, Horatio

When the gravedigger in Shakespeare's *Hamlet* produces the skull of Yorick, the king's late jester, the prince's actual words are: 'Alas, poor Yorick. I knew him, Horatio, a fellow of infinite jest, of most excellent fancy' (V.i.178). To make it easier to quote, presumably, the form 'I knew him *well*' crept into popular use.

YOUTH is too precious to be wasted on the young

Like 'war is too important to be left to the generals', '. . . politics to the politicians', '. . . history to the historians', '. . . broadcasting to the broadcasters', this is a saying in a format that people like to use. The only source I have come across is, 'Youth is a wonderful thing: what a crime to waste it on children' – but where in George Bernard Shaw's voluminous writings it is to be found, I know not.

YOUTH must have its fling

Meaning, 'let the young enjoy themselves while they can', this proverbial saying appears in this precise form in W. S. Gilbert's lyrics for *The Pirates of Penzance* (1879) –

> I pray you, pardon me, ex-Pirate King,
> Peers will be peers, and youth must have its fling

– and *The Mikado* (1885) –

> But youth, of course, must have its fling.

Gilbert greatly enjoyed proverbs and, indeed, wrote two songs completely made up of them. In this case, to my mind, he appears to have created a more memorable version of the older proverbs 'Youth will have his course' (known from the sixteenth century) and 'Youth will be served' (though this latter did not appear until the early nineteenth century).

In *The Water Babies* (1863), Charles Kingsley has: 'When all the world is young lad/ And all the trees are green:/ . . . Young blood must have its course, lad/ And every dog his day.'